Queer Italia

Italian and Italian American Studies

*Series Editor: Stanislao G. Pugliese,
Hofstra University*

Published by Palgrave

Upcoming Titles

Frank Sinatra: History, Identity, and Italian American Culture
edited by Stanislao G. Pugliese

The Legacy of Primo Levi
edited by Stanislao G. Pugliese

Representing Sacco and Vanzetti
edited by Jerome A. Delameter and Mary Ann Trasciatti

Mussolini's Rome: The Fascist Transformation of the Eternal City
by Borden W. Painter Jr.

Carlo Tresca: Portrait of a Rebel
by Nunzi Pernicone

Queer Italia: Same-Sex Desire in Italian Literature and Film

Gary P. Cestaro

QUEER ITALIA
© Gary P. Cestaro, 2004

First published 2004 by
PALGRAVE MACMILLAN™
175 Fifth Avenue, New York, N.Y. 10010 and
Houndmills, Basingstoke, Hampshire, England RG21 6XS
Companies and representatives throughout the world

PALGRAVE MACMILLAN is the global academic imprint of the Palgrave Macmillan division of St. Martin's Press, LLC and of Palgrave Macmillan Ltd. Macmillan® is a registered trademark in the United States, United Kingdom and other countries. Palgrave is a registered trademark in the European Union and other countries.

ISBN 0–312–24024–4 hardback
ISBN 0–312–24026–0 paperback

Library of Congress Cataloging-in-Publication Data
    Queer Italia: same-sex desire in Italian literature and
    film / edited by Gary P. Cestaro.
        p. cm.
    Includes bibliographical references and index.
    Contents: Queer Italia: same-sex desire in Italian literature and film / Gary P. Cestaro— The Dead Sea of sodomy: Giordano da Pisa on men who have sex with men / Bernard Schlager—Bibbiena's closet: interpretation and the sexual culture of a Renaissance papal court / Michael Wyatt—Knots of desire: female homoeroticism in Orlando furioso 25 / Mary-Michelle DeCoste—ACTing UP in the Renaissance: the case of Benvenuto Cellini / Margaret A. Gallucci—Nature is a mother most sweet: homosexuality in sixteenth- and seventeenth-century Italian libertinism / Giovanni Dall'Orto—Tra(ns)vesting gender and genre in Flaminio Scala's Il (finto) marito / Rosalind Kerr—Beauty and the beast: lesbians in literature and sexual science from the nineteenth to the twentieth centuries / Daniela Danna—Desire and disavowal in Liliana Cavani's "German trilogy" / Áine O'Healy—Adapting to heterocentricity: the film versions of Umberto Saba's Ernesto and Giorgio Bassani's The gold-rimmed spectacles / William Van Watson—Reluctantly queer: in search of the homoerotic novel in twentieth-century Italian fiction / Sergio Parussa—Secret wounds: the bodies of fascism in Giorgio Bassani's Dietro la porta / Derek Duncan—Transitive gender and queer performance in the novels of Mario Mieli and Vittorio Pescatori / Marco Pustianaz.
        ISBN 0–312–24024–4 (cloth)—ISBN 0–312–24026–0 (pbk.)
        1. Italian literature—History and criticism. 2. Motion pictures—Italy
    3. Homosexuality in motion pictures. 4. Homosexuality in literature. I. Cestaro, Gary P.

PQ4028.Q44 2004
850.9′353—dc22   2003066427

A catalogue record for this book is available from the British Library.

Design by Newgen Imaging Systems (P) Ltd., Chennai, India.

First edition: July 2004
10 9 8 7 6 5 4 3 2 1

Printed in the United States of America.

For Rob

Contents

Acknowledgments

I'd first like to thank Greg Hutcheson and Joe Blackmore, editors of *Queer Iberia*, who put the idea of a collection of queer essays on Italian literature in my head, and Michael Flamini, editor at St. Martins, for approaching me about the project at the Medieval Studies Congress at Kalamazoo in 1999 (at a session entitled "Queering the Italian Middle Ages"). Members of the Lesbian and Gay Studies Caucus of the American Association for Italian Studies have provided inspiration through the fabulous sessions they have organized over the years. My many queer colleagues in the DePaul LGBT faculty group deserve praise for helping create such a queer-friendly environment there. I am grateful also to the DePaul Humanities Center for giving me the opportunity to discuss the project with wonderful colleagues who generously offered advice and encouragement. My friends in the Department of Modern Languages have provided crucial more support through some tough times, especially Clara Orban and Andrew Suozzo. I'd like to thank Armand Cerbone for listening and for his insight. My thanks also to the many LGBT friends and acquaintances in Italy who have allowed me to spend time with them and learn something about their lives. Finally, love and thanks to my friends in the United States, especially Rob Garofalo, Rich DeNatale, and Arthur Little, for making me to write about – and be part of – queer culture in the first place.

Introduction

Queer Italia: Same-Sex Desire in Italian Literature and Film

Gary P. Cestaro

On July 8, 2000, some 200,000 lesbians and gay men marched on the Italian capital in celebration of World Pride 2000. Although a number of successful and well-attended national pride marches have taken place since, World Pride in Rome continues to be seen as a historically significant event by Italian gays and lesbians, an important turning point in the history of the Italian gay rights movement that for the first time garnered serious national—indeed international—attention. The Rome parade marked the culmination of a week's worth of events in support of gay rights and culture that one reporter defined as "a victorious coming-out parade for Italy's gay community."[1] The note of triumph reflects the event's success despite months of polemics in the Italian press over the appropriateness of such a demonstration in Rome during the Jubilee year and the Vatican's vigorous attempts to have it cancelled. In the end, the participants—a few even clad in togas and laurel wreaths—marched peacefully to the Coliseum and then back to the Circus Maximus for a rally. At once legitimate historical reminder and pure camp, this victory of Italian gays amidst the iconic monuments of their classical past, in the face of stern disapproval from mother Church, neatly introduces themes that inform the essays in this volume. World Pride 2000 and the controversy surrounding it reflect the difficult positioning of Italian culture and Italian literature between the classical and the Catholic, between ancient organizations of human sexual activity that left some space for same-sex desire and Christian efforts to redefine and delimit.[2] Such is the complex history inherited by the first producers of vernacular Italian texts in the middle ages and passed on to Italian literature.

Queer Italia gathers essays on Italian literature and film, medieval to modern. The volume's chronological organization reflects its intention to define a queer tradition in Italian culture. While cognizant of the theoretical risks inherent in transhistoricizing sexuality (not to mention nationality), the contributors to this volume share an interest in probing the multiform dynamics of sexual desires in Italian texts (texts produced by natives of the peninsula in some form of Italian or, in earlier instances, Latin) through the centuries. The volume aims not to promote the mistaken notion of a single homosexuality through history; rather, these essays together upset and undo the equally misguided assumption of an omnipresent heterosexuality through time by uncovering the various, complex workings of desire in texts from all periods. Somewhat paradoxically, a kind of queer canon results. We accept the word "queer" from the contemporary critical vocabulary when it signifies a reading practice that challenges a critical tradition complacent in its heterosexist bias. These queer essays open a much-needed critical space in the Italian tradition wherein fixed definitions of sexual identity collapse. *Queer Italia* is the first and only work of its kind in Italian criticism.[3]

The methodological and theoretical approaches employed in these essays vary as widely as the historical periods they survey. They range from close textual readings that draw significantly on contemporary critical vocabularies and queer theory to more traditional historical and sociohistorical investigations into individual instances of desires that do not conform to a presumed heterosexual norm. Some of the essays in this volume accomplish the important task of shedding light on little-known or marginalized texts. But many engage the sexuality of texts in the most traditional literary histories. And yet mainstream criticism, Italian and American, has largely overlooked and/or stepped around the inherent queerness of so many of the texts at the center of the canon. There are many reasons, then, why a volume such as this is needed and timely— indeed, long past due.

The great projects of gender criticism, feminism, and queer theory have arisen out of a largely French and Anglo-American critical heritage and have thus focused their energies on texts in those traditions. Yet even in this work, Italy is always there as constant point of reference, a comfortable intellectual background, an easy suggestion of origins and source material. But Italian texts are rarely the focus of the critical effort. Of the 15 essays in Jonathan Goldberg's groundbreaking *Queering the Renaissance*, for instance, only one deals with Italian literature.[4] In Louise Fradenburg and Carla Freccero's important *Premodern Sexualities*, Bruce Holsinger's provocative treatment of the homoerotics of the *Divine Comedy* is again the sole Italian offering.[5] These collections focus on the medieval and early modern periods, where attention to Italian texts among comparativists is most likely. As we move into the seventeenth century and beyond, it becomes even harder to find queer critical work on Italian literature. Critical studies and collections of queer readings in other national European literatures exist.[6] In Italian literature, there is no such volume. What follows offers a first attempt to fill this serious lacuna. This is not to say that important queer work on Italy is not being done. Indeed, something of a critical mass has been attained only very recently. Interestingly, much of this studies the medieval and early modern periods and comes from historians—historians of art, law, and theology.[7] Of course, scholarly interest in the construction of sexuality in the ancient world has been long-standing and engaged primarily with ancient Greece, though sexuality in ancient Rome has also been the object of close study.[8] Seldom as idealized as in ancient Greek literature, same-sex desire receives frank— sometimes satirical, sometimes romantic—treatment by Roman poets from Catullus (ca. 84–54 B.C.) to Juvenal (55–140). Virgil (70–19 B.C.) sings the noble love between hero warriors Nisus and Euryalus in the *Aeneid*: Homosexual love is there in the very foundations of empire.[9] Virgil also celebrates the idyllic desire of the shepherd Corydon for the fair young Alexis in the second eclogue. And Byrne Fone has recently called Petronius's *Satyricon* (first century of the common era) "the first gay novel."[10]

John Boswell's pioneering book, *Christianity, Social Tolerance, and Homosexuality: Gay People in Western Europe from the Beginning of the Christian Era to the Fourteenth Century*, includes discussions of sexuality in Rome, and the Latin poetic and theological tradition, some of which is of course Italian.[11] After all, we have the *locus classicus* of the Scholastic condemnation of sodomy, male and female, as the crime *contra naturam* from the hand of an Italian, the saint from Aquino.[12] Mark Jordan's recent work on the complex and confused history of *sodomia* in Latin patristics and Scholastics signals as a crucial chapter in the criminalization of same-sex behavior saint Peter Damian's eleventh-century anti-sodomy harangue, the *Liber gomorrhianus*.[13] In Jordan's reading, this text reflects very real and self-implicating anxieties about homosexual activity in medieval Italian monastic communities. Appropriately, homosexual horror lies at the murderous heart of the monastery in Umberto Eco's best-selling modern thriller, *The Name of the Rose*.[14] In his article on Italian literature in *The Lesbian and Gay Literary Heritage*, **Derek Duncan** cites Eco's construction of homosexuality, the secret crime of the community, as paradigmatic of the Italian tradition in general.[15] In Duncan's reading, homosexual contact is the constant, spectral threat in the homosocial monastic community, typified in Eco's novel by the pedagogical bond between William of Baskerville and Adso. Eco's novel is, in some ways, perfectly medieval in its consistent equation of homosexual activity to the perverse and the monstrous.[16] The well-known ancient practice of adolescent boy love, particularly in a pedagogical context, flourished in the late Middle Ages and Renaissance and casts reflections throughout the Italian tradition. One thinks most readily of Brunetto Latini and Dante.[17] The first panel of Benozzo Gozzoli's cycle on the life of St. Augustine in the church of Sant'Agostino in San Gimignano (1465) shows the innocent young saint being delivered into the hands of the bearded, sinister grammar masters at Tagaste. In the riotous school scene behind them, Gozzoli—in a visual pun that suggests the popular association of the grammar masters with pederasty—frames the naked, upturned buttocks of several of the young boys hoisted on their fellow students' shoulders as they receive a whipping from the master: the notorious mounting-the-horse discipline alluded to by Dante himself in his famous treatise on the Italian vernacular, *De vulgari eloquentia*.[18]

Theological condemnation of sodomy gained popular, vernacular currency in the sermons of Italian preachers such as Bernardino of Siena (1380–1444) and Girolamo Savonarola (1452–1498).[19] The church fathers' arcane and often illogical theorizing about same-sex desire of the sort studied by Boswell and Jordan was thus translated and transmitted to the masses: This constitutes an important first chapter for the history of queer desire in Italian letters. In this volume, **Bernard Schlager** calls our attention to the earlier and somewhat less-celebrated Giordano of Pisa (ca. 1260–1311), a contemporary of Dante. In Giordano's sermons, Schlager unveils a particularly forceful and influential early instance of vernacular discourse on same-sex desire. Thus we discover in medieval and early modern Italy—side by side in a difficult and sometimes destructive counterpoint—aggressive ecclesiastical denial of same-sex desire and tenacious ancient affirmation of sex between men, particularly in an educational context. It was only a matter of time before the new institutions of the rising city-states intervened.

This administrative intervention has been the object of some of the most significant recent scholarship on sexuality in medieval and Renaissance Italy. Michael Rocke's *Forbidden Friendships: Homosexuality and Male Culture in Renaissance Florence* uses legal archives to revive a Florentine society where male same-sex desire and activity was largely commonplace despite draconian attempts to legislate against it; where men over 18 commonly had sometimes long-term sexual liaisons with adolescent boys; where such relationships in no way invalidated or prevented their eventual acceptance of a wife and the civic responsibilities of the heterosexual family unit.[20] Rocke suggests that the Florentine state, unable to eradicate ancient sexual patterns, eventually settled on a policy of containment, surveillance, and even economic profit through fines. Thus, complicating the definition of sodomy in Italy between classical acceptance and Christian condemnation was a secular legal code at once severe and tacitly complicitous.[21]

These important contributions to the critical literature come from historians who look mainly at legal and administrative documents to evoke social history and suggest the lives of individuals. But Rocke is not averse to invoking the occasional "literary" text in his impressive array of evidence and, surely, the male homosexual/homosocial world he describes is relevant to our reading of some well-known early Italian texts. Although the focus of his investigation falls in the fifteenth century, the homosociality he details has its roots in the earlier *comune* and would not have been entirely unfamiliar to Dante (1265–1321), Petrarch (1304–1374), or Boccaccio (1313–1375). Surely it helps provide some historical context for the sodomites of the *Comedy* and for the long parodic tradition that includes such personages as Boccaccio's ser Ciappelletto and Pietro di Vinciolo in the *Decameron*, and in the sixteenth century, Bandello's Porcellio, perhaps the shrewdest advocate for gay love in the Renaissance.[22] When rebuked by his puzzled confessor for denying having had sex with young men, Porcellio dismantles the Scholastic condemnation of sodomy with admirable simplicity: " 'Oh, oh, padre reverendo, voi non mi sapeste interrogare. Il trastullarmi con i fanciulli a mel più naturale che non è il mangiare e il ber a l'uomo, e voi mi domandavate se io peccava contro natura. Andate, andate, messere, ché voi non sapete che cosa sia un buon boccone.' " ("But reverend father, you asked me the wrong question. For me, having fun with the boys is as natural as eating or drinking, and you asked if I had sinned against nature. So go on with yourself mister. You don't know a good thing when you see one.")[23] And while Dante and his Tuscan cohorts were engaged in the intensely heterosexual business of *dolce stil nuovo* love lyric, a smaller—but no less ardent—group of men in central Italy were professing their love and desire for other men in rhetorically innovative verse. Cecco Nuccoli (ca. 1290–1350) and Marino Ceccoli (died ca. 1371) were the leading exponents of the so-called Perugian school, whose homoerotic lyrics have been explained away as sterile rhetorical exercise by many traditional (read: straight) critics.[24]

The Renaissance recuperation of ancient mores opens a significant cultural space for the realization and inscription of same-sex desire. The Florentine humanist Marsilio Ficino (1433–1499) gave renewed philosophical vigor to Plato's notion of an ideal homosexual love that found its way into the Latin and Greek (and occasionally vernacular) lyric of the period by celebrated figures like Poliziano (1454–1494) and, much later, Torquato Tasso (1544–1595), as well as dozens of lesser-known *literati*.[25] Long before Rocke's important work on the subject, **Giovanni Dall'Orto** had posited that the textual profession of an idealized *eros socraticus* among many Renaissance artists and writers was merely a high-minded guise for homosexual desire. What is more, sodomy became the moral and criminal accusation of choice, a charge that artists and authors of the period hurled at one another with notable frequency and from which few escaped unscathed.[26] In his essay for this volume, Dall'Orto affirms the vitality of pedagogical sodomy through the Renaissance and into the Counter Reformation as a component of sixteenth- and seventeenth-century Italian libertinism. He calls our attention to the *Alcibiade fanciullo a scola* (*Alcibiades, Schoolboy*), a little-studied defense—indeed celebration—of pedagogical sodomy written by the priest Antonio Rocco (1576–1653).[27] Through Rocco's extraordinary tract, Dall'Orto argues for a reappreciation of the complexity and seriousness of libertine thought regarding sexuality.

In turn, **Margaret Gallucci** investigates perhaps the most famous and flamboyant of Renaissance defendants, Benvenuto Cellini (1500–1571), the only major artist of the period who was actually tried and convicted for sodomy. Cellini went on to proclaim his love of men in defiance of the Florentine court's attempt to humiliate him and has become a sort of early gay hero frequently anthologized in modern collections of gay verse and literature. For Gallucci, however, Cellini's life and writings represent a truly radical effort to queer gender and sexuality that cannot be contained by facile categorization. The intensely homosocial sexual ambiance of sixteenth-century Florence described by Rocke and elaborated upon by Gallucci again provides the backdrop for **Michael Wyatt**'s essay on the court of Giovanni de' Medici, Pope Leo X (1475–1521). Wyatt begins with the clear intimations of Leo's sodomitic interests found in Paolo Giovio's *Life of Leo X* in order to explore the secret, inner chamber of one of Leo's most prominent courtiers in Rome, Bernardo Dovizi da Bibbiena (1470–1520). Wyatt reads Bibbiena's room—a kind of Vatican sauna with frescoes—as important evidence for the queer erotics of Leo's entire court.

Mary-Michelle DeCoste's essay on female homoeroticism in Ariosto's *Orlando Furioso* (1532) brings us at long last to the almost completely unin-scribed story of female-female desire in the early period.[28] Despite its oddly heterosexualized outcome, the love story between the Spanish princess Fiordispina and the virgin warrior Bradamante challenges and titillates with its representations of lesbian love. For Decoste, Fiordispina is herself a warrior: an early gender warrior who subverts binary heteronormativity as Ariosto probes the fluid relationship between desire and narrative form. Gender and genre again intermingle in **Rosalind Kerr**'s fascinating study of Flaminio Scala's 1617 *Il marito* (*The Fake Husband*), the full-length play version of an earlier *commedia dell'arte* sketch that features a lesbian marriage. Kerr's reading teases out the inherent queerness of the *commedia dell'arte* as a genre that exerted constant, subversive pressure on social norms of class, gender, and sexuality.[29]

At the beginning of the following century, the Franciscan friar Lodovico Maria Sinistrari (1622–1701) in the *Peccatum mutum*, a manual for confessors, puzzles over various definitions of female sodomy in impressive anatomical detail. The good father's obvious befuddlement would be amusing were it not for the deadly seriousness of his moral outrage, which calls for torture and death by fire in the end.[30] In his famous Enlightenment tract on criminal law and punishment, *Dei delitti e delle pene*, Cesare Beccaria (1738–1794) demands the abolition of torture and the death penalty, but he continues to view sodomy, "la greca libidine," as a horrific crime and—much like the Scholastics centuries before him—a fruitless dissipation of nature's forces.[31] By contrast, the libertine adventurer Giacomo Casanova (1725–1798) cannot begin to take love between women seriously (though even he allows the Scholastic commonplace about homosexuality's alleged sterility to creep into his otherwise light-hearted remarks). In the famous history of his life, his young paramour's dalliance with another woman—both of them nuns, no less—serves as source of momentary amusement, mere prelude to the true gratification that only he and his phallus can provide: "At first, I just watched my two bacchantes indulge in their sterile contest, truly excited by their efforts and the contrasting colors, for one was blonde and the other brunette. But before long I, too, was aroused and, burning with every conceivable passion, I threw myself upon them, transporting them one by one to the very limits of desire and bliss."[32]

As we move from early modern to modern proper, it is striking how many canonical literary figures of the Settecento and Ottocento—romantics and Risorgimento revolutionaries alike—left traces of a queer sensibility. Neoclassical tragedian and patriot Vittorio Alfieri (1749–1803) writes rather frankly in chapter three of his autobiography ("First Symptoms of a Passionate Character") of his boyhood love for the adolescent novices in a nearby church.[33] Giacomo Leopardi's (1798–1837) passionate love letters to live-in companion Antonio Ranieri have been the subject of much recent controversy regarding the affective and sexual proclivities of Italy's great Romantic poet. Whatever the nature of Leopardi's attachment to his handsome friend, it seems clear that the amorous rhetoric of his letters surpasses even the conventions of Romantic friendship inasmuch as they were the source of scandal and, for Ranieri, no small embarrassment at the time.[34] Philologist and Risorgimento hero Luigi

Settembrini (1813–1876) left behind in his posthumous papers an extraordinary and erotically explicit tale of Greek love between beautiful young boys, *I neoplatonici*. Settembrini evidently composed this work during his long confinement in a Bourbon prison in Naples, and it was published only many years later in 1977 after decades of successful efforts to suppress it.[35]

But by the end of the nineteenth century, sexual science and recognizably modern notions of sexual identity had begun to take hold. It is to late nineteenth- and early twentieth-century theories of "sexuality" that **Daniela Danna** turns in her sociological assessment of lesbian representation in some dozen novels from the turn of the century through the 1930s. Danna's work places these Italian texts within the larger context of European fiction and social thought, from the reigning positivism of the day to the ground-breaking sexual science of Magnus Hirschfeld, as imported to Italy by the physician Aldo Mieli. Danna's emphasis is everywhere on the social: on editorial history and critical reception, on the public discourses incited by these early portraits of lesbian desire. As such, her piece provides important background for the essays that follow, all of which are engaged in the project of defining queer representation in twentieth-century Italian narrative and film.

A lesbian relationship is the narrative centerpiece of Liliana Cavani's film *The Berlin Affair* (1985), last of the so-called "German trilogy" that begins with *The Night Porter* (1974) and that is the focus of **Áine O'Healy**'s essay. It is again nineteenth-century male friendship and triangulated desire—this time among Nietzche, Paul Rée, and Lou Salomé in the 1880s—that furnishes the historical material for the second film in Cavani's trilogy, the 1977 *Beyond Good and Evil*. O'Healy draws expertly on Eve Sedgwick's reading of Nietzche's sexuality and her consequent notion of disavowal to understand Cavani's Salomé: at once dazzling beauty, stereotypical "mannish woman," and prototypical "fag hag" as she facilitates Rée's (queer) sexual liberation. Thus it is the second film that gives us the most complex and radically queer character in Cavani's trilogy. Queer representation at the turn of the century and then under fascism are the dual points of reference for **William Van Watson**'s exposition of the film versions of two queer classics of modern Italian narrative, Umberto Saba's *Ernesto* (written in 1953) and Giorgio Bassani's *The Gold-Rimmed Spectacles* (1958). Saba's deeply personal account stands in poignant testimony to the endurance of a premodern paradigm of sexual relationships between an older man and an adolescent boy well into the modern bourgeois era. Bassani's novella offers an exceptionally nuanced portrait of the lethal effects of middle-class conformity on Italian "queers" of the 1930s and 1940s, Jews and homosexuals. Bassani's effort is exceptional when one considers the facile, quasi-formulaic identification of queer sexuality *with* fascist tyranny in so much twentieth-century Italian film and fiction.[36]

A frank male homoeroticism finds expression in some of Italy's most celebrated modern poets, from the unabashed Sandro Penna (1906–1977) through Pier Paolo Pasolini (1922–1975) to Dario Bellezza (1944–1996).[37] Twentieth-century narrative and in particular the bourgeois novel have proven a more problematic setting for homosexual desire. Nonetheless, **Sergio Parussa** here argues that something of a queer tradition indeed exists in twentieth-century Italian narrative and can be distinguished not merely by homoerotic situations but by a consistent queering of narrative form that undermines the conventions of the novel. Looking at Saba and Pasolini, as well as less well-known writers such as Filippo de Pisis (1896–1956) and Giovanni Comisso (1895–1969), Parussa argues that it is precisely the lack of the social—of real social space for individual lives—that defines Italian homosexual characters through the century. He thus sees a series of fungible allegories invested, ultimately, in representing homoeroticism per se more than the lives of real people. These queer representations call into question the very notions of generic and national boundaries. Spatial and sexual transgression is again the theme of **Derek Duncan**'s focus on (de-)constructions of masculinity in the postwar novel. On Duncan's reading novelists such as Giorgio Bassani (1916–2000), Alberto Moravia (1907–1992), and Vasco Pratolini (1913–1991) plot normative male subjectivity as strict spatial containment. Duncan here employs recent work in queer theory and geography to consider the complex interactions among sexuality, race, and gender in Bassani's *Dietro la porta* (1964).

The social movements of the 1960s and 1970s witnessed the rise of an ardent theoretical and political feminism, lesbian feminism, and fledgling gay rights movement in Italy as elsewhere.[38] Inseparable from a radical and often utopian leftist politics, the discourse of gay liberation in Italy during this period is perhaps best exemplified by Mario Mieli's 1977 *Elementi di critica omosessuale*, which forwards a Marxist and psychoanalytic critique of patriarchal capitalism as the only true path to sexual liberation.[39] In his essay for this volume, **Marco Pustianaz** discusses the ways in which this revolutionary discourse finds aesthetic expression in two novels of the period, Mieli's own *Il risveglio dei Faraoni* (The Awakening of the Pharaohs) and Vittorio Pescatori's linguistically inventive *La maschia* (She-Male). Pustianaz's reading probes these not entirely successful attempts to unmask gender as performance (with particular regard for the novels' inadequate incorporation of female and lesbian subjectivities) while reevaluating the political and linguistic maneuvers of 1970s revolutionary social discourse.

The final decades of the millenium witnessed the emergence of two widely read gay male novelists, Pier Vittorio Tondelli (1955–1991) and Aldo Busi (b. 1948).[40] More recent generations of lesbian and gay authors and characters have become increasingly visible.[41] Something of a gay publishing industry has begun to develop, with lesbian and gay bookstores in several Italian cities and national gay periodicals in circulation.[42] In the last few years, Italian films with gay themes and characters have met with popularity at home and abroad; a gay television channel was born; Internet sites devoted to issues of interest to lesbians and gays have multiplied.[43] All of this attests to an unprecedented vibrancy and diversity of gay life in contemporary Italy.

As Italian gays and lesbians secure their political footing in that ancient society, cultural and textual identities past and present will continue to make their mark. We began this introduction by suggesting that Italian texts provide a privileged site for the delicate interaction between classical and Christian in the long story of same-sex desire. Further complicating matters much more recently are modern constructions of gay selfhood of Anglo-American and northern European provenance that more and more Italian lesbians and gays have embraced to various degrees. It will come as no surprise to anyone that same-sex desire has a rich history in Italy as elsewhere. But we suspect it may be news for some to learn just how many texts are out there waiting to be explored, how broadly queer desire informs (invades?) the Italian tradition. The present volume aims to provide some sense of the elaborate scope of same-sex desire at play in Italian books and movies. An enterprise such as this is necessarily varied in its themes and interests, but *Queer Italia* is bound together by its contributors' shared commitment to challenge the heteronormative bias of so much Italian criticism to date and to affirm the longevity and prominence of queer desire in Italian culture.

Gary P. Cestaro is Associate Professor of Italian language and literature and Director of the Program in Comparative Literature at DePaul University in Chicago. He is the author of the book *Dante and the Grammar of the Nursing Body* (Notre Dame, IN: University of Notre Dame Press, 2003). He has given talks and published articles on a variety of lesbian and gay topics in Italian literature.

Notes

1. Online article, "Gay Pride Week in Rome Ends with Triumphant Victory Parade" at http://www.cnn.com (8 July 2000). For press reports on more recent Italian pride celebrations (June 2003: Bari; June 2004: Grosseto), as well as other news of interest to the Italian lesbian and gay community, you can often

find links on the websites of the national organizations ArciGay (http://www. arcigay.it; includes a description of the organization's history and mission in English) and ArciLesbica (http://www.arcilesbica.it), as well as Giovanni Dall'Orto's website *La gaya scienza* (http://digilander.libero.it/giovannidallorto: click on "Attualità e vita omosessuale"); for a personal perspective on several recent pride events, see in particular Dall'Orto's "Degustazione alfabetica dei Gay Pride."

2. The June 2002 Pride celebration in Padua included a small but vociferous group of opposition protesters crosstown at the Church of St. Anthony, famed pilgrimage destination. Thus the classical/Catholic binary continues to thrive. For a deeply personal perspective on the thorny issue of homosexuality and the Church, see Marco Politi, *La confessione: Un prete gay racconta la sua storia*, preface by Luigi Bettazzi (Rome: Editori Riuniti, 2000).

3. See, however, the essay by Francesco Gnerre, *L'eroe negato: omosessualità e letteratura nel Novecento italiano*. Milan: Baldini & Castoldi, 2000 [1981]. *Franco-Italica* 6 (1994) is dedicated to homosexuality in modern French and Italian literature.

4. Alan K. Smith, "Fraudomy: Reading Sexuality and Politics in Burchiello" in: *Queering the Renaissance*, ed. Jonathan Goldberg (Durham, NC and London: Duke University Press, 1994), pp. 84–106.

5. *Premodern Sexualities*, ed. Louise Fradenburg and Carla Freccero (New York and London: Routledge, 1996), pp. 243–74.

6. See, for instance, *Homosexualities and French Literature: Cultural Contexts/Critical Texts*, eds. George Stambolian and Elaine Marks (Ithaca, NY and London: Cornell University Press, 1979) or, more recently, Lawrence R. Schehr, *Alcibiades at the Door: Gay Discourses in French Literature* (Stanford, CA: Stanford University Press, 1995); and on Spanish and Portuguese literature, *Queer Iberia: Sexualities, Cultures, and Crossings from the Middle Ages to the Renaissance*, eds. Josiah Blackmore and Gregory S. Hutcheson (Durham, NC and London: Duke University Press, 1999); my thanks to the editors of *Queer Iberia* for the title of the present volume.

7. In art history, see in particular James M. Saslow, *Ganymede in the Renaissance: Homosexuality in Art and Society* (New Haven, CT: Yale University Press, 1986). Saslow has also produced an edition and translation of Michelangelo's poems that corrects earlier, bowdlerized editions that had effaced same-sex desire: *The Poetry of Michelangelo: An Annotated Translation* (New Haven, CT: Yale University Press, 1991).

8. One thinks most readily of the work of the Italian historian Eva Cantarella, *Secondo natura: la bisessualità nel mondo antico* (Rome: Editori Riuniti, 1988); *Bisexuality in the Ancient World*, trans. Cormac Ó Cuilleanáin (New Haven, CT: Yale University Press, 1992); and Craig A. Williams, *Roman Homosexuality: Ideologies of Masculinity in Classical Antiquity* (Oxford: Oxford University Press, 1999).

9. See *Aeneid* V.294–361 and particularly IX.176–449; and John F. Makowski, "Nisus and Euryalus: A Platonic Relationship," *The Classical Journal* 85, 1 (October/November 1989), pp. 1–15.

10. *The Columbia Anthology of Gay Literature: Readings from Western Antiquity to the Present Day*, ed. Byrne R. S. Fone (New York: Columbia University Press, 1998), p. 71; for selections in English from the Latin poets with historical background, see pp. 61–88.

11. John Boswell, *Christianity, Social Tolerance, and Homosexuality: Gay People in Western Europe from the Beginning of the Christian Era to the Fourteenth Century* (Chicago: University of Chicago Press, 1980).

12. For queer perspectives on Aquinas and sodomy, see Boswell, pp. 318–32; see also Mark D. Jordan, *The Invention of Sodomy in Christian Theology* (Chicago: University of Chicago Press, 1997), pp. 136–58.

13. See Jordan; for an English translation, see the *Book of Gomorrah: An Eleventh Century Treatise Against Clerical Homosexual Practices*, ed. and trans. Pierre J. Payer (Waterloo, Ontario, Canada: Wilfrid Laurier University Press, 1982). For an online Italian edition with commentary, see http://www.swif.uniba.it/lei/personali/zavattero/traduzioneLG_a.htm.

14. Umberto Eco, *Il nome della rosa* (Milan: Bompiani, 1980); *The Name of the Rose*, trans. William Weaver (San Diego, CA: Harcourt Brace Jovanovich, 1983).

15. "Italian Literature" (pp. 391–97) in: *The Gay and Lesbian Literary Heritage: A Reader's Companion to the Writers and their Works from Antiquity to the Present*, ed. Claude J. Summers (New York: H. Holt, 1995). On Eco's novel, see also Teresa de Lauretis, "Gaudy Rose: Eco and Narcissism" in: *Technologies of Gender: Essays on Theory, Film, and Fiction* (London: Macmillan, 1987), pp. 51–69.

16. To some extent Eco's novel and particularly Jean-Jacques Annaud's 1986 film featuring a young Christian Slater as Adso comfort the presumed heterosexual reader/viewer by dramatically heterosexualizing Adso in the scene of his copulation with the peasant girl (*Nome della Rosa*, pp. 246–53; *Name of the Rose*, pp. 243–50). Eco's novel, at least, allows the aging narrator Adso his pederastic phantasies (*Nome della Rosa*, p. 143; *Name of the Rose*, p. 137).

17. Dante provides the only significant exception to the general lack of work on Italian texts among critics interested in sexuality. See, for instance, Joseph Pequigney, "Sodomy in Dante's *Inferno* and *Purgatorio*," *Representations* 36 (Fall 1991), pp. 22–42; Bruce Holsinger, "Sodomy and Resurrection: The Homoerotic Subject of the *Divine Comedy*," pp. 243–74 in the *Premodern Sexualities* volume referenced above; the appendix on "Dante and Homosexuality" in the edition and translation of *Inferno* by Robert M. Durling and Ronald L. Martinez (New York: Oxford University Press, 1996), who write, in reference to Dante and sodomy, "It is difficult not to read cantos 15 and 16 as an acknowledgment that Dante had felt such desires (p. 559)." See also Cestaro, "Queering Nature, Queering Gender: Dante and Sodomy" in: *Dante for the New Millenium*, ed. Teodolinda Barolini and H. Wayne Storey (New York: Fordham University Press, 2003), pp. 90–10?. A version of this paper was also presented in a session called "Dante On Fire Island," organized by James Miller, at the Queer Middle Ages conference at CUNY, 5–7 November 1998,

where Michael Camille delivered a keynote address, now published: "The Pose of the Queer: Dante's Gaze, Brunetto Latini's Body" in: *Queering the Middle Ages*, eds. Glenn Burger and Steven F. Kruger [*Medieval Cultures* 27] (Minneapolis and London: University of Minnesota Press, 2001), pp. 57–86.

18. *De vulgari eloquentia* I.vii.2. The mounting the horse image recurred as marginal ornamentation in a number of early printed editions of various grammatical and rhetorical texts. For a closer exploration of this tradition and its relation to sodomy in the grammar classroom, see my forthcoming " 'They all seem to be stained with this vice': Sodomy and the Grammar Masters in Commentaries on Dante's *Commedia*."

19. On Bernardino and sodomy, see the recent study by Franco Mormando, *The Preacher's Demons: Bernardino of Siena and the Social Underworld of Early Renaissance Italy* (Chicago: University of Chicago Press, 1999). One invaluable source on homosexuality in Italian history and literature is Giovanni Dall'Orto's website *La gaya scienza* (http://digilander.libero.it/giovannidallorto), which includes dozens of relatively brief but informative biographies of many of the figures mentioned in this volume, including Savonarola, from a gay perspective. Many of these biographies reprise articles that Dall'Orto wrote for journals such as *Babilonia* and *Sodoma*.

20. Michael J. Rocke, *Forbidden Friendships: Homosexuality and Male Culture in Renaissance Florence* (New York: Oxford University Press, 1996).

21. Although not as focused on same-sex activity as Rocke, Guido Ruggiero has investigated the legislation of sexuality during a similar period in Venice: *The Boundaries of Eros: Sex Crime and Sexuality in Renaissance Venice* (New York: Oxford University Press, 1985); on sodomy, see in particular pp. 109–45. Judith Brown's *Immodest Acts: The Life of a Lesbian Nun in Renaissance Italy* (New York: Oxford University Press, 1986) provides insight into the almost completely uninscribed story of female homosexuality in the early period.

22. See *Decameron* I.i for the anticlerical sodomitic caricature of the Florentine ser Ciappelletto and V.ii, where the Perugian Pietro di Vinciolo eventually comes to an arrangement with his frustrated wife that allows them both to indulge their desire for men. It appears that the sodomite became something of a stock character in the Italian novella tradition. See Rocke, pp. 123–30, who mentions sodomite characters in novellas by Giovanni Sercambi (1347–1424), Gentile Sermini (fifteenth century), Giovanni Sabadino degli Arienti (ca. 1445–1510), and Francesco Maria Molza (1489–1544). For Porcellio, see Matteo Bandello (1485–1561), *Novelle* I.vi.

23. English trans. Cestaro. Matteo Bandello, *Le novelle*, ed. Giuseppe Guido Ferrero (Turin: Utet, 1974). Bandello's character may be modeled on the humanist Giannantonio de' Pandoni, nicknamed "il Porcellio" (before 1409–after 1485); see the biography at Dall'Orto, *La gaya scienza*.

24. For selections in English from both poets, see *The Columbia Anthology*, pp. 139–43. Steven Botterill has taken to task mainstream Italian critics for reading as parody or mere formality what he feels are heartfelt love lyrics between these men in the best classical tradition. See Botterill's article on

"Minor Writers" of the Trecento in: *The Cambridge History of Italian Literature*, ed. Peter Brand and Lino Pertile (Cambridge: Cambridge University Press, 1996), pp. 108–27 and particularly pp. 116–17 ("The *perugini*") and by the same author, "Cecco Nuccoli: An Introduction," *The Italianist* 8 (1988), pp. 16–32 and "Autobiography and Artifice in the Medieval Lyric: The Case of Cecco Nuccoli," *Italian Studies* 46 (1991), pp. 37–57. Fabian Alfie, "Men on Bottom: Homoeroticism in Cecco Angiolieri's Poetry," *Medievalia et Humanistica* 28 (2001), pp. 25–44 explores homoeroticism in the verse of master medieval Italian parodist Cecco Angiolieri (ca. 1260–1312), a nearly precise contemporary of both Dante and Giordano da Pisa. Alfie's essay poses important questions about the rhetoric of a lyric tradition—parodic and otherwise—that formulaically casts the male as passive, penetrated victim. For a thorough scholarly survey of homoeroticism in Italian lyric through Dante that includes discussions of Brunetto Latini and Bondie Dietaiuti, Sienese and Perugian poets, see Giovanni Dall'Orto, "L'omosessualità nella poesia volgare italiana fino al tempo di Dante: Appunti," *Sodoma* 3,3 (Spring–Summer, 1986), pp. 13–37.

25. For Poliziano's several homoerotic Greek epigrams, see Angelo Poliziano, "Epigrammi greci [1471–1494]," ed. Enzo Savino, *Poesia* 7,74 (1994), pp. 4–20 and Giovanni Dall'Orto at *La gaya scienza*, where you can also find Tasso's love sonnet to a young man (as published in Luigi Roncoroni, *Genio e pazzia in Torquato Tasso* [Turin: Bocca, 1896], p. 155) as well as details of Tasso's apparent obsession with the young Luca Scalabrino. On the homoerotics of humanism and Poliziano, see Alan Stewart, *Close Readers: Humanism and Sodomy in Early Modern England* (Princeton, NJ: Princeton University Press, 1997), pp. 3–37. Other Renaissance writers who produced homoerotic lyric include: Pacifico Massimo d'Ascoli (ca. 1400–1500), Niccolò Lelio ("Cosmico," ca. 1420–1500), Giulio Pomponio Leto (1428–1498), Filippo Buonaccorsi (1437–1496), Girolamo Balbi (ca. 1450–1535), Benedetto Varchi (1503–1565), and Francesco Beccuti ("il Coppetta," 1509–1553). For selections in English from many of the above-mentioned, see *The Columbia Anthology*, pp. 131–50.

26. Giovanni Dall'Orto, "Socratic Love as a Disguise for Same-Sex Love in the Italian Renaissance," *Journal of Homosexuality* 16,1/2 (1989), pp. 33–65. Of course, a rich burlesque and satirical literature throughout the Renaissance included intricate (and sometimes obscene) depictions of sodomy and same-sex desire in texts such as Stefano Finiguerri (called "il Za"), "La buca di Montemorello" and "Il gagno" (1407–1412); Antonio Beccadelli (called "il Panormita," 1394–1471), *Hermaphroditus* (1425); Antonio Vignali, *La cazzarìa* (ca. 1525). Many of the satirical verses of Antonio Francesco Grazzini (called "il Lasca," 1503–1584) profess love of young men, as well as at least an occasional poem by Pietro Aretino (1492–1556), particularly in the bawdy *Sonetti lussuriosi*. For scurrilous charges of sodomy against Aretino, see the verses of his disaffected former pupil Niccolò Franco (1515–1570) in the *Priapea* (particularly VII, "Buggera il papa, e tutti i suoi prelati"; "The pope's a bugger and so are all his prelates"); for a selection, see *Poesia italiana: il Cinquecento*, ed. Giulio Ferroni (Milan: Garzanti, 1978), pp. 382–89. For Finiguerri and his

milieu, see D. Guerri, *La corrente popolare nel Rinascimento* (Florence: Sansoni, 1931) and Antonio Lanza, *Polemiche e berte letterarie nella Firenze del primo Quattrocento* (Rome: Bulzoni, 1972), particularly pp. 103–70. There are several modern editions of Beccadelli's text, including a recent bilingual Latin/English edition: *Hermaphroditus*, ed. and trans. Eugene O'Connor (Lanham, MD: Lexington Books, 2001). For Vignali, see Antonio Vignali, *La cazzaria*, ed. Pasquale Stoppelli (Rome: Edizioni dell'elefante, 1984); *The Book of the Prick*, ed. and trans. Ian Frederick Moulton (New York: Routledge, 2003).

27. Antonio Rocco, *L'Alcibiade fanciullo a scola*, ed. Laura Coci (Rome: Salerno, 1988). For selections in English, see *The Columbia Anthology*, pp. 151–56. Italians seem to have enjoyed something of a national reputation for sodomy throughout Renaissance Europe and into the seventeenth century. Rocke, p. 3, reports that *Florenzer* was a synonym for sodomite in fourteenth-century German. In the seventeenth century, see the amusing anecdotes related by Tallement des Réaux (1619–1692), *Historiettes*, ed. Antoine Adam (Dijon: Gallimard, 1961), volume II, pp. 739–41, "Contes d'Italiens Sodomites" ("Tales About Italian Sodomites").

28. On the history of female homoeroticism in the ancient world and early Church, see the important book by Bernadette J. Brooten, *Love Between Women: Early Christian Responses to Female Homoeroticism* (Chicago: University of Chicago Press, 1996). Karma Lochrie has done important work on female same-sex desire in medieval literature and the methodological difficulties posed by such research. Lochrie is particularly interested in the (homo)eroticism inherent in the writings of late medieval female mystics. On Italian texts see, for instance, her discussion of Catherine of Siena (pp. 188–89) in: *Constructing Medieval Sexuality*, eds. Karma Lochrie, Peggy McCracken, James A. Schultz (Minneapolis: University of Minnesota Press, 1997).

29. Giovanni Faustini's libretto for the opera *La Callisto* by Francesco Cavalli (1602–1676) also plays with the lesbian intimations of the Greek myth; see Giovanni dall'Orto, "Orsa cerca orsa," *Babilonia* 137 (October 1995), pp. 68–70.

30. For Sinistrari, see the discussion in Lilian Faderman, *Surpassing the Love of Men: Romantic Friendship and Love Between Women from the Renaissance to the Present* (New York: William Morrow, 1981), pp. 35–37.

31. See paragraph xxxi entitled "Delitti di prova difficile" ("Crimes that are Difficult to Prove").

32. English translation Cestaro from the original French Giacomo Casanova, *Mémoirs*, 3 vols., ed. Robert Abirached and Elio Zorzi (Tours: Gallimard, 1958), vol. I, p. 886: "D'abord simple spectateur du combat stérile que se livraient mes deux bacchantes, je jouissais de leurs efforts et du contraste des couleurs, car l'une était blonde et l'autre brune; mais bientôt, irrité moi-même par tous les feux de la volupté, je me jetai sur elles, et tour à tour je les fis expirer d'amour et de bonheur"; see also Faderman, pp. 26–27.

33. For the text, see Dall'Orto, *La gaya scienza* (click on "Testi gay del passato" and "Secolo XVIII").

34. See the closely reasoned essay by Giovanni Dall'Orto at *La gaya scienza*, which argues that Leopardi was certainly in love with Ranieri, who did not, however, return the sentiment. For recent controversy, see Ansa and Adnkronos (Italian news agencies) news releases for 24 July 2002 on a recently rediscovered letter to Ranieri in the Biblioteca Nazionale in Naples. Professor Giulio Ferroni of the University of Rome dismissed reports of Leopardi's homosexuality as so much nonsense. The Centro Nazionale di Studi Leopardiani threatened a lawsuit against the newspaper *Libero* for alleging that Leopardi was gay.

35. *I neoplatonici*, ed. Raffaele Cantarella (Milan: Rizzoli, 1977), but see also the more recent edition by Sellerio editore (Palermo, 2001) with endnote by Beppe Benvenuto, pp. 57–67, which details the fascinating history of the manuscript, willfully kept secret by illustrious critics like Benedetto Croce and Francesco Torraca as not to sully Settembrini's reputation as a national hero; for more on Settembrini, see also the last essay in this volume by Pustianaz, note 52.

36. One thinks immediately of the Nazi villainess Ingrid in Rossellini's classic Neorealist film *Open City*, of Moravia's novel *Il conformista* and Bertolucci's film of the same. As Duncan comments in his article for the *Gay and Lesbian Literary Heritage* (p. 394): "Fascism is a lesbian." See Duncan's essay in this volume for a more elaborate consideration of the relationship between Italian fascism and (homo)sexuality.

37. For selections in Italian from both Italian and foreign modern gay poetry, see *Il senso del desiderio: poesia gay dell'età moderna*, ed. Nicola Gardini (Milan: Crocetti, 2001). For Sandro Penna in English, see *The Columbia Anthology*, pp. 472–74.

38. For a primer on Italian feminist thought in English, see Lucia Chiavola Birnbaum, *Liberazione della donna: Feminism in Italy* (Middletown, CT: Wesleyan University, 1986) and *Italian Feminist Thought: A Reader*, ed. Paola Bono and Sandra Kemp (Cambridge, MA and Oxford: Basil Blackwell, 1991); see pp. 162–80 on lesbian feminism. On the Italian theorists of sexual difference that emerged in the 1980s, particularly in connection with thinkers from the Diotima research group such as Luisa Muraro and Adriana Cavarero, see the publication of the Milan Women's Bookstore Collective, *Sexual Difference* (Bloomington and Indianapolis: Indiana University Press, 1990), with its valuable introduction by Teresa de Lauretis. On the history of the lesbian and gay rights movement in Italy, see Gianni Rossi Barilli, *Il movimento gay in Italia* (Milan: Feltrinelli, 1999).

39. Mario Mieli, *Elementi di critica omosessuale* (Turin: Einaudi, 1977) and Mario Mieli, *Homosexuality and Liberation: Elements of a Gay Critique*, trans. David Fernbach (London: Gay Men's Press, 1980). Feltrinelli is currently reissuing all of Mieli's works, including an edition of the *Elementi* with accompanying critical essays: *Elementi di critica omosessuale*, ed. Gianni Rossi Barilli and Paola Mieli (Milan: Feltrinelli, 2002); see the essay by Pustianaz in this volume, note seven. The University of Michigan Press is considering an English version of this new edition.

40. Tondelli's final and, from a gay perspective at least, most significant novel, *Camere separate: un itinerario erratico nella memoria e nell'amore* (Milan: Bompiani, 1989), enjoys an English translation, *Separate Rooms*, trans. Simon Pleasance (London: Serpent's Tail, 1992). Several of Busi's satirical and linguistically inventive works have been translated into English; these include *The Standard Life of a Temporary Pantyhose Salesman*, trans. Raymond Rosenthal (London: Faber and Faber, 1989) and *Sodomies in Eleven Point*, trans. Stuart Hood (London: Faber and Faber, 1992).

41. For starters, see Tondelli's Progetto Under 25 Series and the three volumes in the OffSide series published by Edizioni Libreria Croce.

42. Edizioni Libreria Croce in Rome and Zoe in Forlì publish lesbian and gay narrative and general interest books. The Libreria Babele in Milan is also a center for lesbian and gay culture. Their extensive website at http://www.libreriababele.it catalogs and surveys much of their inventory and offers an invaluable, up-to-date source of information on lesbian and gay publishing in Italy. The most significant periodicals at the moment are *Babilonia, Guide, Pride* (Milan) and *Aut* (Rome).

43. Some of the most successful Italian films of recent years involving same-sex desire are by the Turkish-born Ferzan Özpetek (b. 1959): the award-winning *Bagno turco/Hamam* (*Steam: The Turkish Bath*, 1997) the hugely popular *Le fate ignoranti* (*His Secret Life*, 2001), and most recently *La finestra di fronte* (*The Window Across the Way*, 2003). For television, see online http://www.gaytv.it. Other websites of interest include: http://it.gay.com (general and current events), http://www.digayproject.org (site of the Di' Gay Project, Rome), http://www.mariomieli.org (site of the Circolo di Cultura Omosessuale Mario Mieli, Rome), http://www.gayroma.it (site of GayRoma, Rome), http://www.gayamater.cjb.net (site of the lesbian and gay student group at the University of Bologna), http://www.arcigay.it and http://www.women.it/arciles (sites of ArciGay and ArciLesbica, the national associations headquartered in Bologna with chapters in many Italian cities), and http://www.towanda.it (online lesbian review).

The Dead Sea of Sodomy: Giordano da Pisa on Men Who Have Sex With Men

Bernard Schlager

B etween the years 1303 and 1307 and again in 1309, the Dominican friar Giordano of Pisa (ca. 1260–1311) undertook an active and popular preaching ministry in the city of Florence. Some seven hundred of Giordano's Florentine sermons survive from these years (most likely written down by several different recorders as they were being delivered), and they reveal a preacher at the height of his powers. Certainly erudite in their content (Giordano quotes a wide range of secular and religious authorities from the classical era as well as his own), these sermons also reflect the talents of a preaching friar able to sermonize effectively on a wide variety of topics to an audience he understood very well. To the citizens of the Florentine commune Giordano condemned the practice of *vendetta* and urged them to build a city of fraternal love; to bankers and merchants he warned of the dangers of avarice and usury; to women he spoke about the virtues of marriage and the evils of prostitution; and to people of all classes he engaged in catechetical preaching—expounding on the tenets of Christianity and explaining the mysteries of the faith to his listeners.[1]

Now we know relatively little about this Dominican from Pisa: Giordano was born around the year 1260 into the Orlandini family, probably in the Tuscan town of Rivalto. After studies at the University of Paris, he moved to Pisa, where he was received into the Order of Preachers at the priory of Santa Caterina in the year 1280. As a young Dominican, Giordano studied in Bologna and Paris (where he lived again between 1285 and 1288). Some accounts report that he engaged in study and preaching missions throughout various parts of the continent and that he visited the Dominican priory at Cologne. We know, as well, that he was appointed to serve as conventual lector at the priory of Santa Maria Novella in Florence from 1305 to 1306, and it was during this stay in Florence that Giordano preached many of the sermons that have survived. In 1307 he was called back to Pisa to serve as a biblical lecturer at Santa Caterina, and finally in 1311 he was sent to study for his *magister* degree at Paris (a destination he never reached, dying in Piacenza while en route to France).[2]

Giordano's training in Pisa, Bologna, and Paris indicates that he received the best education that the order of his day had to offer. By the time he began his novitiate and early studies at Pisa, the convent school had developed a solid reputation among the friars as one of the most effective preaching schools in the order's Roman province. For much of the thirteenth century, in fact, the convent of Santa Caterina was, according to Mulchahey, "a special place which commanded the best-qualified men in the province as teachers and developed many of the same pedagogical features seen at [the Dominican priory of] Naples";[3] it was also where Thomas Aquinas taught in the early 1270s.[4] The Bologna priory of San Niccolò had achieved the rank of a *studium generale* in 1248, a full generation before the time of Giordano's residence there and, of course, the Dominican school at Saint Jacques in Paris (recognized as the order's first *studium.* In the 1220 Constitutions of the Dominican Order) was located in the city with the most prestigious theology faculty in all of Europe.[5]

Giordano's extant sermons reveal not only the depth of theological training that he received as a friar preacher; they also provide a valuable example of an important and sustained focus of much early Dominican preaching—the salvation of the laity.[6] In a world undergoing profound economic, social, and political upheavals, Dominican preaching friars of the early fourteenth century saw the new urban classes in such cities as Florence, Pisa, and Siena as some of their most important constituencies. Indeed, all of Giordano's Florentine sermons (both those delivered to large congregations assembled in the piazza of Santa Maria Novella and those preached in the more intimate meetings of Dominican lay confraternities) have as their aim the conversion of his urban audiences to a more authentic Christian life.[7]

As is well known, much mendicant preaching in the late medieval period was undertaken with the goal of ridding the urban centers of Europe (such as the communes of late medieval Tuscany) of a wide range of behaviors that churchmen of the day viewed as especially detrimental to Christian living. In line with other Italian mendicant preachers of his era, Giordano was devoted to fostering (one is tempted to say even "creating") the *bene comune*, purged of a whole array of activities that he deemed destructive of good morals and religious faith itself.[8] While the city was the locus of learning, artistic progress, and business opportunity, it was seen by Giordano and many other mendicant preachers of the late medieval period as a haven of ignorance, vice, and economic exploitation as well.[9]

Chief among the urban vices that Giordano discusses in his sermons are those connected with capitalistic enterprise: the lending of money at interest, the exploitation of workers, and the many evils wrought by a cash-based economic system. Perhaps most destructive to urban life was the rampant greed for money that, in turn, led Florentines into social and even military conflict. As Daniel Lesnick points out, Giordano saw the sin of greed as destructive not only to society as a whole but, more ominously for the Christian person, as catastrophic for individual salvation.[10] Incessant violence was another evil confronting residents of early fourteenth-century Italian communes and, as we know, the city of Florence was particularly prone to internal and external strife in the late medieval period. Since the civil war between the Black and White factions of the Guelphs had ended only the year before Giordano's move to Florence in 1303, it is understandable that this Dominican's preaching, if it were to be relevant, had to deal with the poison of civil strife that had so damaged the communal spirit of the city. Quite understandably, then, the interminable feuds between powerful Florentine families were another aspect of urban discord that attracted Giordano's attention, and he argued that such feuds were caused by the sinful pride of their combatants.[11]

Sodomy was another vice that Giordano of Pisa condemned and strove to eradicate through his preaching.[12] While we can agree with Michael Rocke that Giordano's polemical complaint that " 'nearly all . . . or at least the majority' of Florentine men were sodomites"[13] is hardly an objective observation of sexual mores in early fourteenth-century Florence, it is significant that sodomy was seen by this friar as a common enough corruption among the male citizens of this city to warrant its detailed discussion in a most public venue. Indeed, Giordano seems eager to expose what many earlier and contemporaneous preachers were reluctant to put into print, much less preach in public. Several of Giordano's sermons make reference to sodomy among males, but a sermon preached in the open-air piazza of Santa Maria Maggiore on December 28, 1305 (the Feast of the Holy Innocents) includes the most extensive and noteworthy discussion of what he termed the "worst sin of sodomy."[14] A close reading of this sermon is worthwhile because it reveals an early example of the type of virulent antisodomy preaching that will appear in the sermons of later mendicant preachers, such as the Franciscan Saint Bernardino of Siena

(1380–1444) and the Dominican Girolamo Savonarola (1452–1498).[15] More significantly, however, this sermon is a remarkable instance of the transmission to a popular audience of the theological attacks on male homosexual activity that had been crafted by influential thirteenth-century Dominicans.

Giordano's sermon for the Holy Innocents begins in typical fashion with a biblical quotation, in this case a passage from the Book of Jeremiah as quoted in Matthew's account of the slaughter of first-born sons in the town of Bethlehem at the time of Jesus's birth: "A voice is heard in Ramah."[16] After establishing these slain innocents as genuine martyrs (equal in stature, he says, to the early martyrs St. John the Baptist and St. Stephen), the preacher outlines the three chief sins of King Herod who, according to the biblical story, had ordered the murder of these children. In addition to his pride (*superbia*) and lack of faith (*infedelitade*), Herod was guilty of a gross evil (*perversitade*) that led him to attempt to thwart the will of God when he slew the male babies of Bethlehem. The cries of the distraught mothers rose up to heaven and made known to all people the horrendous deeds of this Judean king. Theirs was the "voice heard in Ramah," the voice that God uses at all times and all places as a weapon against those who sin. Giordano continues:

> "*Vox in Rama audita est.* Di questa parola predichiamo stamane: la quale parola chiude tutte le vie onde l'uomo pecca o può peccare. Vedi che ha fatto Iddio, acciocchè non possi peccare, che t'ha chiuse e serrate tutte le vie, onde l'uomo avrebbe materia di peccare; tutte l'ha chiuse Iddio."

> "*A voice was heard in Ramah.* It is this word that I preach on this morning: such a word closes all the ways by which a man sins or is able to sin. You see that God has done this so that you cannot sin, [namely,] he has closed and shut all of the ways by which a man would have the means to sin. All of these has God closed off."[17]

Continuing in scholastic mode by carefully defining his terms, Giordano tells his audience that there are three paths to sin: concealment (*occultatio*), evasion (*evasio*), and depravity (*infamia*). For Giordano, the first of this trio is the most common: "[M]olti peccano perchè non sono veduti da molti" ([M]any sin because they are not seen by many).[18] Without notoriety there is no shame and, hence, the sinner believes that he will not be punished because his actions are unknown. Of course, this is foolish since *all* ways of sinning are ultimately frustrated by God. In Giordano's reasoning, if the sinner realized that his sins were visible, perhaps he would be less apt to commit them.

Giordano is keen to keep before his assembled listeners this unsurprising claim that God sees all sin. Just as the slaughter of the Holy Innocents was made known through the cries of their mothers, so too are all sins (even those thought by sinners to be accomplished in secret) known to God. If only people remembered that God as just judge punishes every sinner, perhaps they would stop sinning. Giordano asks why most people who live under the power of an earthly king fear to offend him in thought, word, or deed lest they be punished and yet, nevertheless, foolishly offend a heavenly and omniscient God by their sins? He concludes his discussion of the illusions and dangers of hidden sin by reminding his audience that punishment will surely follow any and all unforgiven evil-doing:

"Adunque, come é ardito il peccatore di fare il peccato, sappiendo che Iddio il vede, e tutti gli angioli di paradiso e tutti i santi, e sa ch'egli é giudice giusto e che punirà tutto, e non può fuggire nè campare dal giudicio suo?"

"Therefore, how foolhardy is the sinner who commits a sin, since he well knows that God sees it—as do all of the angels of paradise and all of the saints—and he knows that God is a just judge who will punish all sin, and that he can neither flee nor escape His justice."[19]

That there are many people who seem to sin without being punished is no reason, Giordano argues, for the sinner to conclude that he might escape God's wrath. Nor should the promise of God's mercy lead the sinner to hope that his unseen sin might be forgiven.[20] In the end all sin, however small, is known to God and duly punished.

Having argued that no sin can be hidden from God and that punishment for all unforgiven human evil-doing is inevitable, Giordano sensibly notes that there are, in fact, degrees of sin—some sins are indeed more serious than others. Continuing with his image of sin as a voice that is heard, the preacher says that some sins produce a very small sound, while others (like the slaughter of the Holy Innocents) produce a veritable outcry because of their gravity. It is at this point in his sermon that Giordano makes an abrupt and significant shift from a general discussion of sin and punishment to his main topic, the condemnation of the specific sin of male sodomy. "Quale è questo grido così grande?" (What is this cry so great?), Giordano asks his listeners with appropriate rhetorical flourish. "Questo sono i grandi peccati," he answers, "siccome quel grave peccato maladetto contra natura." (It is for the big sins such as that grave and accursed sin against nature.)[21] The implication here is clear: Although sodomites may believe that they sin in secret, theirs is a sin that raises a veritable cry to heaven that God well hears and of which He takes careful notice. In the same way that King Herod's murder of innocent children rose to heaven on the wails of their anguished mothers, so too does the evil of sodomitical vice ascend to heaven.

Drawing once again on urban imagery, Giordano next outlines in detail the fate of the five cities of Sodom for their wicked sin. These cities "of the plain" were destroyed and presently lay at the bottom of the Dead Sea because of the sexual practices of many, or even most, of their male citizens. It is significant for Giordano that these ancient cities now lie at the bottom of a sea named "dead"—so-called because it is a body of water in which no living thing can be born or survive, a sea that emits the constant stink of sulphur. It is said, Giordano relates, that beautiful apples adorn trees that surround the shore of this Dead Sea. These apples are beautiful to the eye but, when opened, reveal insides of smoke and ashes. The preacher concludes:

> "Queste cose si dicono del Mare morto, che significano direttamente le condizioni di quello pessimo peccato della sodomia, il quale è sterile e sanza frutto nullo, il quale pute a Dio e a tutto l' mondo."

> "These are the things that are said about the Dead Sea, which signify directly the conditions of that worst sin of sodomy, which is sterile and without any fruit and which stinks before God and the whole world."[22]

Addressing the audience assembled before him on the Feast of Holy Innocents, Giordano warns that all those in his own day who are guilty of the sin that destroyed the citizens of Sodom so long ago deserve both the name "sodomite" and their punishment of eternal fire. Many Florentines have become sodomites, the preacher claims, and he warns all of the citizens assembled before him in dire tones, calling upon them to acknowledge and repent of this great sin in their midst:

> "O quanti ci ha di quelli cittadini in questa cittade! Anzi tutti o la maggior parte ne sono cittadini; anzi quasi è convertita questa cittade in Soddoma. Non pensate che i loro sieno maggiori peccati ch' e' nostri, no, o che noi siamo meno peccatori di loro; anzi potremo dire con verità, che più abbondano oggi in noi, e spezialmente in questa cittade, che non fece in loro."

> "O how many of those citizens [of Sodom] are in this city! All—or at the very least, the majority of us—are citizens and it is as if this city has been changed into Sodom. And do not think that they were greater sinners than we are. For it is not so. Nor should you believe that we are lesser sinners than they were. Rather, I can truthfully say that there are more of them among us today in this city than there were among them."[23]

As with the sins of usury, hatred, and murder (against which Giordano says he has preached tirelessly to the people of Florence), sodomy for this Dominican is an insidious sin that, left unchecked, will multiply quickly among the populace.[24] And yet, Giordano points out to his listeners that sodomy is of a different order altogether than other sins rampant among Florentines because of the intensity of divine wrath that it elicits. The preacher recalls for his congregation that the destruction of the city of Sodom came after the destruction of nearly all humanity in the Great Flood as described in *Genesis*. But whereas the people of Noah's day had been forewarned of their impending doom, no such warning was granted to the citizens of Sodom: "[M]a di subito mandò angeli e profondolli in nabisso; ma prima venne fuoco dal cielo, che gli arse tutti" ([R]ather [God] sent his angels all of a sudden to cast them into the abyss; but first came fire from heaven which burnt them all).[25] Nor were the miseries of these ancient peoples to end with the destruction of their cities and their lives, for they were destined to endure an infinitely worse fire—once again, the fires of hell in which they would burn forever.

The sin of sodomy was ranked by Giordano of Pisa among the most damning of sins—indeed, it ranked on par with the murder of innocent children by the wicked King Herod and deserved the same unannounced, sudden, and total destruction visited upon the people of Sodom. Giordano gives three reasons for naming male sodomy such a horrible sin: It had been unequivocally condemned in the Bible; it was deemed contrary to nature; and it was, in the preacher's own words, "sterile e sanza frutto nullo" (sterile and devoid of fruit)—that is, it is sexual activity that produces no offspring.[26]

One need not look far to find the source of Giordano's views on male sodomy; in fact, his religious order counted among its members friars who had contributed significantly to the refinement of a theology of sodomy in the later Middle Ages. While sodomy received increasing attention from Christian theologians from various quarters of the church in the later medieval period, Giordano had at hand some of the most thorough and detailed writings on sodomy ever produced by Christian thinkers— Dominican friars eager to combat a vice that, they had argued, was especially heinous in the sight of God.[27] One such friar whose thoughts on sodomy may well have informed Giordano's own preaching on the matter is Paul of Hungary, an early recruit into the Order of Preachers by its founder, the charismatic Dominic de Guzmán. Although Paul's date of entry into the order is not known for certain, we do know that he was teaching law at the University of Bologna when he joined the Dominicans and that he attended the order's General Chapter held in that same city in 1221, when Dominic chose him to serve as superior of the newly established Province of Hungary.[28]

Paul of Hungary wrote a *Summa de penitentia* that holds the distinction of being the first handbook of penance written expressly for use by members of the Order of Preachers; it may, in fact, have been composed at the specific request of St. Dominic.[29] Drawn up, no doubt, with the recent rulings of the Fourth Lateran Council on the Sacrament of Confession in mind and designed to aid the Dominicans in their papally approved ministry as itinerant confessors, this work provided the friars with practical suggestions on how to deal with penitents.[30] It is also a manual that contains a surprisingly extensive discussion of sodomy, which may reflect, as Mark Jordan argues, the author's concern that his fellow confessors take seriously the gravity of this sin among their penitents.[31] Composed sometime in the year 1221, this work was destined to become, after Raymond of Penyafort's *Summa*, "the most popular handbook of penance written during the 13th century."[32] It is not difficult to believe, therefore, that this handbook might well have been known by Giordano of Pisa and consulted in his own ministry as a confessor and preacher. There are striking similarities between Paul's *Summa* and Giordano's Holy Innocents homily of 1305 in terms of the imagery employed to describe sodomy and the theological justification used in both works for the view that sodomy should be understood, quite literally, as the very worst of sins.[33]

Within Paul's typically broad medieval definition of sodomy (that is, any sexual activity involving the emission of semen outside of a vagina) is included sexual activity between men: This early Dominican, it should be noted, makes explicit reference to men who are sexually abused by other men, and he describes male sodomites as effeminate.[34] His statement that certain courtiers and some spiritually corrupt clerics and monks are two groups particularly susceptible to sodomitical practices also reflects his personal concern with the evils of sex between men.[35]

The first similarity between the *Summa de penitentia* and Giordano's sermon regards the imagery of the Dead Sea of sodomy. While Giordano does not repeat Paul's statement that the flood described in Genesis was due, at least in part, to the sin of sodomy, Giordano's description of the beautiful apples that hang on trees surrounding the Dead Sea may well, in fact, have been inspired directly by Paul of Hungary, who says the same in his work: These apples, while delectable to the eyes, reveal insides of ash when touched by the human hand.[36] More significantly, however, Paul provides a theological justification for viewing sodomy as such a deplorable sin: Sodomy is so awful, he argues, because it endangers the human–divine relationship itself and because it can sever irrevocably the bond between humanity and God.[37] Note how astounding this claim is: Nonreproductive sexual behavior causes nothing less than a radical alienation between God and all those who engage in a wide variety of sexual practices.

How can Paul make such a claim, a claim that seems to elevate sodomy to a level surpassing incest and even mass murder, a sin that causes God to abandon a human being? Paul believes that sodomitical practices fundamentally violate and frustrate the divine plan that links all human sexual activity to the end of human reproduction. Those who partake of sexual activity not ordered toward this end risk not only falling into sin but upsetting the very order of creation ordained by God. Paul emphasizes that sodomites willfully subvert the divine plan for human reproduction and they rightfully deserve such names as "God's enemies" and "destroyers of the human race."[38]

Paul of Hungary did not create a new understanding of sodomy for the medieval church, but his views on the matter were spread far and wide by his fellow Dominican confessors as they expanded the reach of their order throughout Europe. Similar arguments would be used to support subsequent Christian theological views that male homosexuals were the worst of all sodomites and that they deserved to be listed among God's chief enemies. Moreover, once the term "sodomy" came to be understood primarily (and, in time, exclusively) as the sin of male homosexual behavior (and this was the view espoused by weighty Dominican theologians in the later thirteenth century), the stage was set for the construction of a theological rationale that justified the stigmatization, punishment, and damnation of men who had sex with men.

More immediate and more significant sources for Giordano's own preaching on the evils of male homosexual activity can been found in the thought of two of the most influential Dominicans of the late thirteenth century, Albert the Great and Thomas Aquinas, men whose writings were to receive early acclaim and quick practical application within the Order of Preachers. By the early fourteenth century, aspects of their thought began to reach a much wider audience in the church through the preaching, pastoral care, teaching, and missionizing of friars who worked across the European continent. Their writings on human sexuality have long been described by medieval historians as pivotal to the understanding of sodomy as same-sex activity and to the construction of the male sodomite in Western thought.[39]

The German Dominican Albert of Lauingen (ca. 1200–1280), known as "the Great" even in his own day, wrote about homosexual activity as early as 1249 in his *Quaestio de luxuria* and as late as 1270 when he compiled his *Summa theologiae* (only a decade before Giordano's entrance into the Dominican order at Pisa).[40] A truly prodigious and unusually well-rounded scholar for his times, Albert excelled in the study of medicine, ethics, philosophy, and theology. Moreover, his was a mind voracious in its quest to investigate the world about him (in true Aristotelian fashion) and eager to reconcile this knowledge with his Christian faith and Dominican vocation.

In the *Summa* Albert explains his views on sodomy, views that represent an important stage in the development of what would become official Roman Catholic church teaching on homosexuality from the thirteenth century to the present day. For Albert, sodomy—by which he meant sexual activity between members of the same sex—was sinful because it affronted grace, reason, and nature.[41] Sodomy was a sin against grace because biblical revelation (as Albert, of course, read both the Old and New Testaments) had clearly condemned it; sodomy offended human reason because the passion that it aroused in men made them abandon their use of reason; finally, sodomy defied nature because it did not lead to human reproduction.[42] This last reason was of particular concern to Albert and, in fact, like Paul of Hungary and many others before him, Albert taught that the only legitimate form of human sexual activity was that which led to the conception and birth of children.[43] But why should God single out male homosexuality for such harsh treatment among the many types of nonreproductive sexuality? Albert's most succinct response can be found in his *Commentary on the Gospel of Luke*, specifically in his explication of *Luke* 17:28–29.[44] Albert lists reasons for the awful punishment that God meets out to sodomites: Sodomy, he argues, involves an ardor, a burning desire so fierce that it overpowers the operation of reason; moreover, this sin produces a stench (akin to that produced by corpses) that rises up to the heavens; thirdly, this sin takes hold so firmly of men that it almost never leaves those whom it afflicts; and, finally, sodomy spreads from one man to another like an infectious disease.[45]

Albert's pupil, Thomas Aquinas (1225–1274), also taught that only sexual activity ordered toward the reproduction of the species was legitimate for humans in his *Summa Contra Gentiles*.[46] Once again we hear the argument that sodomy is a sin against nature because sexual activity between members of the same sex (like many other forms of human sexual activity) does not lead to the begetting of children. Thomas also states (in his *Summa Theologiae*) that sodomy is particularly grievous in the eyes of God since, like all sins contrary to nature, "the very order of nature is violated, [and] an injury is done to God, the Author of nature."[47] Elsewhere in this same work the Dominican speaks of homosexual behavior as unnatural when he argues that sodomy is one of the vices against nature (along with masturbation, bestiality, and all forms of heterosexual intercourse that do not lead to conception) and that these vices comprise the most sinful kinds of lust. Recalling Paul's condemnation of homosexual activity in *Romans* 1:27, Aquinas also argues that homosexual behavior serves to subvert the divinely-ordained order that legitimates only sexual desire and sexual activity between members of the opposite sex.[48]

Thomas followed directly in the footsteps of his mentor Albert in singling out male homosexual behavior as a particularly loathsome vice and, indeed, as the preeminent sin against nature. As John Boswell pointed out over twenty years ago, however, Aquinas intensified quite dramatically the theological rhetoric on homosexuality by "classifying homosexual acts as . . . worse than comparable heterosexual ones"[49] and, specifically, by equating male sodomy with several abhorrent human behaviors.[50] Again, Boswell:

> "Aquinas . . . [linked] homosexuality to behavior which was certain to evoke reactions of horror and fear. He compared homosexual acts . . . with violent or disgusting acts of the most shocking type, like cannibalism, bestiality, or eating dirt. Indeed, by suggesting subliminally to his thirteenth-century readers that homosexual behavior belonged in a class with actions which were either violently antisocial (like cannibalism) or threateningly dangerous (like heresy), Aquinas subtly but definitively transferred it from its former position among sins of excess or wantonness to a new and singular degree of enormity among the types of behavior . . . most severely repressed by the church."[51]

As a student at the prestigious priory schools of Santa Caterina in Pisa, San Niccolò in Bologna, and San Jacques in Paris, Giordano availed himself of an excellent Dominican education. While it is true that the *Sentences* (1155–1158) of Peter Lombard still served as the basic textbook of theology in Giordano's day, this work is utterly silent on the topic of male homosexual behavior.[52] The sources that informed Giordano's sermons on sodomy are the theological works of his own religious brothers, works designed to be used in the education of friars whose ministries of preaching and teaching would lead them beyond the walls of their priories and into the thick of lay urban life.

Although Giordano mentions Thomas Aquinas only once by name in his several hundred extant sermons, scholars have long known that a variety of Thomistic principles and ideas imbue Giordano's preaching, such as references to God as pure act and the good as the ultimate end of all human action.[53] It is certainly likely that Giordano might also have been well versed in Aquinas's theology of human sexuality as the result of his studies under scholars in Paris, who were themselves Thomist in their theological orientation.[54] In addition, the fact that the Dominican schools at Pisa and Naples (where Aquinas taught in the last years of his life) were considered the best training centers in the order's Roman province at the end of the thirteenth century increases the likelihood that Thomas's writings on the Christian life would have been known, if not directly consulted, in those regions. Finally, Giordano might well have taken advantage of the popular handbooks of Thomistic moral theology that had been assembled from "excerpts and abbreviations of the *Secunda secundae* [of Thomas's *Summa Theologiae* that] had begun circulating in the order within a very few years of [Thomas's] death."[55]

In Giordano of Pisa's sermon for the Feast of the Holy Innocents, we witness an example of the transmission of recently elaborated theological concepts from the schoolroom of a Dominican priory to the outdoor pulpit of a Dominican church. In preaching against the sin of sodomy, the skilled and popular preacher Giordano was communicating to his audience what he had undoubtedly learned in his years of training as a young friar preacher (whether from such works as Paul of Hungary's manual for confessors or the thought of Albert and Thomas). Formulated by intellectual leaders in the first century of the Order of Preachers' existence, this new theology of sodomy was proclaimed aloud in the piazza outside the church of Santa Maria Maggiore in Florence late one December morning in the year 1305. The message that his listeners heard was one that would be repeated with increasing intensity by countless preachers throughout the remaining decades of the late medieval period—namely, that sodomy (understood now primarily as the sin of men who had sex with men) was a sin supremely abhorrent to God and that sodomites rightfully deserved the most serious of divine punishments.

Bernard Schlager currently teaches at the Pacific School of Religion (PSR) in Berkeley, California, and is Director of National Programming for the Center for Lesbian and Gay Studies in Religion and Ministry at PSR. Co-editor of the forthcoming *Encyclopedia of Homosexuality, Religion and American Culture* (Sharpe Press, 2004), he has published articles in *Viator*, the *Greek Orthodox Theological Review*, and the *Reader's Guide to Lesbian and Gay Studies*.

Notes

1. From the point of view of sources, structure, and delivery techniques, the sermons of Giordano were composed and delivered according to the popular *sermo modernus* style, originating in the early thirteenth century and heavily favored by Dominican preachers of Giordano's day. For instance, his vernacular sermons contain four of the five items of the *sermo modernus* (theme, introduction, division, and clause—like other Dominicans of his era, he omits the protheme that announced a subtheme and followed the theme). Giordano's sermons also reveal his expert use of *florilegia* (manuals of handy authoritative quotations) and *exempla* (collections of pithy moral stories), both of which were favorite sources used by early mendicant preachers in their sermon-making. On the *sermo modernus*, see Daniel R. Lesnick, *Preaching in Medieval Florence: The Social World of Franciscan and Dominican Spirituality* (Athens,

GA: University of Georgia Press, 1989), pp. 96–108. See M. Michèle Mulchahey, "First the Bow is Bent in Study . . .": Dominican Education Before 1350 (Toronto: Pontifical Institute of Mediaeval Studies, 1998), n. 20, p. 406, on the structure of Giordano's vernacular sermons. On Giordano's Florentine audiences and for a good overview of themes in his preaching, see Carlo Delcorno, Giordano da Pisa e l'antica predicazione volgare (Florence: L. S. Olschki, 1975), pp. 43–80.

2. For basic biographical information on Giordano of Pisa, see Bibliotheca Sanctorum (Rome: Istituto Giovanni XXIII della Pontificia Università Lateranense, 1961–1970), s.v. "Giordano da Pisa." See also Delcorno, pp. 3–28.

3. Mulchahey, p. 184.

4. Aquinas was assigned to the Neopolitan priory in 1272 to oversee the establishment of a studium generale, and it was here that he wrote, in the last years of his life, the third part of his Summa Theologiae. On Aquinas's years in Naples, see James A. Weisheipl, Friar Thomas D'Aquino: His Life, Thought, and Work (Garden City, NY, Doubleday, 1974), pp. 293–322.

5. Mulchahey, p. 351.

6. Lesnick, Preaching in Medieval Florence, p. 113.

7. Cities were a natural environment for the mendicant orders, of course, and Italian Dominicans of the thirteenth and fourteenth centuries found receptive and enthusiastic audiences for their preaching among the growing well-to-do merchant classes there. On the urban-related themes and content of Giordano's sermons, see Cecilia Iannella, Giordano da Pisa: Etica Urbana e Forme della Società, Studi Medioevali 8 (Pisa: ETS, 1999).

8. D. L. D'Avray, The Preaching of the Friars: Sermons Diffused from Paris before 1300 (Oxford: Clarendon Press; New York: Oxford University Press, 1985), pp. 30–36 discusses the urban focus of mendicant preachers and the relatively high level of religious and secular education among late-medieval Italian preaching audiences. A focused study of mendicant preaching in one city is offered by Bernadette Patton, Preaching Friars and the Civic Ethos: Siena, 1380–1480 (London: Centre for Medieval Studies, 1992), pp. 307–35. For book-length studies of Italian cities where late-medieval religious leaders strove to address the new religious needs of urban populations, see David Herlihy, Medieval and Renaissance Pistoia: The Social History of an Italian Town, 1200–1430 (New Haven, CT: Yale University Press, 1967) and William M. Bowsky, A Medieval Italian Commune: Siena under the Nine, 1287–1355 (Berkeley: University of California Press, 1981).

9. On late-medieval views of the city, including mention of Giordano's use of urban imagery in his sermons, see Chiara Frugoni, A Distant City: Images of Urban Experience in the Medieval World, trans. William McCuaig (Princeton, NJ: Princeton University Press, 1991), pp. 97–101, 177–78, and 186–88.

10. Lesnick, p. 123.

11. Ibid., p. 116.

12. The term "sodomy," referring primarily to male homosexual acts, was coined by Peter Damian in his Book of Gomorrah (ca. 1050 C.E.), a work especially concerned with what the author believed was rampant homosexual activity

between clerics. See Mark D. Jordan, *The Invention of Sodomy in Christian Theology* (Chicago: University of Chicago Press, 1997), pp. 29–30 and 45–51 and John Boswell, *Christianity, Social Tolerance, and Homosexuality* (Chicago: University of Chicago Press, 1980), pp. 210–12.

13. Giordano of Pisa quoted in Michael Rocke, *Forbidden Friendships: Homosexuality and Male Culture in Renaissance Florence* (New York: Oxford University Press, 1996), p. 27.

14. Giordano da Pisa, Sermon 91, in Giordano da Rivalto, *Prediche Inedite del b. Giordano da Rivalto dell'ordine de' predicatori, recitate in Firenze dal 1302 al 1305*, ed. Enrico Narducci (Bologna: G. Romagnoli, 1867), pp. 441–50. See also Sermon 30 in *Prediche del beato fra Giordano da Rivalto dell'ordine dei predicatori, recitate in Firenze dal MCCCIII al MCCCVI*, ed. D. Moreni (Florence: Magheri, 1831), vol. 1, p. 230, in which the preacher rails against Florentine men who prostituted their sons: According to Giordano, some men encouraged their sons to seek gifts from older male suitors.

15. For a discussion of Bernardino of Siena's extensive comments on sodomy, see Franco Mormando, *The Preacher's Demons: Bernardino of Siena and the Social Underworld of Early Renaissance Italy* (Chicago: University of Chicago Press, 1999), pp. 109–63. On Savonarola and his role in the persecution of male homosexual activity, consult Rocke, *Forbidden Friendships*, pp. 204–23.

16. *Gospel of Matthew* 2:18: "A voice is heard in Ramah, weeping and great mourning, Rachel weeping for her children and refusing to be comforted, because they are no more."

17. Giordano da Pisa, Sermon 91, *Prediche Inedite*, pp. 444–45. English translations are my own unless otherwise indicated.

18. Ibid., p. 445.

19. Ibid., p. 446.

20. Ibid., p. 448. Giordano argues that the *Book of Maccabees* demonstrates that God often displays just mercy when he punishes people in this world who have sinned.

21. Ibid., p. 448. In this sermon Giordano assumes that his audience understands the "sin against nature" as male homosexuality.

22. Ibid., pp. 448–49.

23. Ibid., p. 449.

24. Ibid., p. 449.

25. Ibid., p. 450.

26. Ibid., p. 449.

27. See, for instance, Michael Goodich, *The Unmentionable Vice: Homosexuality in the Later Medieval Period* (Santa Barbara, CA: ABC-Clio, 1979).

28. On Paul of Hungary, see William A. Hinnebusch, *The History of the Dominican Order* (New York: Alba House, 1973), vol. 2, p. 238.

29. Paul of Hungary, *Summa de penitentia* in: *Bibliotheca Casinensis seu Codicum manuscriptorum qui in tabulario casinensi asservantur series per paginas singillatim enucleata; notis, characterum speciminibus ad unguem exemplatis*

aucta, cura et studio monachorum ordinis S. Benedicti, abbatiae Montis Casini (Monte Cassino: Typographia Casinensis, 1880), vol. 4, pp. 191–215.

30. See canon 21 of the Fourth Lateran Council (1215), which mandated yearly confession for the laity and called for the training of confessors skilled in compassionate and informed pastoral care.

31. Jordan, p. 95.

32. Hinnebusch (vol. 2, p. 238) also writes that: "[M]ore than fifty manuscripts [of Paul's *Summa de penitentia*] survive, though some of them contain only the first half."

33. I follow here the interpretation of Paul of Hungary on sodomy offered by Mark Jordan, pp. 93–103.

34. Paul of Hungary, *Summa de penitentia*, pp. 207–08.

35. Ibid., p. 210. Recent church legislation had expressed concern over homosexual activity among the clergy. See, especially, canon 11 of the Third Lateran Council (1179): "Let all who are found guilty of that unnatural vice for which the wrath of God came down upon the sons of disobedience and destroyed the five cities with fire, if they are clerics be expelled from the clergy or confined in monasteries to do penance; if they are laymen they are to incur excommunication and be completely separated from the society of the faithful" in: *Decrees of the Ecumenical Councils*, ed. and trans. Norman P. Tanner (London: Sheed & Ward; Washington, D.C.: Georgetown University Press, 1990), vol. 1, p. 217.

36. Paul of Hungary, *Summa de penitentia*, p. 208. Paul points to the third-century Greek Christian author Methodius as an authority who posited sodomy as a cause of the flood; on the apples of Sodomy, Paul writes: "Ibi sunt poma pulcerrima exterius; interius autem plena favilla et cinere." (Here you will find apples that are extremely beautiful on the outside, but inside they are filled with ash and cinder.)

37. Paul of Hungary, *Summa de penitentia*, p. 207. "[V]iolaretur quippe ipsa societas que cum deo nobis esse debet." (The very bond we should maintain with God is completely violated.)

38. Ibid., p. 209: "Item sodomite sunt adversarii dei et homicide et destructores generis humani. Videntur enim deo tu creasti homines ut multiplicarent. Nos vero operam damus ut tuum opus deperaet." (Sodomites are also enemies of God, murderers, and destroyers of the human race. For they are seen by God, and You created men that they should multiply, but we are bent on bringing your creation to ruin.)

39. See, especially, Boswell, pp. 316–331. On attempts by medieval Christian church authorities to demonize male homosexual activity and the 1200s as a pivotal century in the persecution of male homosexual behavior, see R. I. Moore, *The Formation of a Persecuting Society: Power and Deviance in Western Europe, 950–1250* (New York: Blackwell, 1987), pp. 91–94. Although Giordano may not have been acquainted with Albert's teaching in any detailed sense, he would have known it indirectly given Albert's role as an especially influential teacher of Thomas.

40. On Albert's understanding of the sin of same-sex intercourse in his *Quaestio de luxuria*, see Jordan, p. 126.
41. Albertus Magnus, *Summa theologiae*, 2.18.122.1.4 in: *Alberti Magni Ratisbonensis episcopi, ordinis praedicatorum opera omnia*, ed. A. Borgnet (Paris: Vives, 1890–1895), vol. 33, 400–01.
42. See Jordan, pp. 126–27: "As Albert had already said elsewhere [i.e., in his *Summa de bono*, 5.1.3., and not in his *Summa theologiae*], sin against nature is sin against 'nature's order in the manner of generation, which is the starting point for the whole of nature.' "
43. For a succinct outline of the medieval church's insistence that all sexual intercourse have a procreative purpose, see John T. Noonan, *Contraception: A History of Its Treatment by the Catholic Theologians and Canonists* (Cambridge, MA: Harvard University Press, 1966), pp. 246–57.
44. Jordan, p. 133, describes this as "Albert's fullest explicit discussion of same-sex copulation as sin."
45. Albert the Great, *In evangelium Lucae*, 18:29 (Borgnet, *Opera omnia* 23: 488).
46. *Summa contra gentiles*, 3:122.9. See Thomas Aquinas, *Summa contra gentiles*, trans. C. J. O'Neil (Notre Dame, IN: University of Notre Dame Press, 1975), vol. 4, p. 146: "[T]he inordinate emission of semen is incompatible with the natural good; namely, the preservation of the species. Hence, after the sin of homicide whereby a human nature already in existence is destroyed, this type of sin appears to take next place, for by it the generation of human nature is precluded."
47. Thomas Aquinas, *Summa theologiae*, 2–2.154.12 ad 1, trans. Fathers of the English Dominican Province (New York: Benziger, 1947), vol. 2, p. 1826. See also Jordan, p. 146.
48. Ibid., 2–2.154.11–12.
49. Boswell, p. 321.
50. See, for instance, Thomas Aquinas, *Summa theologiae*, 1–2.31.7, in which homosexual sex is compared with bestiality and cannibalism.
51. Boswell, p. 329. On Aquinas and homosexuality, see also Vern L. Bullough, "The Sin Against Nature and Homosexuality" in: *Sexual Practices and the Medieval Church*, ed. Vern L. Bullough and James Brundage (Buffalo, NY: Prometheus Books, 1982), pp. 64–66.
52. See Boswell, pp. 227–28.
53. On the singular mention of Aquinas in Giordano's writings, see Delcorno, p. 77. Thomistic ideas in the preaching of Giordano are discussed by Enrico Narducci in *Prediche Inedite*, pp. 33, 235, and 296–97.
54. Delcorno, pp. 9–10.
55. Mulchahey, p. 216. See also Leonard E. Boyle, "The *Summa Confessorum* of John of Freiburg and the Popularization of the Moral Teaching of St. Thomas and Some of His Contemporaries" in: *St. Thomas Aquinas 1274–1974: Commemorative Studies*, foreword by Etienne Gilson (Toronto: Pontifical Institute of Mediaeval Studies, 1974), pp. 245–68, who notes on p. 245 that John of Vercelli, the Dominican General, ordered the production of "an abbreviated version of the *Secunda secundae*" sometime between the years 1280 and 1288.

2

Bibbiena's Closet: Interpretation and the Sexual Culture of a Renaissance Papal Court

Michael Wyatt

In his 1697 *Dictionnaire Historique et Chronique*—a large portion of which, in Craig Brush's words, "is devoted to the investigation and certification of facts"[1]—Pierre Bayle makes the following observation about the occasion of Giovanni de' Medici's election as Pope Leo X in 1513: "Nothing contributed more to his elevation to the papacy, than the wounds he had earlier received in Venerean combat."[2] Leo's nineteenth-century English biographer William Roscoe, outraged at Bayle's assertion, accused him of manipulating his sources—Pierre Varillas's 1685 *Les Anecdotes de Florence ou L'Histoire Secrete de la Maison des Medicis*, and Viet Ludwig von Seckendorf's 1692 *Commentarius historicus et apologeticus de lutheranismo*—for partisan Protestant motives.[3] But Bayle foresaw this line of criticism and makes a point, which Roscoe neglects to note, of also citing Catholic historians and commentators in substantiation of his assertion. Roscoe's dismissal of Bayle's allegation of the newly elected pope's preceding sexual adventures also fails to take fully into account Bayle's own extended footnote to the controversial phrase, in which he gingerly distances himself from claiming authoritative evidence in the matter. Roscoe fails as well to mention a similar case in Bayle's *Dictionnaire*, which sheds some light on his treatment of Leo.

A former colleague of Bayle's at the French Reformed Faculty in Rotterdam, the Calvinist theologian Pierre Jurieu repeats an anecdote in his *Préjugez legitimes contre le papisme*[4] regarding Sixtus IV, whom he describes as "having been debauched and vicious beyond all imagining." According to Jurieu, an unnamed "papist author . . . wrote that a request had been presented to the pope on the part of the family of the Cardinal of Sainte-Lucie that they be allowed during the hottest months of the year, June, July, and August, to practice the act of sodomy."[5] Bayle carefully examines all available accounts of the allegation—seven in number—presents each point of view, its means of transmission, and the reliability of its reporter. In the end he concludes that "the accusation against [Sixtus] is highly unlikely, so unlikely that no responsible author would make it."[6] Other examples of Bayle's evidentiary caution in the *Dictionnaire* are so widespread that it is reasonable to suppose that he was not one to jump to wildly unfounded conclusions, even in the religious arena that his Calvinist-tinged skepticism caused him to regard with suspicion.[7]

This essay will be concerned with issues related to the representation and interpretation of the sexual culture of the papal court of Leo X. But as some of the territory it traverses is not perhaps as self-evidently *queer* as that of other contributions to this volume, I begin by citing several aspects of the *Oxford English Dictionary* definition of the term: "Of doubtful [etymological] origin . . . cross, oblique, squint, perverse, wrongheaded . . . 1a. Strange, odd, peculiar, eccentric, in appearance or character. Also of questionable character, suspicious, dubious. 1b. Of a person (usu. a man): homosexual . . . hence of things: pertaining to homosexuals or homosexuality."[8] Both senses of *queer* come into play here: the latter most clearly in regard to Pope Leo's posthumous reputation and the former insofar as historical criticism has evaded, often blatantly, the patent evidence of the Renaissance fascination with the erotic. I mean to examine how the Renaissance interpretive tradition has frequently displayed its own *queer* taxonomy at the same time that it has attempted to draw a veil across the *queer* objects of its critical disdain. I see the various traces of sexuality in the Leonine court under consideration here as diverse manifestations of a culture that, given the ostensibly celibate stamp of its *dramatis personae*, can be regarded as fundamentally *queer* howsoever the pope and his immediate subordinates might have practiced their sexual choices.[9]

In his notes about Giovanni de' Medici's affliction, Bayle cites at length Varillas's description of both the cardinal's suffering from a fistula—acquired, he maintains, through what we might now call unsafe sex—at the time of the conclave that would eventually elect him to the papacy and its eventual explosion while de' Medici was resident in the very cramped quarters shared with his fellow conclavists. But whereas Varillas suggests the location of the problematic condition as Giovanni's genitals, Bayle points out that Paolo Giovio, in his *In vitam leonis decimi*, locates it on his ass and adds, perhaps ironically, that this "does not necessitate the presumption of a disgraceful cause."[10] Were it true, this would be the only occasion I know of in which the effect of a sexually transmitted disease would have determined the outcome of a papal election. But other explanations of Giovanni's fistula have been suggested, most recently, by Ingrid Rowland, who writes of "an anal fistula, an imperfection of the spinal column that leaked fluid and subjected [the pope] to chronic and embarrassing discomfort,"[11] a life-long ailment that would not appear to be congruent with the receptive sexual practices Varillas implies but that conveniently lets Bayle off the hook. The apparent contradiction between these historiographical and physiological readings of Giovanni's affliction can, of course, in part be ascribed to the inadequate state of premodern medical knowledge. But simply applying modern medical diagnostics to conflicting earlier accounts of the fistula does not entirely clarify its signifying role in the genesis of Leo's papacy. For whatever the explanation of its origin, the older cardinals who initially blocked de' Medici's candidacy were eventually convinced that due to the fistula he would not be long for the world, and they voted for him under the assumption that his would be a brief transitional pontificate that would buy them time to find a more suitable long-term successor. Leo would reign, however, for nine years, during which time he sustained a glittering but progressively corrupt court culture, practically bankrupted the Church in both literal and figurative senses, and provoked through a lack of prudence and strategic vision the events that would lead to the Reformation.

Giovio's biography—commissioned by Giovanni's illegitimate cousin Giulio (who succeeded him as Pope Clement VII) and published in 1549—is the earliest source for all subsequent accounts of this first Medici pope. It is interesting that Roscoe should have attacked Bayle for reviving the issue of Leo's sybaritic inclinations in terms of the disputed fistula, for later in his article Bayle states quite unequivocally that Giovio himself:

> cannot be accused of being too sparing in his criticism of Leo X; quite the contrary, in fact, for he explains himself clearly enough in regards to the vices of this pope, and not to leave the intelligent reader in suspense: the pleasures, says he [Giovio], into which he [Leo] too frequently plunged himself, and the lewd actions ascribed to him, tarnished the luster of his virtues. Giovio adds that a tempter more easy and complacent than vicious led him into this abyss, having surrounded himself with people who little recommended him to his duties but talked to him only of diversions . . . a little after [Giovio] notes, regrettably, that this pope was accused of the crime of sodomy.[12]

Giovio does indeed write that "the pope did not escape the accusation of infamy, for the love he showed several of his chamberlains—among the most high-born of Italy—smacked of scandal in its playful liberality."[13]

He goes on to say that Leo was nevertheless a great leader, comparable to the greatest princes the world has seen, but then dissemblingly suggests that what occurs in the dark of night is better left unexamined. For Giovio, the weight of the pope's public responsibilities allow him a degree of freedom in his personal life that should be regarded as off-limits to those prone to snooping—the earned privilege of the closet, as it were.

The presence of a conspicuous sexual culture within the context of the Renaissance papacy—cohabitating there with other more predictable cultures: ecclesiastical, artistic, political, and economic—should come as no surprise to anyone familiar with the histories of Leo's immediate predecessors. But apart from Bayle's encyclopedic project there has until quite recently been a striking elision in the study of the erotic in the historiography that deals with the papacy in the period just preceding what John O'Malley now describes as Early Modern Catholicism following the Council of Trent, when the papal office went through a radical makeover. The possibility that the inflection of the sexual culture of Leo's pontificate was markedly homoerotic has been either studiously avoided by his modern chroniclers or dismissed as so appalling—a position that assumes the prospect to be true—as to warrant silence regarding the matter.[14] Recent work on the history of sexuality in early modern Europe, and in particular Michael Rocke's *Forbidden Friendships: Homosexuality and Male Culture in Renaissance Florence*,[15] has made possible a fuller understanding of the nature of what Valerie Traub usefully distinguishes as early modern "sexual practices" over and against the more recent notion of "sexual identity,"[16] allowing us a glimpse into a social history that from this perspective looks significantly different from previous historiographical accounts of the Florentine *quattrocento*. As Rocke demonstrates, the Florentine world that produced Giovanni de' Medici was throughout the fifteenth century a profoundly homosocial one in which men rarely married before their mid-thirties, and in which male–male penetrative sexual acts that were characterized as "sodomy" played a significant, though for the most part impermanent, role in the socialization of Florentine men of all classes. Rocke marshals a singular and voluminous body of archival evidence—the fifteenth-century records of the Florentine "Night Officers," the only court ever constituted in early modern Europe to adjudicate sodomy cases alone—in support of his argument, material that, because it did not fit the investigative parameters of earlier historiography, was largely ignored until the questions only it could answer were ultimately posed.[17]

Given that Medici ascendency in Florence coincided simultaneously with the period of the most intense activity of the "Night Officers," it is hardly surprising that the family is most associated in its records as judges and not as plaintiffs. But Rocke notes two moments in *quattrocento* Medici history that are suggestive of the environment into which the future Leo X was born and in which his sensibility was formed.[18] Cosimo de' Medici (Florence's *pater patriae*, Giovanni's great-grandfather) and his partisans abstained from the vigorous 1415 effort to repress sodomitical practices between men in Florence that led by 1432 to the institution of the "Office of the Night." Whether an agnostic position or one that aimed to protect Medici interests Rocke says is difficult to determine, but one consequence of this stance was the dedication in 1425 to Cosimo of a collection of Latin epigrams, the *Hermaphroditus*, by Antonio Beccadelli, the first book of which celebrates male–male sexual practices. Rocke writes of Beccadelli's work that it:

> scandalized moralists across Italy, and Bernardino [of Siena] himself publicly burned it and effigies of its author in various cities. . . . [R]eputed a sodomite, Beccadelli lived in Florence in 1419 and 1420, when he was about twenty-five, and frequented the brilliant circle of humanists around Cosimo. By dedicating the book to Cosimo, he probably hoped to gain the eminent benefactor's patronage, perhaps not so much because he would have fully approved of its subjects or shared its sentiments as out of appreciation of its elegant Latin form and imitation of the classics. Nonetheless, Beccadelli must have had good reason to believe that Cosimo would have found the sexual content and message of the *Hermaphroditus* inoffensive.

The confluence here of humanism, neo-Latinity, and sodomy was reiterated in the period during which Giovanni's father Lorenzo consolidated his control over Florence in the 1480s, after the Pazzi Conspiracy that nearly took his life and the subsequent war with Pope Sixtus IV (who was likely in cahoots with two of his nephews responsible for the assassination plot). This same decade marked a significant drop-off in the high rate of condemnations for male homosexuality by the "Night Officers" during the years of Lorenzo's ascendancy even as it brought several of his closest intellectual friends—among them Luigi Pulci, Bacio di Domenico Martelli, and Angelo Poliziano—under the scrutiny of the court. Both of these moments, however, ended under the threat of fanatical religious persecution, the second of them coinciding with Savonarola's rise to power and the imminent expulsion of the Medici from Florence, a decisive time in Giovanni's development.

Though the neo-Platonic brand of humanism that Lorenzo encouraged through his capacious patronage has been increasingly identified in the modern era with a homosexual ethos, be it in the idealized ephebi of Sandro Botticelli or in the barely sublimated raptures of Marsilio Ficino and Cristoforo Landino, there has also been a corresponding effort on the part of some scholars to employ the rhetoric of neo-Platonism to either mask or explain away the erotic in Renaissance culture.[19] The ambiguous moral valence of Lorenzo's learned companions—latent threats to the objects of their elevated attentions—provoked an anxiety that Clarice de' Medici, the Magnifico's wife and Giovanni's mother, shared with the "Night Officers," a concern first noted by Antonio Fabroni in his 1784 biography of Lorenzo, further elaborated by John Addington Symonds in his 1875–1876 *Renaissance in Italy*, and most recently examined by Alan Stewart in *Close Readers: Humanism and Sodomy in Early Modern England*.[20]

As Stewart shows, Poliziano is a crucial figure for both the delineation and occlusion of sentiment regarding homosexuality and its implications within the orbit of the Medici, for apart from the central place he held in Lorenzo's inner circle, Poliziano also served from 1475 until 1479 as tutor to both Piero and Giovanni, a role the boys' mother resisted almost from the beginning and in the end succeeded in terminating.[21] Stewart, however, challenges the shared assumption of both Fabroni and Symonds that Clarice's apprehension regarding Poliziano was exclusively of a sexual character, arguing that she feared a much more comprehensive loss of her maternal authority through the forfeiture of her right to determine how and by whom they should be educated. Clarice's anxiety over Poliziano, in this reading, has as much to do with the fear of a woman's legitimate domestic place being colonized by a man—Poliziano had already insinuated himself securely into Lorenzo's inner circle—as it does, in potentially sexual terms, with the fear of her sons being compelled to play women's parts by the same dominant elder. Stewart does not ignore the imputations regarding Poliziano's sexual practices, as he grounds his discussion of Clarice's wider concerns in a comparative reading of the divergent accounts of Poliziano's death offered by Giovio and by Pietro Bembo. Giovio ascribes Poliziano's demise to a fever he contracted while singing in public to a beautiful boy. According to Bembo, Poliziano died while composing a funeral lament for Lorenzo and expired shortly after his patron. As Stewart puts it, "Both [versions] have their adherents . . . and are impossible to prove": The one evidently aimed to memorialize Poliziano within the parameters of the central patronal relationship of his life; the other clearly intended to shock with its unbridled rehearsal of forbidden desire.[22] Though, as Stewart notes, both accounts were published together in 1546, they had circulated in manuscript form for some time before, and it is likely that similarly conflicting versions of Poliziano's death (as well as his life) had some currency in the oral culture the young Giovanni de' Medici inhabited.

But there were other forces at work in the formation of Lorenzo's and Clarice's children, and in Giovanni's case, as Roscoe piquantly has it, "his youthful mind . . . was not wholly left to the chance of promiscuous cultivation."[23] Among those who emerged in the wake of Poliziano's removal was Bernardo Dovizi da Bibbiena (1470–1520), who had come to Florence in the company of his brother Piero in 1479 and who by 1488 was employed by Lorenzo in increasingly important tasks as one of his private secretaries.[24] When, in 1489, Giovanni was appointed cardinal at the age of 13 by Pope Innocent VIII, he was compelled (at least temporarily) to terminate his humanistic studies in order to pursue canon law at the University of Pisa, and it was Bibbiena who accompanied him there to manage his household. From that point onward, Bibbiena's role in the fortunes of his younger charge, and of the Medici in general, was fixed. He would come to play a critical part in the political designs that restored the Medici to Florence in 1512 (following 18 years of exile and, after the death of Julius II, he brought about Giovanni's election to the papacy in 1513.

Unlike Poliziano, Bibbiena seems never to have aroused the same sort of anxiety of influence. If his later letters to Pietro Bembo are any indication, it would appear that his own sexual inclinations were more normative than transgressive. As he grew older and more established in his advisory capacity to the Medici, Bibbiena developed a reputation for prankish behavior that earned him the nickname *moccicone* ("whipper-snapper" or "snot-head") and a featured role in Baldassare Castiglione's *Il cortegiano*, where in Book Two he is the interlocutor who describes and theorizes the practice of joking. There, Castiglione's Bibbiena defines "laughter" as being natural to mankind alone:

"testimonio d'una certa ilarità che dentro si sente nell'animo, il qual da natura è tirato al piacere ed appetisce il riposo e 'l recrearsi; onde veggiamo molte cose dagli omini ritrovate per questo effetto, come le feste e tante varie sorti di spettaculi."

"a token of a certain jocundnesse and merry moode that he feeleth inwardly in his minde, which by nature is drawne to pleasantnesse, and coveteth quietnesse and refreshing. For which cause we see men have invented manie matters, as sportes, games and pastimes, and so many sundrie sortes of open shewes."[25]

In a passage that segues into the equivocating one cited above regarding the pope's chamberlains, Giovio singles out Bibbiena for thinly veiled criticism, describing him as a man

skilled not only in negotiating difficult matters but also expert in staging games. To this end, as a scholar of both poetry and the Tuscan language, he wrote comedies filled with witticisms, encouraged the younger cardinals' theatrical ambitions, and organized performances in the Vatican's stately halls. On the occasion of Isabella d'Este's visit [in January 1515], having been asked to stage his delectably witty comedy *Calandria* with several courtier-actors, Bibbiena succeeded in persuading the pope to honor the performance with his presence. It was the same Bibbiena who was extraordinarily adept at driving men mad who were otherwise noted for their seriousness. The pope so delighted in these sorts of men that praising them, compelling them to believe fantastic things, and egging them on he tended to make lunatics of those who were already unbalanced and foolish.[26]

First performed in Urbino in 1512 just prior to the Medici restoration in Florence, *Calandria* has long been considered among the finest examples of early sixteenth-century Italian comedy modeled after the recently repopularized Latin comedies of Plautus and Terence. It is a cleverly constructed story of lost twins, confused as well as exchanged identities, a pathetic old man and an ingenious younger one, the whole clothed seamlessly in both the comedic and linguistic dress of Boccaccio. Ronald Martinez has compellingly described Bibbiena's literary strategy in *Calandria* as a commingling of the *beffe* ("jesting") that Castiglione's Bibbiena represents, and that Giovio regrets, with a subtle but toughminded critique of his Medici patrons.[27] Closely involved in practically every major move in Medici politics from the late Laurentian period forward, Bibbiena appears, in this reading, to have cast in his comedy something of an ironic glance at the powers whose success he had to a significant extent engineered and at the culture that they sustained. As Martinez notes, "it is well to keep in mind that Bibbiena's role in furthering and in many cases originating the maneuvers of Medici policy need not imply his complete approval of the Medici themselves."[28] Two further aspects of Martinez's take on *Calandria* are of particular interest for our purposes here.

The action of the play is organized to effect the reunion of twins, Lidio and Santilla, who had been separated at birth. The two are put through the typical paces of mistaken-identity comedy, and along the way issues of androgyny, homosexuality, adultery, incest, and gender reversal are played to great comedic effect. In the end, the play's various transvestisms are apparently undone, the twins reunited and promised in marriages. But the seemingly tidy manner in which the comedy's loose ends are drawn together at its conclusion betray what Martinez identifies as the "sudden full emergence of political and economic motives" at its core. Accordingly, the reunion of the twins is not presented by the author—speaking through the voice of Fessenio, the central manipulator of the play's action, a role similar to the one Bibbiena exercised for his Medici patrons—as a goal in itself but as the means to a richer material end. In *Calandria*'s concluding scene, Fessenio cuts off the exuberant chattering of brother and sister by telling them that

"Di ciò a bell'agio parleremo. Attendasi oggi a *quel che piú importa*. Dissi là drento a Fulvia questa esser Santilla tua sorella: di che ella si mostrò oltra modo contenta; e conchiusemi al tutto volere che sia moglie a Flaminio suo figliuolo."

"Of all that [the means through which the twins have been reunited] we can talk later at length. For the time being we must turn our attention to *what matters most*. I've told Fulvia [Lidio's lover] that this is Santilla, your sister, news that she greeted so happily that I am convinced that she wants nothing better than for Santilla to marry her son, Flaminio."

Fessenio then prompts Santilla to suggest, " 'che Lidio, da noi instrutto, in loco mio entri e pigli per moglie la figliuola di Perillo la qual voglian dare a me' " ("that Lidio, instructed by us, should in my place go and take as his wife the daughter of Perillo" [in whose home Lidio has been living, disguised as a woman]). Lidio asks, " 'Ed è chiaro, questo?' " ("Is this clear?"). And Santilla answers, "'Clearer than the sun, truer than the truth.'"[29] As Martinez suggests, " 'più chiaro ch'el sole, più vero ch'el vero' here represents a situation more advantageous than the mere truth; although it requires a fraud, it benefits the protagonists . . . truth produced is superior to truth discovered."[30] Dissimulation is the force that triumphs at the play's conclusion, for the desire that earlier deceptions had engendered is now turned to the material advantage of the undisguised twins, and in the case of Fulvio it would look as if he can have his cake and eat it too as there seems to be nothing standing in the way of continuing his adulterous relationship with Fulvia after his marriage.

Central to the *Calandria*'s gritty economic politics is what Martinez identifies as Bibbiena's correction of a neo-Platonic misreading of the myth of the hermaphrodite. The play is constructed around a series of fractured halves, most obviously in the separated twins but evident as well in the name of the comedy's principal architect Fessenio, derived from *fesso* ("split" or "cleft"). Whereas Plato, in the *Symposium*, has the gods splitting the originally hermaphroditic human in order to both control him/her and squeeze further profits out of the resulting increase, Ficino in his commentary on the passage entirely ignores "economic self-interest and vengeance as motives of the gods," consequently denuding Plato's narrative of its political import.[31] In resolving his hermaphroditic comedy in the profit motive, restoring to Plato what Ficino had elided, Bibbiena signals in this instance his critical distance from the tradition of neo-Platonism with which his early career in Florence had brought him into contact. Ficino himself had expressed his admiration for Bibbiena's intellect in an exchange of letters with the younger man late in his life,[32] but such an association should not ipso facto be construed as an endorsement or as advocacy of the mystagogic doctrine of the Florentine neo-Platonists. Indeed, the significance of restoring to the Platonic myth the elements erased by Ficino is emphasized in Santilla's evocation of both sun and truth, key elements in Platonic and neo-Platonic imagery. Citing them at the end of the play when its economic ends have been exposed, Bibbiena makes clear his preference for the originally politicized Platonic hermaphrodite, for even "if Lidio and Santilla cannot fuse as bodies, they can fuse as wealth, as two fortunes: the monetary 'offspring' that is interest (*tokos* in Aristotle) can join with similar offspring from another household and add up, as Everett Dirkson used to say, to real money."[33]

Fessenio is a particularly fitting figure for Bibbiena himself, divided as he was between his respectably middle-class Tuscan roots—his father was a notary in the small provincial Tuscan town of Bibbiena—and the significant fiscal and diplomatic responsibilities he shouldered for his Medici bosses. After managing Giovanni's election to the papacy and his own elevation to the cardinalate, Bibbiena was in need of a Roman residence of his own, but (perhaps uniquely among his fellow *porporati*) lacking the personal fortune necessary to purchase and sustain a villa suitable to his new rank, he was assigned a suite of rooms on the third floor of the Vatican palace. Raphael was entrusted with the task of redesigning the rooms, located directly above those that then served as the papal household, and among them was a small, square space with a window opening out onto the Cortile del Pappagallo that has come to be known as the *Stufetta*, or bath-closet. The site of a Venerean fresco cycle, the *Stufetta*'s genesis, preservation, and interpretative history provide further evidence of the difficulty Renaissance historiography has had in dealing with the erotic, even when, as in this instance, there are tangible material vestiges conveying an erotically-charged visual narrative that can only be construed otherwise through tortuous critical distortions.[34] And the financial dividend Martinez identifies at the heart of *Calandria*, entwined as it is there with the sexual politics of the comedy, is also central to the meaning of the *Stufetta*, for while the space constituted part of the recompense for indispensable services rendered to the Medici, it is also a sign of Bibbiena's dependence on the largesse of the newly enthroned pope.

The six extant *Stufetta* frescoes (originally eight) are now in very poor condition, and this fact alone should signal the need for a cautious appraisal of their meaning. Little is known of what the room was used for in the period following Bibbiena's death in 1520, but it was later requisitioned as a storage space and eventually utilized as a private chapel, the frescoes covered over by pieces of cloth nailed into them. There are other signs of disfigurement, in particular graffiti etched into several of the images, indicating an obvious lack of approval of what they represent.[35] The design of the room, as well as its original purpose (revealed in the last restoration of the space conducted in the early 1970s),[36] replicates the form and decoration of an ancient Roman *calidarium*, another of the contemporary efforts at recreating in early sixteenth-century Rome the artistic achievements of classical Rome.[37] Raphael and his apprentices made several visits to the remains of the Domus Aurea, the Emperor Hadrian's villa at Tivoli, and the Baths of Titus at the same time that the *Stufetta* was being painted, from 1515 through 1516, and the fruits of these excursions are evident in its design. The vaulted square shape of the room, its use of deep red and black background fields, the mythographic character of the fresco panels, and the copious use of decorative amorous and grotesque figures demonstrate an affinity with those elements of Renaissance culture that aimed at leap-frogging backwards over the preceding millenium and a half of Christian history in order to arrive at an unmediated encounter with antiquity. However illusory such a project might now appear to have been, it is particularly striking that the *Stufetta* is located just one floor above the Vatican *Loggie* facing onto the Cortile San Damaso that Raphael and his studio were also then occupied in decorating with a series of biblical scenes.

The literary program behind Raphael's conception, inspired by Ovid's *Metamorphoses* and Servius's commentaries on Virgil, was evidently elaborated by Bibbiena in two phases, the second of which Pietro Bembo brokered with the artist due to Bibbiena's protracted absence from Rome on diplomatic business. All that can be said with any certainty, on the basis of the correspondence between Bibbiena and Bembo, is that the first group of panels were completed very quickly, and the artists awaited further instructions before proceeding.[38] That the literary program was not entirely worked out in advance, is never described in the surviving letters, and its principal author was away from Rome during much of its realization should serve as a further check against attempting any exhaustive reading of the *Stufetta* frescoes.

But in the most excessively totalizing interpretation of their significance to date, Franco Ruffini in the first chapter of his 1986 study of the *Calandria* argues that the entire fresco cycle is to be taken as a transparent and powerful reelaboration of the mythology of Venus, a transformation of the erotic into the triumph of reason over passion, a conclusion he attempts in the remainder of his book to extract from the comedy. Ruffini's argument regarding the *Stufetta*, which he repeatedly describes as Bibbiena's "secret space," is predicated not on the extant frescoes themselves, but on utilizing engravings made in the period by Marco

Dente and Marcantonio Raimondi, images that it is generally accepted were made from the artists' preparatory drawings. Ruffini postulates that these engravings are "truer" to Bibbiena's original project than the frescoes as they were executed.[39] An additional clue to the decontextualized reading that Ruffini offers of the *Stufetta* is evident when he writes that its "most iconographically organic area is the upper walls . . . [and] we will therefore limit ourselves to examining only the wall-cycle [of frescoes]."[40] But to ignore the elaborate surrounding decoration of the room, worked out in exquisite approximation of its ancient Roman models (and in considerably better repair than the frescoes), is to misunderstand entirely the *Stufetta*'s original function as a bath-closet after the ancient Roman fashion whose walls, like those of the original *calidaria*, were heated to promote sweating.[41] The thematic unity of the entire space is emphasized by Redig de Campos when he notes that many of the animals depicted coupling together in the decorative detail of the vaulted ceiling are usually considered to be enemies, a sign of the absolute force of Venerean love within the parameters of the *Stufetta*.[42]

One detailed example of Ruffini's method will serve to demonstrate the problems produced when an interpretive point of view is privileged over its evidence. The first of the original eight frescoes is an image of the *Birth of Venus*, in which the goddess is depicted with her back turned to the viewer, the seashell on which she stands the only other discernible detail in the panel. But in Marco Dente's print of the same scene there is a great deal more going on: Two sea monsters swim nearby the goddess in the midst of a foaming sea; above are two crowned figures, one of them in the act of assaulting the other, his genitals exposed, with a curved sword. Ruffini posits that this is an image of *Venus Anadiomene*—one of the two Venuses Plato identifies in the *Symposium*—who was born from the sea into which the castrated genitals of Uranus fell, severed by his son Chronos (Saturn in the Latin pantheon).[43] There is, however, a problem for Ruffini in the engraver's depiction of the upper scene, for the figure about to be castrated is shown holding a sheaf of grain, an iconographic signifier not associated with Uranus but typical in images and descriptions of Saturn, who in the Latin cult was associated with agriculture and abundance. Though Ruffini fails to acknowledge them, sheaves of grain also adorn the two satyrs in the marble bas-reliefs found in the lower north and south walls of the *Stufetta*, an element in Bibbiena's coat of arms. This reading might be considered plausible, providing we recall that the image Ruffini interprets here is not the image painted on the wall of the *Stufetta*, rather an engraving of a formative sketch of it. But he then makes an interpretive leap by asserting that the upper scene is a depiction of the castration of Chronos by Zeus and, hence, that the goddess pictured below cannot be either *Venus*

Anadiomene or Plato's other *Venus Pandemia* (born of the union of Jupiter and Dione), but rather a newly minted *Venus Saturnia*, the daughter of Saturn/Chronos and as such the *daughter of reason*, given that Saturn "symbolized reason, the mediatrix between nature and the intellect." That there is no precedent in antiquity for such a genealogy is never acknowledged,[44] and while much later in the chapter Ruffini notes that this third Venus is a product of Pico della Mirandola's thinking, he sidesteps the question of Bibbbiena's acquaintance with this particular aspect of Pico's system by asserting that "it is superfluous to ask if and how Pico's mythogram would have been known to [him]."[45] But characterizing his hypotheses as "absolutely certain" suppositions, Ruffini then goes on to identify the two sea monsters in Dente's engraving: The one on the left is a dolphin, but the other is more problematic, exhibiting features unknown among sea creatures in the period, an unnatural commingling of fish and, "unequivocally," pig or boar. This latter detail is confirmed for Ruffini in the tale of Adonis, who dies mauled by a boar (the symbol of concupiscence) he had been warned against by his lover Venus, who thereafter becomes the sworn enemy of all swine. So in Dente's image, Venus turned from the viewer is a rebuke to the pig/boar that represents unchecked passion. For Ruffini, this Venus is unimaginable as "low or plebeian"—or, in a word, sexual—though he does admit to the "sensuality of the image." He sees her as "pure, burnished, the friend of light and splendor;" Venus is the embodiment of reason who "rides herd on lust."

The contingent manner in which Ruffini's argument is constructed, however, betrays its credibility. Elements such as the right sea creature's necessarily porcine features are clearly arguable, to say nothing of the fact that his analysis is here completely organized around pictorial clues missing (perhaps never present in the first place) from the remains of the painted image in the *Stufetta*.[46] He sees her as but even were we to concede that Dente's engraving could conceivably be read as a facsimile of the fresco, Ruffini's refusal to pay attention to anything in the room but the frescoes as he assumes they should have been painted forces him to disregard the fastidious attention to antique pictorial detail everywhere in evidence in the *Stufetta*, and that, one might suppose, extended as well to its narrative program.

While there are simply too many gaps in our knowledge of the articulation of the *Stufetta* by those involved in its decoration to reach conclusions as sweeping as Ruffini's, the culmination of his analysis of the *Birth of Venus* lays bare the motivation for such an overdetermined approach: "Neither *Venus Pandemia*, which would be blasphemous for even a lay-cardinal; nor *Venus Anadiomene*, who would be 'out of place' in a cardinal's bath closet; but *Venus Saturnia*, that is human love . . . the impulses of the body, *but tamed by* the bridle of reason. Venus, *but* subdued by Saturn. Something not unworthy of a *calidarium* and similarly not unbecoming of a prelate."[47] So the point of Ruffini's exercise is—as was the case for much of the medieval allegorical tradition with regard to classical literature—to situate the *Stufetta* within a didactically moralizing space that rescues it from the scurrilous imputations that have dogged its reception and interpretation. But with an eye to both the historical realities of the moment in which the room was conceived, the character of its patron, and contemporary artistic practices we are not by any means compelled to accept Ruffini's interpretation as authoritative. His reading of the *Stufetta* is as imaginative as it is *queer*; anxious as he is to save its images from their manifestly erotic import, he turns them into a neo-Platonic fantasy of sexual sublimation. For Ruffini, the *Stufetta* must be considered a "secret space" because of the dirty secrets that it contains for the scandalized post-Renaissance viewer embarrassed by the period's easy conflation of pagan and Christian tropes. It is certainly incorrect to collapse these categories into one another, as Ruffini's analysis attempts, and as these remarks of Pope Clement VII to an unidentified artist-correspondent warn against: "In regard to [antique] stories and fables I prefer a varied menu. I am particularly partial to Ovid, of whom you write; however, see to it that you choose the most beautiful of those tales that I send you . . . nothing obscure, but varied and choice. As for the Old Testament, leave those stories to Our Lord's *Loggie*."[48]

There is little in Bibbiena's own profile to suggest his identification with the sober humanist program Ruffini's reading of the *Stufetta* would suggest. Bembo, of course, did serve as intermediary between Bibbiena and Raphael during much of the period in which work on the room was carried out, but it is equally (perhaps even more) significant that Giulio Romano—who within a few years would have to flee Rome following the unauthorized circulation of the erotic drawings that have come to be known as *I modi*—was closely involved in the actual painting of the space.[49] Though Bibbiena acquired a solid humanistic preparation early in life that led to his rapid advancement with the Medici, he developed as an ambitious man of action with a widely noted love of complicated jokes and games, and there is nothing to suggest, as Ruffini repeatedly implies, that his appointment as Cardinal of Santa Maria in Portico effected anything other than a significant change in his status. Despite a lengthy discussion of Bembo's neo-Platonism and Castiglione's representation of it in the *Cortegiano*, Ruffini ignores the possible implications that Bibbiena's role as jokester in that text (as well as Giovio's image of him in his biography of Leo) might have for understanding the *Stufetta* images as he contemplated them from the comfort of his warm tub.[50] Given that cigars are sometimes only cigars, it would seem reasonable to interpret the series of erotic images adorning the walls of Bibbiena's bath-closet as nothing other than an innovative experiment in the Renaissance revival of Roman antiquity. For as Dollmayr writes:

> "[A]ntique in their form, erotic in their content, the images in the tiny room are a monument characteristic of their patron . . . similar in temperament to the pope he had known since childhood, he was (like him) a man of the world who, in spite of occasional careless lapses that compromisingly exposed his fatuous side, nevertheless also cultivated an informed interest in art and in the literature of antiquity. While this cardinal has often been accused of frivolity for having had his bath-closet decorated with pagan scenes little becoming of a prince of the Church, judgments of this sort are not made according to the standards of his own time."[51]

Dollmayr's final point here is a crucial one for the assessment of the polyvalent forms of early modern sexuality by underscoring the alterity of this historical moment in relation to our own. And it is this recognition of the distance we must travel in interpreting the evidence of a culture so remote from ours that explains why I submit the heterogeneous threads of the preceding examination for consideration under the rubric *queer*. In the course of this essay, I have moved from an examination of the controversial (homo)sexual practices of Giovanni de' Medici and others in his family's circle to the apparently (hetero)sexual frame of reference of his chief counselor, Bernardo Dovizi da Bibbiena, and in doing so I have aimed at outlining a degree of contiguity in the sexual culture of the papal court that they inhabited. But my parentheses here emphasize more than just a semantic problem by drawing attention to the inadequacy of even our most highly theorized contemporary critical categories in accounting for as elusive a panther as human sexuality. *Queer*, in its broadest sense, seems as apposite a taxonomy as any for this phenomenon within the space of the Renaissance papal court, in terms not only of its homoerotic character with regard to Leo X but also in referring to the whole range of sexual practices, their representation, and occlusion within the context of a professedly celibate culture. The contested histories of both Leo's sexuality and the meaning of the ciphers painted on the walls of Bibbiena's bath-closet attest to the manifold ways in which the *queer* space of the Renaissance papacy has hitherto so often been circumscribed.

Michael Wyatt studied philosophy and theology at the Università Gregoriana in Rome and holds a Ph.D. in Italian Studies from Stanford University. His book *The Italian Encounter with Tudor England: A Cultural Politics of Translation* is forthcoming from Cambridge University Press.

Notes

1. Craig B. Brush, *Montaigne and Bayle, Variations on the Theme of Scepticism* (The Hague: Martinus Nijhoff, 1966), p. 252.
2. Pierre Bayle, *Dictionnaire Historique et Critique* (Paris: Desoer, 1820–1824), vol. IX, p. 145: "Rien ne contribua davantage à l'élever à la papauté, que les blessures qu'il avait reçues dans les combats vénériens"; unless otherwise indicated, all translations are my own.
3. See William Roscoe, *The Life and Pontificate of Leo X* (Philadelphia: Lorenzo Press, 1806), vol. 2, pp. 202–04.
4. The remainder of the title is telling: *Ouvrage où l'on considere l'Eglise Romaine dans tous ses dehors, & où l'on fait voir par l'histoire de sa conduite qu'elle ne peut être la veritable Eglise, à l'exclusion de toutes les autres communions du christianisme, comme elle prétend* (Amsterdam: Chez Henry Desbordes, 1685).
5. Cited by Bayle, vol. XIII, p. 326: "débauché et vicieux au delà de tout ce qui se peut imaginer . . . un auteur papiste a écrit qu'on lui présenta une requête de la part de la famille du cardinal de Sainte-Lucie, à ce qu'il leur fût permis d'exercer l'acte de sodomie durant les trois plus chauds mois de l'année, juin, juillet, et août."
6. Brush, p. 254 and pp. 252–54 for a discussion of the careful scrutiny Bayle devotes to this accusation.
7. Bayle has often been accused of an untoward dependence on scabrous material in the *Dictionnaire*, but Ciro Senofonte argues in *Pierre Bayle dal Calvanismo all'Illuminismo* (Naples: Edizioni Scientifiche Italiane, 1978) that [Bayle] "was as apt to collect as to reject rumors of this nature, depending upon the particular exigencies of his research," p. 159; see pp. 158–66 for a thorough discussion of Bayle's strategic deployment of the erotic and obscene in the *Dictionnaire*.
8. *OED Online* (http://dictionary.oed.com).
9. On same-sex desire and Leo X, see also the biography by Giovanni Dall'Orto at *La gaya scienza* (http://digilander.libero.it/giovannidallorto), which cites several sixteenth-century *pasquinate* and a somewhat reticent passage from Francesco Guicciardini, *Storia d'Italia* XVI.xii: "[C]redettesi per molti, nel primo tempo del pontificato, che e' fusse castissimo; ma si scoperse poi dedito eccessivamente, e ogni dí piú senza vergogna, in quegli piaceri che con onestà non si possono nominare." ("[P]articulary at the beginning of his ponitificate, many people believed him to be chaste; but he soon revealed himself a devotee—more shameless with each passing day—of those pleasures which we cannot honorably name," trans. Cestaro.)
10. Bayle, vol. IX, pp. 145–46: "ce qui ne marquerait pas une origine honteuse."
11. Ingrid Rowland, *The Culture of the High Renaissance: Ancients and Moderns in Sixteenth-Century Rome* (Cambridge: Cambridge University Press, 1999), p. 240.
12. Bayle, vol. IX, pp. 146–47: "On ne peut pas accuse Paul Joue d'avoir épargné l'encens à Leon X; mais d'autre côté on doit convenir qu'il s'explique assez

nettement sur les vices de ce pape, pour ne lasser pas en peine un lecteur intelligent. Les plaisirs, dit-il, où il se plongeait trop souvent, et les impudicités qu'on lui objectait, ternirent l'éclat de ses vertus. Il ajoute qu'un naturel plus facile et plus complaisant que corrompu le fit tomber dans ce précipice, n'ayant eu auprès de lui que des gens qui, au lieu de l'avertir de son devoir, ne lui parlaient que de parties de plaisirs. . . . Un peu après il avoue que ce pape fut diffamé pour le crime de sodomie."

13. Paolo Giovio, *In vitam leoni decimi* in *Opera VI, Vitarum* (Rome: Istituto Poligrafico e Zecca dello Stato, 1987), p. 95.

14. The former position is best exemplified by Roscoe, *op. cit.*, the latter by Herbert Vaughan in *The Medici Popes* (New York: G. P. Putnam's Sons, 1908).

15. Michael J. Rocke, *Forbidden Friendships: Homosexuality and Male Culture in Renaissance Florence* (New York: Oxford University Press, 1996).

16. See Valerie Traub, "Desire and the Differences it Makes" in: *The Matter of Difference: Materialist Feminist Criticism of Shakespeare*, ed. Valerie Wayne (Ithaca, NY: Cornell University Press, 1991), pp. 81–114.

17. For other significant work on sexuality in the period relevant to this essay, see James M. Saslow, *Ganymede in the Renaissance: Homosexuality in Art and Society* (New Haven, CT: Yale University Press, 1986), " 'A Veil of Ice between My Heart and Fire': Michelangelo's Sexual Identity and Early Modern Constructs of Homosexuality," *Genders* 2 (Summer 1988), pp. 77–90, and Bette Talvacchia, *Taking Positions: On the Erotic in Renaissance Culture* (Princeton, NJ: Princeton University Press, 1999).

18. For what follows here, see Rocke, pp. 42–43 and 197–201.

19. In "Sacred Erotica: The Classical *figura* in Religious Painting of the Early Cinquecento," *International Journal of the Classical Tradition* 2, 2 (Fall 1995), pp. 238–64, Robert W. Gaston examines the considerable reticence of art historians, beginning with Vasari, in confronting the clearly erotic import of a great deal of Renaissance religious art. I am grateful to John Paoletti for bringing this essay to my attention (and for his helpful critique of an early version of this essay).

20. Alan Stewart, *Close Readers: Humanism and Sodomy in Early Modern England* (Princeton, NJ: Princeton University Press, 1997).

21. Ibid., pp. 19–34.

22. Ibid., pp. 8–19; he notes, however, that Bembo's account does rewrite what can be established with regard to the funeral ode Poliziano did indeed finish (it was set to music at the time by Heinrich Isaac) several years before his own death. Stewart also rightly criticizes Lauro Martines (p. 17) for eliding the sexual politics inherent in Renaissance love poetry, specifically the omission such a misreading creates as to the possibility of "seeing" male–male sexual relations in the period, one further example of the historiographical occlusion/collusion at the heart of this essay's inquiry.

23. Roscoe, vol. I, p. 74.

24. See the *Dizionario biografico degli italiani* (Rome: Istituto della Enciclopedia Italiana, 1960–), vol. 41, pp. 593–600 for a summary of Bibbiena's life and career.

25. Baldassarre Castiglione, *Il libro del cortegiano*, ed. Ettore Bonora (Milan: Mursia, 1972), II.xlv. I quote from the translation of Thomas Hoby, *The Book of the Courtier* (New York: E. P. Dutton, 1928), p. 137.

26. See Giovio, p. 94.

27. Ronald Martinez, "The Triumphs of Calandria," unpublished essay; I thank the author for his permission to cite from his text here.

28. Ibid., p. 3.

29. Bernardo Dovizi da Bibbiena, *La calandria*, ed. Paolo Fossati (Turin: Giulio Einaudi, 1982), V.xii, p. 96.

30. Martinez, pp. 5–6.

31. Ibid., pp. 9–10.

32. See Deoclicio Redig de Campos, "La *Stufetta* del Cardinal Bibbiena in Vatico e il suo restauro," *Römisches Jahrbuch für Keunstgeschichte* (1982), p. 235; and see pp. 225–37 for images of the space, currently among the rooms occupied by the Vatican Secretariat of State.

33. Martinez, p. 6.

34. I use the term "fresco" as a convenience, as have most of the art historians who have written about the *Stufetta*, but the images were not painted onto wet plaster, a fact that partially accounts for their poor state of preservation.

35. See Redig de Campos, p. 235.

36. Redig de Campos, pp. 238–39, and see pp. 239–40 for his argument in support of Raphael as the principal designer of the *Stufetta*'s decorative scheme. Redig de Campos feels that Raphael may have also been responsible for painting several of the the the panels, particularly *Venus and Amor* (the second of the series and widely regarded as the most refined of the surviving six frescoes), as well as some of the imitative Roman antique detail elsewhere in the space, the remaining work left primarily to Giulio Romano and Giovanni da Udine. For the best discussion of the architectural plan of the space, see Stefano Roy, "La *Stufetta* del Cardinal Bibbiena" in: *Raffaello architetto: linguaggio artistico e ideologia nel Rinascimento romano* (Rome: Editori Laterza, 1974), pp. 160–64.

37. Which Leonard Barkan has examined with regard to sculpture in *Unearthing the Past: Archaeology and Aesthetics in the Making of Renaissance Culture* (New Haven, CT: Yale University Press, 1999).

38. The letters can be found in Vincenzo Golzio, *Raffaello nei documenti, nelle testimonianze dei contemporanei e nella letteratura del suo secolo* (Città del Vaticano, 1936), pp. 44–48.

39. For the relationship of the engravings to the frescoes, see the exhibition catalog *Raffaello in Vaticano* (Milano: Electra, 1984), pp. 205–07; for Ruffini's elaboration of this relationship, see his *Commedia e festa nel Rinascimento* (Bologna: Mulino, 1986), pp. 36–37, especially note 9.

40. Ruffini, p. 34.

41. Water issued from the satyr's mouth in the bottom half of the north wall into a free-standing tub; see Heikki Malme, "La *Stufetta* del Cardinal Bibbiena e l'iconografia dei suoi affreschi principali," in: *Quando gli Dei si spogliano: Il bagno di Clemente VII a Castel sant'Angelo e le altre stufe romane del primo*

cinquecento (Rome: Romana Società Editrice, 1984), p. 34, and Redig de Campos, p. 225.

42. Redig de Campos, p. 235.
43. The following discussion is based on Ruffini's discussion, pp. 36–50.
44. Though as Malme notes, the tradition of representing the castration from which this Venus was generated arose in the medieval period, and it was then that the shift from Uranus/Chronos to Saturn/Jupiter occurred; see pp. 40–41.
45. Ruffini, pp. 82–85.
46. Art historians are divided over whether or not the original fresco could have contained the castration scene. Dollmayr writes as if he had seen it, p. 276, but given the restricted space over Venus's head in the fresco it is difficult to imagine how the episode would have fit into the image's overall composition.
47. Ibid., pp. 49–50.
48. Cited by Dollmayr, pp. 278–79.
49. The "Bath of Venus" that Giulio Romano painted in the Sala di Psiche of the Palazzo del Te in Mantua is, according to E. H. Gombrich, a "coarsened" version of a similar scene found in the 1499 *Hypnerotomachia* published in a sumptuous edition by Aldo Manuzio. Whether coarser or not, the Mantuan scene is a Venerean shrine entirely in keeping with the images in the *Stufetta*. For Gombrich, see "*Hypnerotomachiana*," *Journal of the Warburg and Courtauld Institutes* 14 (1951), pp. 119–25.
50. Ruffini, pp. 87–92.
51. Dollmayr, p. 278.

3

Knots of Desire: Female Homoeroticism in *Orlando furioso* 25

Mary-Michelle DeCoste

In the final episode of Matteo Maria Boiardo's *Orlando innamorato*, the maiden warrior Bradamante finds herself in a tricky situation. Dressed in her armor and suffering from a head wound for the treatment of which her hair was shorn, Bradamante stops to rest along the bank of a stream, where she is spotted by the beautiful Fiordispina, out with a hunting party. Fiordispina takes Bradamante for a man and immediately falls in love with her. When Bradamante wakes up, she realizes from the look on Fiordispina's face what has happened, and she says to herself: " 'Qualche una mal contenta / Serà de noi e ingannata alla vista / Ché gratugia a gratugia poco acquista' " (3.9.11.6-8).[1] ("One of us won't be happy! She's / Deceived by what she sees: small gain / Comes when grates grate on grates, not cheese!") Boiardo's epic ends with the two women at this impasse: "Però vi lascio in questo vano amore / De Fiordispina ardente a poco a poco / Un'altra fiata, se mi fia concesso, / Raccontarovi il tutto per espresso" (3.9.26.5-8). (So I will leave this hopeless love / Of simmering Fiordispina. / Some other time, if God permits, / I'll tell you all there is to this.)

Later poets who continued Boiardo's epic had to figure out what to do with the lovesick Fiordispina.[2] Ludovico Ariosto, whose *Orlando furioso* (1532) is the best known continuation of the *Innamorato*, pays most attention to the princess, devoting some of canto 22 and more than half of canto 25 to her story. Ariosto's placement of these two parts of the story within his epic lends the tale additional weight. As Giulio Ferroni points out, "the two moments come one to anticipate and the other to follow, with more or less the same textual distance, the episode of the madness of

Orlando (at the perfect center of the poem)."³ Orlando's madness, the result of his frustrated desire, has obvious and important resonances with the story of Fiordispina. What follows is a reading of Fiordispina's desire against that of Orlando, with a particular emphasis on the role that narrative, and who controls it, plays in these two stories. I am especially interested in what I consider to be the radical nature of Fiordispina's desire, and the ways in which narrative is used ultimately to squelch its subversive potential.

In Ariosto's story, as in Boiardo's, Fiordispina is in the woods with a hunting party when she sees Bradamante, sleeping beside a stream and dressed in the costume of a knight. Believing the maiden warrior to be a man, Fiordispina immediately falls in love with her. Upon waking, Bradamante recognizes Fiordispina's error and explains that she is a woman. This revelation does nothing to change Fiordispina's desire. The entire episode is recounted by Bradamante's twin brother and gender double, Ricciardetto:

"Per questo non si smorza una scintilla
del fuoco de la donna inamorata.
Questo rimedio all'alta piaga è tardo:
tant'avea Amor cacciato inanzi il dardo.

Per questo non le par men bello il viso,
men bel lo sguardo e men belli i costumi;
per ciò non torna il cor, che già diviso
da lei, godea dentro gli amati lumi"
                    (25.32.5-8; 33.1-4).⁴

"These revelations did not abate love-struck Fiordispina's
passion one jot; Cupid had thrust in his dart to make so
deep a gash that this remedy was now too late.

To Fiordispina my sister's face seemed no less beautiful for
this, her eyes, her movements no less graceful; she did not
on this account retrieve mastery over her heart, which had
gone out to Bradamant to bask in her adorable eyes."

The repetition of the adjective *bello* in lines 1 and 2 of octave 33 echoes the description earlier in the canto of Ricciardetto by Ruggiero, Bradamante's fiancé: "'Veggo (dicea Ruggier) la faccia bella / e le belle fattezze e 'l bel sembiante / [...] / [...] de la mia Bradamante'" (25.20.1-4). ("I am looking at the comely face and beautiful figure of my Bradamant.") This echo serves three purposes. First, it highlights the ease with which the twins can be mistaken for one another by using the same adjective to describe them both. Second, it introduces the possibility of male same-sex desire (also based on mistaken identity) to complement Fiordispina's desire for Bradamante. Finally, by assuming the language Ruggiero uses to describe the knight whom he thought was Bradamante, Fiordispina also assumes Ruggiero's role as the subject desirous of Bradamante. The possible disruption of the love between Bradamante and Ruggiero has great subversive potential since this couple is destined to marry and generate the line of the Este family, Ariosto's patrons and the family to which he dedicates his poem.

Lines 3 and 4 of octave 33, with their clear Petrarchan echoes, further establish Fiordispina in the role of the desiring subject that poetic tradition had reserved for men. In fact, the sort of language Fiordispina uses to describe her erotic impulses appears elsewhere in the poem to describe a man's sexual possession of a virgin. Fiordispina says, " 'D'ogn'altro amore, o scelerato o santo, / il desïato fin sperar potrei; / saprei partir la rosa da le spine' " (25.34.5-7). ("Were it a question of any other love, evil or virtuous, I could hope to see it consummated, and I should know how to cull the rose from the briar.") In the first canto of the poem, the knight Sacripante expounds upon the importance of a girl's virginity:

"La verginella è simile alla rosa,
ch'in bel giardin su la nativa spina
mentre sola e sicura si riposa,
[. . .]
[. . .]
La vergine che 'l fior, di che piú zelo
che de' begli occhi e de la vita aver de',
lascia altrui côrre, il pregio ch'avea inanti
perde nel cor di tutti gli altri amanti."
(1.42.1-3;43.5-8)

"A virgin is like a rose . . . while she remains on the thorn
whence she sprang, alone and safe in a lovely garden . . . .
[. . .]
[. . .]
The virgin who suffers one to cull her flower—of which she
should be more jealous than of her own fair eyes, than of
her life—loses the esteem she once enjoyed in the hearts of
all her other wooers."

A similar turn of phrase is used to describe the first mating of Angelica, the main object of desire of the first half of the poem, and Medoro: "Angelica a Medor la prima rosa / coglier lasciò" (19.33.1-2). ("Angelica let Medor pluck the first rose.") Fiordispina's appropriation of this male language and the fact that this language recalls Fiordispina's name itself

("rosa da le spine" echoes Fiordispina), establishes her in the role of the
sexually aggressive subject desirous of a woman, a position held elsewhere
in the poem only by men. Yet the same name that emphasizes her position
also serves to destabilize it. "Fiordispina" might also indicate a flower that
has already been plucked: a "deflowered" girl. Or it might mark her as a
virgin waiting to be deflowered, the object rather than the subject of
desire. Like the semantic instability of her name, Fiordispina's love blurs
the boundaries between subject and object, male and female.

Despite, or perhaps because of, the flexibility of her desire, Fiordispina
believes that it can never be satisfied: " 'Vedendola in quell'abito, l'è aviso /
che può far che 'l desir non la consumi; / e quando, ch'ella è pur femina,
pensa, / sospira e piange e mostra doglia immensa' " (25.33.5-8). ("Seeing
her accoutred as a man, she had imagined that there would be no need for
her passion to remain unassuaged; but now the thought that her beloved
was also a woman made her sigh and weep and betray boundless sorrow.")
Addressing Love, Fiordispina describes why she is sure Bradamante can
never satisfy her:

"Né tra gli uomini mai né tra l'armento,
che femina ami femina ho trovato:
non par la donna all'altre donne bella,
né a cervie cervia, né all'agnelle agnella.

In terra in aria, in mar, sola son io
Che patisco da te sí duro scempio;
E questa hai fatto acciò che l'error mio
Sia ne l'imperio tuo l'ultimo esempio.
La moglie del re Nino ebbe disio,
il figlio amando, scelerato et empio,
e Mirra il padre, e la Cretense il toro:
ma gli è piú folle il mio, ch'alcun dei loro.

La femina nel maschio fe' disegno,
speronne il fine, et ebbelo, come odo:
Pasife ne la vacca entrò del legno,
altre per altri mezzi e vario modo.
Ma se volasse a me con ogni ingegno
Dedalo, non potria scioglier quel nodo
che fece il mastro troppo diligente,
Natura, d'ogni cosa piú possente."
                              (25.35.5-8;36;37)

"Neither among humans nor among beasts have I ever
come across a woman loving a woman; to a woman another
woman does not seem beautiful, nor does a hind to a hind, a
ewe to a ewe.

By land, sea, and air I alone suffer thus cruelly at your hands—you have done this to make an example of my abberation, the ultimate one in your power. King Ninus' wife was evil and profane in her love for her son; so was Mirra, in love with her father, and Pasiphae with the bull. But my love is greater folly than any of theirs.

These females made designs upon the males and achieved the desired consummation, so I am told. Pasiphae went inside the wooden cow, the others achieved their end by other means. But even if Daedalus came flying to me with every artifice at his command, he would be unable to untie the knot made by that all-too-diligent Maker, Nature, who is all-powerful."

Fiordispina's insistence on her desire as unique notwithstanding, there is an obvious literary precedent for a woman desiring another woman. While Ariosto's tale of Fiordispina's love for Bradamante comes from Boiardo, the language of his verses clearly echoes that of Iphis, a girl in love with another girl who thinks Iphis is a boy, in Book 9 of Ovid's *Metamorphoses*.[5] Fiordispina, while declaring her ignorance of the story of Iphis, uses language taken almost directly from Ovid. There is a disjuncture between desire and narrative: Fiordispina claims that she is outside of any narrative tradition while at the same time Ariosto inscribes her into one. Allusion to the story of Iphis foreshadows the change of gender in the Fiordispina story while it hints at the way in which Fiordispina's desire—subversive because it claims to be outside of narrative—will ultimately be controlled by it.

Fiordispina's desire is potentially subversive not only because Bradamante must be free to marry Ruggiero but also because it could overshadow Fiordispina's filial obligations. In Ovid's story, Iphis desires Ianthe and longs to be able to fulfill the role of her husband according to the wishes of their families. The goddess Isis changes Iphis into a boy, who goes happily to his wedding. Iphis's desire, although for another girl, is clearly within the heterosexual paradigm of marriage and family, and as such, it lacks the subversive potential of Fiordispina's desire, which is a lust for " 'la faccia e le viril fattezze' " (25.28.5) ["the face and manly build"] of Bradamante, a lust for sex that is not necessarily accompanied by desire for marriage. With this lust, Fiordispina occupies the position of desiring subject, the same position that Iphis occupies in Ovid's tale, yet Fiordispina's wish is different. Iphis immediately sees a sex change for either her or Ianthe as the answer to her problem: " '[I]pse licet revolet ceratis Daedalus alis, / quid faciet? num me puerum de virgine doctis / artibus efficiet? num te mutabit, Ianthe?' " ("[T]hough Daedalus himself should fly back on waxen wings, what could he do? With all his learned arts could he make me into a boy from a girl? or could he change you, Ianthe?")[6] Fiordispina never expresses such a wish. Her wish is more complicated: she would have Dedalus " 'scoglier quel nodo che fece . . . Natura' " ("untie the knot made by . . . Nature").

"Quel nodo" refers to two things: Bradamante's lack of desire for Fiordispina, which is an impediment to Fiordispina's satisfaction, and the boundary that Fiordispina is certain even Dedalus himself is powerless to help her cross, the boundary of sexual difference. If there were not two sexes, the construction of which Fiordispina attributes to Nature, Fiordispina could desire whomever she chose and hope for satisfaction. It is Fiordispina's wish to "untie the knot" that will be her eventual undoing.[7]

Despite what she sees as the hopelessness of the situation, Fiordispina does her best to seduce an unwilling Bradamante through her powers of persuasion. As Fiordispina laments her plight, Bradamante " 'per pietà ne piange, / et è a sentir di quel dolor constretta' " (25.38.5-6) ("wept for pity and felt embarrassed as she listened to her grieving"). When Fiordispina invites Bradamante to spend the night at her family's castle, " 'non le seppe negar' " (25.40.1) ("she was unable to refuse"). Fiordispina uses this influence to try to awaken some desire in Bradamante. As Ricciardetto relates, when they arrive at the castle, " '[f]ece là dentro Fiordispina bella / la mia sirocchia accarezzar non poco, / E rivestita di feminil gonna' " (25.40.5-6). ("Fiordispina made much of my sister; she dressed her once more in feminine attire.") That Fiordispina dresses Bradamante in female attire and continues to try to seduce her suggests that she is not necessarily after a man. The two sleep in the same bed, and, according to Ricciardetto, Fiordispina repeatedly dreams that Bradamante has been turned into " 'il miglior sesso' " (25.42.8) ("a preferable sex"). Fiordispina touches Bradamante repeatedly throughout the night: " 'Si desta; e nel destar mette la mano, / e ritrova pur sempre il sogno vano' " (25.43.7-8). ("She would wake and reach out, only to find that what she had seen was but an empty dream.") Yet Bradamante wants no part of an affair with Fiordispina. She leaves Fiordispina's castle, proceeds to her family's house, and tells everyone there the story.

Among those listening is Ricciardetto, who looks so much like his sister that even the family can't tell them apart. He had seen Fiordispina before on a number of occasions and had found her very attractive. He sees in Fiordispina's desire for his sister the opportunity to satisfy his own desire for the princess. Telling no one of his plan, Ricciardetto dresses in his sister's armor and rides to the Spanish castle. When he arrives, Fiordispina takes him for Bradamante, and showers him with attention:

"Le belle braccia al collo indi mi getta,
e dolcemente stringe, e bacia in bocca.
Tu puoi pensar s'allora la saetta
dirizzi Amor, s'in mezzo il cor mi tocca.
Per man mi piglia, e in camera con fretta
mi mena; e non ad altri, ch'a lei, tocca
che da l'elmo allo spron l'arme mi slacci;
e nessun altro vuol che se n'impacci.

Poi fattasi arrecare una sua veste
adorna e ricca, di sua man la spiega,
e come io fossi femina, mi veste,
e in reticella d'oro il crin mi lega."
                                    (25.54;55.1-4)

"Throwing her graceful arms around my neck, she softly
hugged me and kissed me on the lips. You can imagine
after this how Love guided his dart to pierce me at the heart
of my heart! She took me by the hand and quickly led me
into her bedroom; here she would suffer none but herself to
undo my armour, from helmet to spurs; no one else was to
take a hand.

Next she sent for a dress of hers, richly ornate, which she
herself spread out and put on me as though I were a
woman; and she caught my hair in a golden net."

With this passage, the narrator Ricciardetto begins to erase Bradamante
from the story of Fiordispina's desire, substituting himself instead. At this
point, Ricciardetto simply steps into Bradamante's place, allowing himself
to be (and apparently enjoying his role as) the feminized object of
Fiordispina's passion. Indeed, Ricciardetto's cross-dressing only serves to
highlight the queerness of the princess's desire. His position as the object
of Fiordispina's ministrations is emphasized by his repetition of the pronoun *mi*, which also effectively shifts the focus of the story to Ricciardetto,
forcing the reader (as well as the listener, Ruggiero) to consider
Ricciardetto's increasing involvement in a tale that began as the story of
Fiordispina's love for Bradamante. By repeating the scene in which
Fiordispina dresses Bradamante in women's clothes, but in much greater
detail and substituting himself for his sister, Ricciardetto cancels out
Bradamante's presence in the story, at least for Ruggiero.
    Ricciardetto, who understands the specificity of Fiordispina's desire
enough to continue the fiction he has invented, then begins his work of

*un*queering this desire. Still pretending to be Bradamante, Ricciardetto explains to Fiordispina that after leaving her castle, he saved a nymph from being devoured by a stag, and the nymph in return promised to give him whatever he wanted. He says that he did not ask for riches or power or victory and honor in war, " 'ma sol che qualche via donde il desire / vostro s'adempia, mi schiuda e disserre: / né piú le domando un ch'un altro effetto, / ma tutta al suo giudicio mi rimetto' " (25.63.5-8). ("but that she would show me some way I could fulfill your desire; I did not ask to achieve this in one way or in another, but left the method up to her own discretion.") According to Ricciardetto's story, the nymph turned Bradamante into a man. Ricciardetto thus realigns Fiordispina's desire with the penis by insisting that he is actually Bradamante, except now a man. Furthermore, he insists that he did not ask to be changed into a man, but only that he be granted the means to satisfy Fiordispina's desire. Ricciardetto thus tricks Fiordispina into believing that the satisfaction of her desire depends on Bradamante's (once absent, now present) penis and that the nymph, who has the power to " 'far cose stupende, / e sforzar gli elementi e la *natura*' " (25.62.1-2, emphasis mine) ["to perform miracles, to coerce *nature* and the elements"], wills it thus. The devouring stag can be read as nature perverted (since in nature stags do not prey on other animals) as well as love perverted (since in the literary *topos* of the hunt, the hunter normally represents the lover and the stag, his quarry, the beloved). By killing the stag, Ricciardetto restores both nature and love to their proper course.

Certainly Fiordispina is pleased with what she assumes to be a change in Bradamante. Ricciardetto would have the reader believe that Fiordispina is pleased because "Bradamante" acquires the penis necessary to satisfy Fiordispina's desire: " 'la donna [. . .] tocca e vede / quel di ch'avuto avea tanto desire' " (25.67.1-2). ("she saw and touched the object she so craved.") Yet "Bradamante" has also acquired the desire to satisfy Fiordispina's passion. Fiordispina had spent the previous evening groping Bradamante, trying to arouse her desire. On this second night, "Bradamante" takes Fiordispina's hand and places it on his/her genitals (25.65.7-8). From Fiordispina's point of view, where once Bradamante slept through Fiordispina's advances, now Bradamante is taking the initiative.

By presenting himself as Bradamante with a newly acquired male organ, Ricciardetto aligns the satisfaction of Fiordispina's desire with Bradamante's possession of a penis. He thus makes allowances for Fiordispina's very specific desire for *Bradamante* while diminishing the subversive potential of that love by changing it into desire for Bradamante as a man. Ricciardetto recognizes what makes Fiordispina so dangerous: that she desires Bradamante across gender boundaries. She loves the

Bradamante who is a woman but who appears to be a man, the Bradamante whom she knows to be a woman, and the man she believes to be Bradamante (really Ricciardetto) turned into a man. To ask whether or not Fiordispina's love is homosexual, as many critics have, is to ask the wrong question. Fiordispina's love is subversive because it defies such categorization.[8]

Fiordispina's desire renders irrelevant not only the categories of homo- and heterosexual, but also man and woman. Because her desire is so specifically for Bradamante, she is not interested in what body parts Bradamante possesses; Bradamante's gender is unimportant to her. The differentiation and naming of sexual body parts is essential to gender distinction and, by extension, to the organization of heterosexuality itself. As Judith Butler writes, "that penis, vagina, breasts, and so forth, are *named* sexual parts is both a restriction of the erogenous body to those parts and a fragmentation of the body as a whole. Indeed, the 'unity' imposed upon the body by the category of sex is a 'disunity,' a fragmentation and compartmentalization, and a reduction of erotogeneity."[9] Fiordispina's desire celebrates instead what she perceives as the fluidity of Bradamante's gender, which, in her eyes, changes from male to female and back to male again.

When Ricciardetto directs Fiordispina's desire away from "la faccia e le viril fattezze" of Bradamante and towards his penis, he is reaffirming the naming of body parts that defines sexual difference and heterosexuality. He literally reconstructs Fiordispina's desire, and she is drawn back into the order of a binary gender system, the knot tied by Nature that Fiordispina sought to undo. Monique Wittig argues that this "natural" system is not natural at all. She feels that sex, like race, "is taken as an 'immediate given,' a 'sensible given,' 'physical features,' belonging to a natural order. But what we believe to be a physical and direct perception is only a sophisticated and mythic construction, an 'imaginary formation,' which reinterprets physical features (in themselves as neutral as any others but marked by the social system) through the network of relationships in which they are perceived."[10] Ricciardetto squelches Fiordispina's attempt to interpret physical features in her own way, outside of the heterosexual imperative, and insists that she, too, organize her desire according to the dominant paradigm.

Ricciardetto has Love Himself on his side in his efforts to tighten the knot of sexual difference. He says of his plan to take Bradamante's place: " 'Di questa speme Amore ordisce i nodi, / che d'altre fila ordir non li potea' " (25.50.1). ("Out of this hope, Love prepared bonds for me, having no other cord with which to capture me.") On one level, the "altre fila" refer to the slim hope Ricciardetto had of satisfying his desire with

Fiordispina, as opposed to the great hope he has now. They also refer to Bradamante. Ricciardetto asserts that love between two women is impossible: Love cannot work with such material. When Ricciardetto goes to Fiordispina that night, "'Amore è duce'" (25.52.1) ("Cupid is guide"), and in the end Fiordispina is completely bound by these knots that Ricciardetto and Love have contrived: "'Non con piú nodi i flessuosi acanti / le colonne circondano e le travi, / di quelli con che noi legammo stretti / e colli e fianchi e braccia e gambe e petti'" (25.69.5-8). ("Never did twisting acanthus entwine pillars and beams with more knots than those which bound us together, our necks and sides, our arms, legs, and breasts in a close embrace.")

Ricciardetto also has narrative on his side—an ally at least as powerful as Love. It is Ricciardetto who tells the entire story of Fiordispina and is in complete control of the narrative. It is therefore crucial to remember that the reader hears the story of Bradamante and Fiordispina third-hand: Bradamante tells Ricciardetto, and Ricciardetto tells Ruggiero. The reader is privileged to listen in on this second telling. Furthermore, Ricciardetto has a lot at stake in telling this story to Ruggiero. He is greatly in debt to Ruggiero for saving his life; he can begin to repay that debt by entertaining his companion to make their journey less tiresome. Ricciardetto also promises Ruggiero a good story: "'Io non credo che fabula si conte, / che piú di questa istoria bella fosse'" (25.27.5-6). ("I don't believe there can be a story more beautiful than this one.") Having made such a promise, he must deliver. Finally, by telling Ruggiero a story that showcases his own ingenuity and sexual prowess, Ricciardetto can shore up his masculinity, compromised by having had to be rescued by Ruggiero in the first place.

For all of these reasons, Ariosto casts the truth of Ricciardetto's words in doubt from the beginning. Although Ricciardetto introduces his tale as *istoria*, a true story, he compares it to a *fabula*, an invented fable. Furthermore, because he was not a witness to the unfolding of Fiordispina's love for Bradamante, the reader must doubt everything he says regarding the princess. Particularly suspicious are exclamations like "'Quanti prieghi la notte, quanti voti, / offerse al suo Macone e a tutti i dèi, / che con miracoli apparenti e noti / mutassero in miglior sesso costei!'" (25.44.1-4). ("How many prayers and vows did she not offer that night to Mahomet and all the gods, asking them to change Bradamant's sex for the better by a clear and self-evident miracle!") This is a self-serving affirmation on Ricciardetto's part to strengthen his case that Fiordispina's true desire is for a penis. Logically, he could not know what Fiordispina had said unless Bradamante told him, and she was supposedly asleep at the time. Similarly, Ricciardetto claims that after being left by Bradamante,

Fiordispina returned to her castle in tears. Again, Ricciardetto could not know this because Bradamante was not with Fiordispina at that time.

A reading of the Fiordispina story must take into account not only Ricciardetto's shortcomings as a narrator, but also the position of the story within the larger narrative of the poem as a whole. Ariosto presents the Fiordispina episode in two parts: In canto 22, Ruggiero comes upon one of Fiordispina's ladies crying in the woods, who tells him that she fled the castle because a young man who had been sleeping with the princess had been caught and was to be burned. Ruggiero and Bradamante agree to save the young man, and the three set off. In canto 25, Ruggiero rescues Ricciardetto, whom he soon learns is Bradamante's twin brother. Ricciardetto proceeds to tell Ruggiero the story of Fiordispina's love for Bradamante and, eventually, for him. The fact that the Fiordispina story sandwiches the poem's central incident has important ramifications for its interpretation.[11] The episode of Orlando's madness, a story of narrative and its relationship to desire, provides useful clues for a reading of canto 25.

Orlando goes mad in canto 23 upon learning that Angelica, the object of his desire, is in love with someone else. Angelica and Medoro have written their names together all over a small grove: "Angelica e Medoro con cento nodi / legati insieme, e in cento lochi vede" (23.103.1-2). (He saw 'Angelica' and 'Medor' in a hundred places, united by a hundred love-knots.) These "nodi," which Orlando is desperate to loosen, prefigure the knot in canto 25 that Fiordispina would have Dedalus untie. In both instances, the knots point to a truth within the poem. Angelica and Medoro are in fact bound together; they have consummated their love with sexual union. Ricciardetto forces Fiordispina to accept the knot of sexual difference as a prerequisite for the satisfaction of her desire; he refers to his penis as the "veritade espressa," proof that his story about the faun is true, proof that Bradamante needs a penis to satisfy Fiordispina's desire.[12]

Orlando tries to dissuade himself of the truth he sees: "Va col pensier cercando in mille modi / non creder quel ch'al suo dispetto crede" (23.103.5-6). (He searched in his mind for any number of excuses to reject what he could not help believing.) "Usando fraude a se medesmo" (23.104.6) (thus deceiving himself), Orlando tries to convince himself that someone else is lying: "[P]ensa come / possa esser che non sia la cosa vera: / che voglia alcun cosí infamare il nome / de la sua donna" (23.114.1-4). ([H]e hoped against hope that it might simply be someone trying to besmirch his lady's name this way.) He proceeds to an inn, where he finds the "odiato scritto" (23.117.3) (hateful inscriptions) covering the walls. A shepherd confirms the truth about Angelica and Medoro, showing Orlando the jewel that Angelica had given him in thanks for his hospitality.

This last bit of evidence is incontestable. Orlando goes mad and rages through the forest, destroying the graffiti of Angelica and Medoro: "Tagliò lo scritto e 'l sasso, e sin al cielo / a volo alzar fe' le minute schegge" (23.130.1-2). ([he] slashed at the words and the rock-face, sending tiny splinters shooting skywards.) As Millicent Marcus points out, "He kills the writing, vainly hoping, by a kind of magical transference, to destroy the referents of the offending script."[13] Orlando tries desperately to disassociate his desire from narrative truth, both the narrative of the "cento nodi" as well as the narrative of canto 21, through which the reader already knows of Angelica's marriage to Medoro. In the end, it is Orlando's unwillingness or inability to interpret narrative correctly that drives him mad.

The story of Fiordispina can be read in much the same way. Fiordispina's willingness to believe Ricciardetto's narrative draws her into a kind of madness, in which she believes a nymph has turned her beloved Bradamante into a man in order to satisfy her desire. She hovers in a liminal state between sleep and wakefulness, between belief and incredulity. When she touches Ricciardetto's penis, "agli occhi, al tatto, a se stessa non crede, / e sta dubbiosa ancor di non dormire; / e buona prova bisognò a far fede / che sentia quel che le parea sentire. / 'Fa, Dio (disse ella), se son sogni questi, / ch'io dorma sempre, e mai piú non mi desti' " (25.68.3-8) ("she could not believe her eyes or her fingers or herself, and kept wondering whether she were awake or asleep. She needed solid proof to convince her that she was actually feeling what she thought she felt. 'O God, if this is a dream,' she cried, 'keep me asleep for good, and never wake me again!' "). Fiordispina wants to believe that her dream has come true, that a love such as hers, which ignores boundaries of gender, can be fulfilled because gender itself is a transient, changeable quality. As Giulio Ferroni writes, "The fantasy of a happy indistinctness between masculine and feminine, between truth and trick, solidity and illusion, in an erotic universe without boundaries, is the impulse that guides the eternal dreaming of Fiordispina, her impossible identification with an object of desire in which opposite sexual valences contradict and reconcile with one another."[14] Yet to Fiordispina, her desire was not impossible; as far as she knew, she had found what she wanted. But such belief in the changeability of gender is dangerous indeed, and, once again, narrative intervenes to put Fiordispina in her place. The dominant paradigm of sexual organization reasserts itself in the form of the king's dungeon, where Ariosto leaves Fiordispina to rot, never to be heard from again. However, even though she is left behind, Fiordispina is still a source of pleasure in the form of the story Ricciardetto tells to Ruggiero to make their journey less tiresome.

Although Ruggiero expresses his desire to hear the story, the reader already knows that stories told for such reasons can be dangerous.

The shepherd tells Orlando about Angelica and Medoro to lighten the knight's burden: "Il pastor che lo vede cosí oppresso / da sua tristizia, e che voria levarla, / l'istoria nota a sé, che dicea spesso / di quei duo amanti a chi volea ascoltarla, / ch'a molti dilettevole fu a udire / gl'incominciò senza rispetto a dire" (23.118.3-8). (The herdsman, who saw him so downcast and sad and wanted to cheer him up, embarked, without asking leave, upon the story of those two lovers: he knew it well, and often repeated it to those who would listen. There were many who enjoyed hearing it.) With this tale, Orlando is driven into madness. He is, however, given another chance after the knight Astolfo journeys to the moon, collects Orlando's wits, and restores them to him. His sanity having been recovered, Orlando rejects desire, the original cause of his madness:

> "Poi che fu all'esser primo ritornato
> Orlando piú che mai saggio e virile,
> d'amor si trovò insieme liberato;
> sí che colei, che sí bella e gentile
> gli pare dianzi, e ch'avea tanto amato,
> non stia piú se non per cosa vile.
> Ogni suo studio, ogni disio rivolse
> a racquistar quanto già amor gli tolse."
> (39.61)

> "His old self once more, a paragon of wisdom and manliness, Orlando also found himself cured of love: the damsel who had seemed hitherto so beautiful and good in his eyes, and who he had so adored, he now dismissed as utterly worthless. His only concern, his only wish now was to recover all that Love had stolen from him."

His wisdom restored, Orlando is beyond the influence of desire and, therefore, of narrative. Fiordispina, still desiring, still under the influence of Ricciardetto's tale, does not manage to sort out the relationships between desire and narrative, between narrative and truth.[15] With these two examples, Ariosto has offered the reader different possibilities for the interpretation of narrative and, thus, for reading his own poem. It is up to each reader to decide how much of the lying Ricciardetto is in the poet and how much of the believing Fiordispina is in the reader.

Mary-Michelle DeCoste an Assistant professor of Italian Studies at the University of Guelph, received her PhD from Cornell University in Medieval and Renaissance Italian Literature. She is currently at work on a study of the meanings of food in Italian Renaissance literature.

Notes

1. Boiardo published Books 1 and 2 of the *Innamorato* in 1483. It took him until 1494 to write the nine cantos of Book 3, at which time failing health prevented him from continuing with his writing. The apparently incomplete Book 3 was released by the poet's widow after his death in 1494. See the introduction to Matteo Maria Boiardo, *Orlando Innamorato*, with facing-page trans. by Charles Stanley Ross (Berkeley: University of California Press, 1989). Quotations from the *Innamorato*, both the Italian and the English translation, are taken from this edition.

2. For descriptions of the different editions and continuations of the *Innamorato*, see Neil Harris, *Bibliografia dell'Orlando Innamorato*, vol. 2 (Ferrara: Franco Cosimo Panini, 1991).

3. "Da Bradamante a Ricciardetto: Interferenze testuali e scambi di sesso" in: *La parola ritrovata: Fonti e analisi letteraria*, ed. Costanzo Di Girolamo and Ivano Paccagnella (Palermo: Sellerio editore, 1982), p. 140. The English translation is my own.

4. All Italian quotations are taken from Ludovico Ariosto, *Orlando furioso*, ed. Lanfranco Caretti (Turin: Giulio Einaudi, 1966). All English translations are taken from Ludovico Ariosto, *Orlando Furioso*, trans. Guido Waldman (New York: Oxford University Press, 1983).

5. See Pio Rajna, *Le fonti dell'Orlando Furioso* (Firenze: Sansoni, 1900), pp. 368–69.

6. Ovid, *Metamorphoses*, with facing page trans. by Frank Justus Miller (Cambridge, MA: Harvard University Press, 1968), 9.742–744.

7. In *The Lady Vanishes: Subjectivity and Representation in Castiglione and Ariosto* (Stanford, CA: Stanford University Press, 1992), p. 208, Valeria Finucci argues that "quel nodo" refers to the "male organ"; this makes little sense to me given that this noun is the object of the verb *sciogliere* (to untie or to loosen).

8. For example, Ferroni, p. 148, writes that Fiordispina's advances are "circling insidiously around the suggestion of homosexual desire, a desire that grows stronger to the extent that it lacks any possibility of satisfaction or release" (trans. Cestaro). Finucci, pp. 212–13, insists that "the absent penis has to be the narrative center" and that because the penis is the true object of Fiordispina's desire, her wish is "heterosexual and normative."

9. *Gender Trouble: Feminism and the Subversion of Identity* (New York: Routledge, 1990), p. 114.

10. *The Straight Mind and Other Essays* (Boston: Beacon Press, 1992), pp. 11–12.

11. See Elissa Weaver, "Letture dell'intreccio dell'*Orlando Furioso*: il caso delle tre pazzie d'amore," *Strumenti Critici* 34 (1977), pp. 384–406 and, in particular, p. 384: "L'intreccio dell'*Orlando Furioso* attua una consapevole valorizzazione delle possibilità significative dell'*entrelacement*, tecnica ereditata dalla tradizione cavalleresca italiana e da quella francese più antica, che interrompe e divide sequenze di narrazione per collegarle a un livello associativo; episodi vengono approfonditi o complicati per analogie implicite con altri

episodi. . . . Quando il lettore ha apprezzato il singolo episodio, prescindendo dalla tecnica dell'*entrelacement*, è invitato a notare le risonanze di quell'episodio in altri prossimi o simili (per struttura, per tema, o per linguaggio) e di conseguenza i significati aumentano, si complicano, si completano." ("The plot of the *Orlando Furioso* makes conscious use of the signifying possibilities of *entrelacement*, a technique handed down from the Italian—and before that French—chivalric tradition that interrupts and divides narrative sequences in order to link them back up on an associative level. Episodes are enriched and complicated through implicit analogy with other episodes. . . . Once the reader has grasped a single episode, he or she is invited to take note of the ways in which the episode resonates with others near it or like it in structure, theme, or language and as a result meanings multiply as they complicate and complete one another"; trans. Cestaro).

12. See 25.65.7-8, where Ricciardetto invites Fiordispina to verify his masculinity by touching it: "Cosí le disse; e feci ch'ella istessa / trovò con man la veritade espressa." ("Thus I spoke to her, and I guided her hand to test the truth for herself.")

13. "Angelica's Loveknots: The Poetics of Requited Desire in *Orlando Furioso* 19 and 23," *Philological Quarterly* 72 (Winter 1993), pp. 33–51; quotation on p. 43.

14. Ferroni, p. 157; the English translation is my own.

15. A number of readers have been dissatisfied with Ariosto's handling of the situation. In "Androgyny and the Epic Quest: The Female Warrior in Ariosto and Spenser," *Postscript* 2 (1985), pp. 29–37, Elizabeth J. Bellamy refers to the "glaring irresolution of Fiordispina's sexual impulses" (p. 32). Giulio Ferroni, pp. 144–45, also feels that there is something not entirely satisfying about the conclusion of the story: "E la chiusura della vicenda (per la quale non c'è bisogno di nessuna agnizione, di nessun rientro in scena di Bradamante) non propone ricomposizioni, sintesi di contrari, ma lascia, come vedremo, un residuo di 'martire' e di 'dolor' non facilmente dialettizzabile." ("And the episode's close—which requires no unmasking, nor that Bradamante return to the scene—proposes no restructuring or synthesis of opposites, but leaves behind as we shall see a residue of "martyrdom" and "suffering" that is difficult to resolve"; trans. Cestaro.) Similarly, in "*Orlando Innamorato*, Book III: An Appreciation," *Italian Studies* 36 (1981), pp. 27–40, C. E. J. Griffiths writes, "Although, on the one hand, Ariosto's resolution may be considered extremely skillful, on the other hand it may be said to diffuse the dramatic tension of the situation, which exists in Boiardo's poem, with the two women face to face. Ariosto, by allowing Ricciardetto, Bradamante's twin brother, to become the narrator-protagonist, puts the story at one further remove from the reader and relegates it to the role of a mildly bawdy 'filler' " (pp. 37–38).

4

ACTing UP in the Renaissance: The Case of Benvenuto Cellini

*Margaret A. Gallucci**

In the introduction to his English translation of *The Life of Benvenuto Cellini* (1888), the Victorian John Addington Symonds characterized Cellini's sexual relations with boys as partaking of " the darker lusts which deformed Florentine society in that epoch." In a footnote, he clarified these darker lusts as that "unnatural vice"—commonly understood to signify sodomy—something so unpleasant that Symonds himself could not even name it. Elaborating further, Symonds claimed that Cellini's desires were "animal, licentious, almost brutal."[1] Symonds was not the first to note that there was something strange, what we would now call queer,[2] about Cellini's sexual behavior, particularly when compared to that other favorite of the Victorian imagination, Michelangelo, whose sonnets Symonds had translated a decade earlier. Symonds joined a long line of famous men that included Stendhal and Goethe who were simultaneously fascinated and repulsed by Cellini's sexual misdeeds. Of course, that such invective against Cellini should come from Symonds—himself homosexual—suggests a queerness beyond the scope of this brief essay.

In this essay, I propose a queer reading of the body of texts and materials that make up the life and work of the famed Renaissance artist Benvenuto Cellini (1500–1571).[3] In my reading, Cellini represents a moment of resistance to the dominant cultural discourse of heterosexuality. He envisioned alternative models for male sexual experience and desire that took shape alongside the enforced script of heteronormativity. To this end, I will employ Cellini as a kind of case study within a wider context of sodomitical sex, homoerotic desire, and homosocial bonds in Renaissance

Florence. I will argue that Cellini's words and deeds confirm that there were other possibilities for sexuality and desire in the Renaissance besides heteronormativity. As we shall see, Cellini's case both exemplifies and qualifies the notion that homosexual sodomy was widespread, tolerated, and temporary in Renaissance Florence. I am using the term *queer*, as first proposed by Teresa de Lauretis, to signify a reading practice that looks for tensions and discontinuities in discourses of sex in order to construct "another discursive horizon, another way of thinking the sexual."[4] In performing my queer reading, I will also consider what I believe to be some of the limitations of queer theory when applied to Cellini in particular and to Renaissance sexuality and desire in general. I would like to conclude by examining the current fascination with Cellini as a kind of gay icon, as attested by his appearance in numerous anthologies of gay literature.

Cellini stands in Renaissance history as the world's most famous sodomite. Although many of his contemporaries—including Michelangelo, Agnolo Bronzino, and Pietro Aretino—were rumored to be sodomites, there is no evidence that any other artist or man of letters of their stature was formally charged and convicted of this illegal sexual act. Michelangelo lived within the same constraints of desire—aware that "his feelings [for Tommaso de' Cavalieri were] at odds with theological and civil morality"[5]— and the same official restrictions on male same-sex eroticism as Cellini. Unlike Cellini, however, Michelangelo probably never acted on his desires. Michelangelo "may never have consummated his desire (there is no evidence that he did, and good reason to believe that his own internal resistance would have prevented him)."[6] Cellini's bold declarations stand in stark contrast to Michelangelo's frequent proclamations of orthodoxy and what appears to be a life of total sexual abstinence.

A brief summary of the judicial records of Cellini's sex crime is illustrative.[7] In 1557 the Florentine criminal court convicted Cellini of "the nefarious vice of sodomy." In particular, they charged him with having sexual relations "very many times" with Fernando, a male adolescent most likely between the ages of 13 and 18, who worked in his goldsmith's shop, probably as an apprentice. In the official sentence housed in the state archives in Florence, the authorities claimed that Cellini kept Fernando "in his bed as his wife." The magistrates sentenced Cellini to pay a fine and serve four years in prison and stripped him of the privilege of holding public office. Upon a successful petition to Duke Cosimo I de' Medici, the magistrates commuted the prison term to house arrest.

The authorities viewed sodomy as a transgressive sexual act. In Florence as in other Italian cities, sodomy was a crime punishable by harsh penalties, including death by burning. Although in theory sodomy encompassed a broad range of nonprocreative sexual acts, including anal sex between men and women, sexual intercourse with the woman on top, and bestiality, in practice the authorities overwhelmingly prosecuted anal intercourse between males. Sodomitical sex in Cellini's day was perceived as transgressive because it violated Nature as well as the strict gender roles prescribed in sexual intercourse. In sodomy between males, the older man took the active role of penetrator, the young boy the passive role of being penetrated. The active, dominant role was gendered masculine by the culture; the passive role was gendered feminine. Thus, in the criminal records of Cellini's 1557 case, the magistrates feminized Fernando, referring to him as Cellini's "wife."

This was Cellini's second conviction for sodomy, and since it provides evidence that Cellini probably had a life-long erotic interest in male adolescents, I will briefly provide the details of the first case.[8] This first conviction for the sex crime of sodomy occurred in 1523 and also took place in Florence. The magistrates charged Cellini and a certain Giovanni di Ser Matteo Rigoli with committing sodomy on Domenico di Ser Giuliano da Ripa.[9] The authorities sentenced him as the adult and active partner to a fine paid, not in cash, but as 12 bushels of flour.

In his life and writings, Cellini provides evidence for the sodomitical sexual norms of his day. Sodomitical sex as practiced by Cellini, in particular, or more generally between Florentine men and boys, challenges the notion that heterosexuality is normative and universal. In Renaissance Florence many men chose boys as their object of desire, and at times these men were perceived as dangerous to the social order. Over a twenty-four-year period (1478–1502), for instance, the Florentine magistracy known as the *Ufficiali di Notte* (The Night Officers) prosecuted over four thousand men for homosexual sodomy.[10] Moralists were afraid that boys would have trouble unlearning their passive, feminine role in sex and never become "real" men. Sodomites clearly threatened what we would call compulsory heterosexuality.[11] The authorities of the time feared that men who had sex with boys would destroy the very foundations of civil society by rejecting marriage and fatherhood: "Sodomy threatened to undermine the basic organizational units of society—family, male–female bonding, reproduction."[12] But what if Cellini, who was unmarried at the time of the conviction, felt that Fernando *was* his wife? For gender is not so much a "role" as an ideology that invested a host of institutions, including marriage. Femininity and masculinity were "thus not the product of a choice, but the forcible citation of a norm, one whose complex historicity is indissociable from relations of discipline, regulation, punishment."[13]

In his writings Cellini not only refused to keep silent about, but indeed celebrated, the pleasures of sodomitical sex and the joys of male love. In his sonnet "Porca fortuna" (Damn, Cursed Fortune), for instance, Cellini celebrates his reputation as a "whoremonger" who unceremoniously abandons Fortune, presented in the guise of an earthly woman lover, for a male lover, his beloved Ganymede.[14] The openness about male love and sexual pleasure between males evident in Cellini's poetry stands in stark contrast to the silence and defensiveness about these subjects found in the artist's autobiography. This notion that the artist's choice of genre in some sense conditions what he can or will express is strengthened by Cellini's use of the lyrical and mythological term "ganymede" in his sonnets to signify sexual intercourse between males that may include love or desire. By contrast, in the *Vita* Cellini tends to use the legal term "sodomy" when referring to these same acts or desires. This is not surprising when we consider how, as I have argued elsewhere, Cellini's autobiographical text has a forensic quality, as if he were defending himself before a tribunal.[15] We know that the artist was well aware of the differences in age and social status between male sexual partners. Cellini staged the marble sculptural group *Apollo and Hyacinth* (ca. 1546–1548) as an adult male with a young boy.

Cellini's appearance in the history of sodomy poses new challenges for scholars of queer theory and history. What is the precise relationship between someone like Cellini, an adult man who had sex with boys in the Renaissance, and men who have sex with men in our own (modern Western) culture?[16] As has been shown by both Ruggiero and Rocke, sexual relations between men and boys in Renaissance Italy adhered to rigid codes of behavior organized around the twin axes of power and gender: old–young, active–passive, masculine–feminine.[17] The sex act between an adult man and a boy or woman was not viewed as a mutual exchange between social equals based on (modern) notions of respect and reciprocity. This does not mean that sexual pleasure was not possible for the passive partner in sodomitical sex, merely that it was not considered necessary. Similarly, Cellini used his female models for sexual pleasure, a body of matter to be manipulated by the master: "[P]erché io sono uomo, me ne son servito ai mia piaceri carnali." ([S]ince I'm a man, I used her for my sexual pleasure.)[18]

In Cellini's day, engaging in male–male sodomy did not preclude sexual relations with women, or even marriage. Indeed, the evidence strongly suggests that most contemporary sodomites did, in fact, have relations with both boys and women. Cellini certainly fit this pattern: His sexual exploits with women before his marriage resulted in several illegitimate children; more children followed marriage to his lover of several years ca. 1562. Although Cellini was technically unmarried in 1557, he might have been living with his future wife at the time, suggesting that one could be both homosexual sodomite and husband simultaneously. This evidence is well documented in sources besides the *Vita*. In the Renaissance, then, a male's choice of sexual partner did not necessarily condition the other choices he made or roles he assumed. It is important to underscore in this regard that engaging in homosexual sodomy in no way detracted from Cellini's masculinity because he took the active, dominant role, whether with boys or women. The cultural connection between (active) homosexuality and effeminacy is not evident in these early modern documents. Cellini's case further suggests that desire was fluid and dynamic rather than fixed and stable. The possibilities for desire in the Renaissance seem more open than we might expect since—by choosing both boys and women as objects of desire—men like Cellini avoided the homosexual/ heterosexual binary of our own day.

The problem of early modern sodomy is extremely complex and highly charged, fraught with tensions and ambiguities. Sodomy was illegal and subject to harsh penalties, including capital punishment. In early modern Italy, officials went to great lengths to police sexuality and control perceived deviant sexual behavior. And yet, the prosecution of sodomitical acts between males did not follow a linear course: At times it was aggressively prosecuted, at others it appears to have been relatively tolerated. These patterns were clearly tied to the larger social, religious, and political climate of a particular city and its rulers. In Renaissance Florence, homosexual sodomy may have been tolerated because it was widely considered a part of normal manhood: "Sexual relations between males were more or less tolerated as long as they were expressed within culturally defined and accepted conventions."[19] As a result, although prosecutions were common, convictions were far less so; moreover, penalties were relatively mild for both active and passive partners when compared to other cities in Italy or Europe.

But Cellini's case both exemplifies and qualifies this assertion. On the one hand, Cellini can be seen as the most famous and articulate representative of the widespread homosocial/sexual world Rocke describes. At the same time, however, his "normative" sodomitical sex with Fernando was not tolerated. Cellini's sodomy clearly fit the paradigm of an older, active male involved in sexual intercourse with a young, passive boy and, thus, was expressed within recognized cultural norms. Why, then, if the artist was just one more Florentine committing a normal form of sodomy, did he receive the full measure of the law—long-term incarceration, a fine, and the loss of office-holding privileges granted to citizens? The answer might lie in the changing climate of mid-sixteenth century Florence: a new regime, a new sodomy law, a new disciplining institution on the horizon called the Inquisition. Within the normal parameters of sodomy, the authorities made careful distinctions, and one of these applied to Cellini. The law clearly singled out some sodomites like Cellini as more dangerous because their involvement with boys was not "fleeting or casual" but rather "more culpable and subject to greater stigma" because their "illicit erotic activity was more intense or habitual."[20] A special provision of the 1542 sodomy law (applied to Cellini) allowed the authorities to impose harsher penalties on these older male sodomites. The details of Cellini's case seem to suggest that feelings of affection or even love might have existed between Cellini and Fernando: "For about the last five years" the unmarried artist "kept" Fernando "in his bed as his wife" and sodomized him "very many times."

Offering up alternative formulations for male desire and male sexual expression does not prevent a Renaissance man from donning less subversive cultural cloaks: Queering Cellini means that he can be both polymorphously perverse in his sexual behavior and desire and a violent misogynist. In his writings, Cellini tells us much about his feelings of love and desire for various women he meets in the course of his life; but he also tells how he acted toward these very women, and the contrast is striking. The details he relates of these alleged amorous relationships are fraught with violence and abuse. For instance, Cellini seems quite nonchalant when he recounts how he punched and kicked his model and occasional sex partner Caterina, dragging her around the room by the hair, in a rage at her for having sex with his assistant Paolo: "[D]atomi in preda all'ira, la pigliavo pe' capegli e la strascicavo per la stanza, dandogli tanti calci e tante pugna insino che io ero stracco." ([G]iving in to my wrath, I grabbed her by the hair and dragged her around the room, giving her so many kicks and so many punches until I was exhausted.)[21] The cycle of sex and violence that this scene sets in motion between the two, as related by Cellini, borders dangerously on rape. When Caterina returns, the master's primary concern is that, having rendered her unusable as a model, he has temporarily lost an occasion to display his honor through her beauty: "Ancora vedevo lei esser tutta lacerata, livida e enfiata, pensando che, se pure lei tornassi, essere di necessità di farla medicare per quindici giorni, innanzi che io me ne potessi servire." (Besides, I saw that she was all lacerated, bruised and swollen, and I thought that, even if she came back, it would be necessary to have her treated for fifteen days before I could use her.)[22] By contrast, boys working as apprentices in his *bottega* do not appear to have suffered physical abuse at his hands. In addition, these boys had the possibility of becoming journeymen, a professional option denied to women.

The artist's *bottega* was one of many sites for male–male erotics in the Renaissance. The nature of this professional relationship meant that the master's male assistants and apprentices often slept in the workshop itself, often in the same beds. This does not necessarily imply sexual intimacy, but the workshop surely provided a place/space for male sexual activity and experimentation. It also helped forge the homosocial bonds, in this case between the goldsmith and his male assistants, that structured society and male culture in the Renaissance. Homoerotics color images of the *bottega* in Cellini's *Vita*. Cellini's youthful male friendships and relations with young assistants and apprentices teem with homoerotic overtones, if not overt sexual potential. What Barkan identifies as the *Vita*'s many "lovingly described homoerotic sentiments"[23] includes Cellini's adolescent love for Francesco Lippi: "Nel praticare insieme generò in noi un tanto amore, che mai, né dì né notte, stavamo l'uno senza l'altro." (In working together such a great love was born between us, that never, neither day nor night, were we apart.)[24] In addition, instances of the homoerotic potential of male friendships are evident in many places in the *Vita*, such as the bond between Cellini and Piero Landi, of which the artist writes, "ci volevamo bene più che se fratelli fussimo stati" (we loved each other more than if we had been brothers),[25] and that between the artist and a certain Albertaccio del Bene, about which Cellini reported "a me voleva bene quanto a sé medesimo" (he loved me as much as himself).[26]

We also find expressions of Cellini's homoeroticism in the homoerotic content of his art. Besides his famous *Perseus* (completed 1554), other male nudes of the artist include the three marble statues of *Ganymede* (ca. 1548–1550), *Narcissus* (ca. 1548–1565), and *Apollo and Hyacinth*. For Saslow, Cellini's choice of the *Ganymede* in particular was "ideally suited to embody the principal patterns of homosexuality at the time."[27] On more than one occasion Cellini celebrates male beauty in his writings. In the *Vita*, Cellini describes his model Diego—a Spanish boy whom the master dresses up as a woman and brings to a party in Rome as his date— as "bello di persona, maraviglioso di color di carne; lo intaglio della testa sua era assai più bello che quello antico di Antino, e molte volte lo avevo ritratto" ([Diego was] beautiful and had a marvelous skin tone; the profile of his head was even more beautiful than the ancient one of Antinous, and many times I had drawn him).[28]

Turning from Cellini's art to our own cultural fascination with the great artist, Cellini has, in recent years, been resurrected as a kind of gay icon. He appears, for example, in the 1995 *Penguin Book of International Gay Writing* and the 1998 *A History of Gay Literature*.[29] In the Penguin anthology, Cellini's date with the cross-dresser Diego was chosen by the editor because it "illuminate[s] the experience of love between men, explore[s] the nature of homosexual identity, or investigate[s] the kinds of relationships gay men have with each other, with their friends, and with their families."[30] In *A History of Gay Literature*, Cellini is invoked on two occasions, first as a central figure in the pantheon of gay men from the past and then again briefly in the section concerning Marcel Proust's "homo-erotic set pieces" involving Swann's dreamy vision of a young footman in the Sainte-Euverte household who resembles an " 'angel or sentinel' by the bisexual Benvenuto Cellini."[31] The artist also appears in a number of online lists of famous queers, for instance, in the list of "Famous or Distinguished Gays, Lesbians, and Bisexuals" compiled by the Gay and Lesbian Task Force of the American Library Association.[32] Whether sodomite or bisexual, Cellini is considered part of a queer constituency because his sexuality was not considered "normal or sanctioned."[33]

Establishing a taxonomy of queer literature represents a challenge for queer theorists and historians. What texts make up a gay or queer canon? Does queer literature comprise all those works that articulate "artistic expressions of same-sex love"[34] or that express "a language for a male homosexual orientation"?[35] Are queer texts those with homoerotic themes, or is simply transgressing any established boundary sufficient to being labeled a queer writer? Is the queer reader more important than the texts themselves? Woods suggests just that when he takes refuge in "read-erly" texts, claiming that he is not concerned with "whether William Shakespeare was 'gay' or 'queer' or a 'homosexual' or a 'sodomite' or if he and the male addressee of his sonnets were 'just good friends.' All of this is irrelevant if any of the sonnets are amenable to being read by a gay reader *as if they were* 'gay poems.' If they work as if they were, they *are*. The reader's pleasure is paramount."[36]

Not all modern cultural artifacts about Cellini have sought out the deviant.[37] The 1934 Hollywood film *The Affairs of Cellini*—starring Fredric March in the title role, Frank Morgan as the duke of Florence (Alessandro de' Medici), Constance Bennett as the duchess, and Fay Wray as Angela, a female model—portrays our hero as a hot-tempered swash-buckler in the Errol Flynn tradition [figure 4.1]. Flynn's Robin Hood (*The Adventures of Robin Hood*, 1938) and March's Cellini are look-alikes: Both sported a belted tunic and tights, a sword hung diagonally across the body and a pointed goatee. The film inscribes Cellini in a purely heterosexual love story—with the duchess, after the duke runs off with Angela—and presents him as a composer of love lyrics to women. Directed by Gregory La Cava, it is classified generically in film databases as a historical romance comedy. The romantic heterosexual love story seems to have captivated American viewers. It was chosen by American Movie Classics to be shown on Valentine's Day in 1992 as one of three "amorous" films.

Nor was Cellini's sex appeal (presumably with women) lost on writers of the 1966 Audrey Hepburn comedy, *How to Steal a Million*. The story centers around a statue of Venus on loan to a Paris museum from the collection of Charles Bonnet (Hepburn's father in the film, played by

Figure 4.1   *The Affairs of Cellini* (1934), starring Fredric March and Constance Bennett. Photo courtesy of The Museum of Modern Art/Film Stills Archive.

Hugh Griffith), a legendary art collector. The small marble statue of the goddess was not sculpted by our famed Renaissance artist but forged instead by Bonnet's father. Directed by William Wyler, the film stars Peter O'Toole as the burglar hired to steal the million-dollar forgery from the museum before it can be appraised as a fake. When Charles tries to persuade his daughter Nicole that the Cellini carved by her grandfather is better than any crafted by Benvenuto, he jibes: "If it was genuine, what would it be? A piece of sculpture made centuries ago by an over-sexed Italian."

Cellini's resurrection as a homosexual, gay, bisexual, or queer hero brings us to a troublesome area for queer theory: terminology. Although most scholars who have studied Cellini's oeuvre have argued against the notion of a queer genealogy (in other words, a historical continuum of homoerotic experience), even a scholar like Pope-Hennessy, who often tried to minimize the relevance of an artist's sexuality, felt obliged to admit that Cellini was "bisexual."[38] The consequence of using (post)modern terms such as *homosexual, lesbian, or bisexual* to describe persons living in the early modern world is to imply a linear development of transhistorical identifications based on familiarity and sameness rather than difference and strangeness. As we have seen with Cellini, it is instructive to trace the contours of same-sex eroticism through history in its specific social forms at different times, taking care to underscore how such acts or subjects are not "just like us," however politically unpopular this might be. As such, Cellini provides scholars of queer theory and history with a model of alternative formulations for sex and desire in the Renaissance.

Margaret A. Gallucci earned a Ph.D. at the University of California, Berkeley. She has taught at the University of Michigan; the University of California, Berkeley; and Syracuse University in Florence. A Fulbright scholar, she is a published author and translator and has held postdoctoral fellowships at Columbia University's Italian Academy and, most recently, at Harvard University's Villa I Tatti in Florence. She is the author of *Benvenuto Cellini: Sexuality, Masculinity, and Artistic Identity in Renaissance Italy,* (New York: Palgrave Macmillan, 2003) and coeditor, with Paolo L. Rossi, of *Benvenuto Cellini: Sculptor, Goldsmith, Writer,* forthcoming from Cambridge University Press.

Notes

* I would like to thank Gary Cestaro, Carole Gallucci, Elizabeth Leake, Michael Rocke, and James M. Saslow for their thoughtful comments and suggestions on a draft of this essay.

1. John Addington Symonds, *The Life of Benvenuto Cellini* (Rpr. London: MacMillan, 1920), p. xxxv.

2. *Oxford English Dictionary*, vol. 8 (Oxford: Clarendon, 1914), p. 41. The entry for "queer" reads: "strange, odd, peculiar . . . of questionable character, suspicious, dubious."

3. A few words about the great artist are in order: Cellini is famous for a bronze statue of Perseus, commissioned by Duke Cosimo I de' Medici and displayed in the Loggia dei Lanzi in Florence, and infamous for his outrageous *Vita*, in which he recounts acts of murder and narrates tales of assault with a disarming nonchalance. He created works of art in marble, bronze, and gold, both large and small; composed in verse and prose; and worked at various courts: the papal court in Rome, the royal courts of Francis I in Paris and Fontainebleu, and the ducal and granducal courts of the Medici in Florence. For more on Cellini's life and work, see Antonio Paolucci, *Cellini* (Florence: Giunti, 2000).

4. Teresa de Lauretis, "Queer Theory: Lesbian and Gay Sexualities. An Introduction," *Differences* 3,2 (1991), p. iv.

5. James M. Saslow, *Ganymede in the Renaissance: Homosexuality in Art and Society* (New Haven, CT: Yale University Press, 1986), p. 48.

6. Ibid., p. 48.

7. For a fuller account of the 1557 sodomy case, see my "Cellini's Trial for Sodomy: Power and Patronage at the Court of Cosimo I" in: *The Cultural Politics of Duke Cosimo I de' Medici*, ed. Konrad Eisenbichler (Aldershot, England: Ashgate, 2001), pp. 37–46. A note on terminology: following Ruggiero, Rocke, and Brackett, I will use "homosexual sodomy" and

"heterosexual sodomy" to refer, respectively, to anal intercourse between males and anal intercourse between males and females. In this essay I am avoiding referring to Cellini as a "homosexual" because I believe the term carries too many modern connotations.

8. Extant documentation on this earlier case is very slight; to my knowledge only the very brief sentence survives. For more on Cellini's two convictions for sodomy as well as the claim he makes in the *Vita* that he was hauled into court in Paris in ca. 1543 on the charge of heterosexual sodomy with his model and occasional sex partner Caterina, see Paolo L. Rossi, "The Writer and the Man. Real Crimes and Mitigating Circumstances: *il caso Cellini*" in: *Crime, Society and the Law in Renaissance Italy*, eds. T. Dean and K. J. P. Lowe (Cambridge: Cambridge University Press, 1994), pp. 157–83 and particularly 174–80.

9. In these documents, the title "ser" most likely indicates a notary, although it was sometimes used rather generically as a sign of respect to mean simply "Mister" (messer). In addition, the preposition "di" that precedes it stands for "son of," i.e., Giovanni, son of the notary Matteo Rigoli.

10. Michael J. Rocke, *Forbidden Friendships: Homosexuality and Male Culture in Renaissance Florence* (New York: Oxford, 1996), p. 10.

11. I take this term from the now-classic essay by Adrienne Rich, "Compulsory Heterosexuality and Lesbian Experience," *Signs: Journal of Women in Culture & Society* 5, 4 (1980), pp. 631–60.

12. Guido Ruggiero, *The Boundaries of Eros: Sex Crime and Sexuality in Renaissance Venice* (New York: Oxford, 1985), p. 109.

13. Judith Butler, *Bodies that Matter: On the Discursive Limits of "Sex"* (New York: Routledge, 1993), p. 232.

14. Benvenuto Cellini, *Opere*, ed. Bruno Maier (Milan: Ricciardi, 1968), pp. 900–01. For more on this sonnet, see my "A New Look at Benvenuto Cellini's Poetry," *Forum Italicum* 34, 2 (2000), pp. 343–71 and particularly 350–54.

15. See my "Cellini's Trial for Sodomy," pp. 37–38.

16. For a discussion on how, epistemologically, to characterize different types of homosexual relations throughout history, see David Halperin, "Questions of Evidence: Commentary on Koehl, DeVries, and Williams" in: *Queer Representations: Reading Lives, Reading Cultures*, ed. Martin Duberman (New York: New York University Press, 1997), pp. 39–54 and particularly 40–41.

17. Ruggiero, pp. 121–25 and Rocke, pp. 101–09. See also John K. Brackett, *Criminal Justice and Crime in Late Renaissance Florence, 1537–1609* (New York: Cambridge University Press, 1992), pp. 131–32.

18. Benvenuto Cellini, *La Vita*, ed. Lorenzo Bellotto (Parma: Bembo/Guanda, 1996), p. 545. Unless otherwise noted, English translations are mine.

19. Rocke, pp. 101–02.

20. Ibid., p. 234.

21. Cellini, *Vita*, p. 562.

22. Ibid., p. 563.

23. Leonard Barkan, *Transuming Passion: Ganymede and the Erotics of Humanism* (Stanford, CA: Stanford University Press, 1991), p. 105.

24. Cellini, *Vita*, p. 46.

25. Ibid., p. 63.
26. Ibid., p. 261.
27. James M. Saslow, "Homosexuality in the Renaissance: Behavior, Identity, and Artistic Expression" in: *Hidden from History: Reclaiming the Gay and Lesbian Past*, eds. Martin B. Duberman et al. (New York: New American Library, 1989), pp. 90–105; quotation on p. 101.
28. Cellini, *Vita*, p. 107. The technical term "intaglio" makes possible another rendering of the second sentence as "the engraving of his head was even more beautiful than the ancient one of Antinous, and many times I had portrayed him/it." Antinous was the beautiful Bithynian boy loved by the Emperor Hadrian. I would like to thank Patricia Reilly for discussing this passage with me.
29. *The Penguin Book of International Gay Writing*, ed. Mark Mitchell (Harmondworth, England: Penguin, 1995); Gregory Woods, *A History of Gay Literature: The Male Tradition* (New Haven, CT: Yale University Press, 1998).
30. Ibid., p. xiii.
31. Woods, pp. 4, 198.
32. http://calvin.usc.edu/~trimmer/famous_names.html.
33. Annamarie Jagose, *Queer Theory: An Introduction* (New York: New York University Press, 1996), pp. 98, 112.
34. *The Gay and Lesbian Literary Heritage: A Reader's Companion to the Writers and their Works from Antiquity to the Present*, ed. Claude J. Summers (New York: Henry Holt, 1995), p. x.
35. Joseph Cady, " 'Masculine Love,' Renaissance Writing, and the New 'Invention' of Homosexuality," *Journal of Homosexuality* 23 (1992), pp. 9–40; quotation on p. 9.
36. Woods, pp. 8–9.
37. Indeed, some scrupulously avoid history, such as two made-for-TV biopics on Michelangelo and Cellini produced by Italian state television that make no mention of homoeroticism; see Giovanni Dall'Orto, "Le bugie della RAI," *Babilonia* 85 (January 1991), pp. 14–16.
38. John Pope-Hennessy, *Cellini* (London: MacMillan, 1985), p. 254.

5

"Nature is a Mother Most Sweet": Homosexuality in Sixteenth- and Seventeenth-Century Italian Libertinism

*Giovanni Dall'Orto**

In his book *Homosexuality and Liberation,* a fundamental text of the Italian gay rights movement, Mario Mieli entitled one chapter on the history of homosexuals "How Homosexuals—From One Burning Stake to the Next—Became Gay."[1] Even at the risk of overdramatizing a bit, in 1977 it was essential to uncover and denounce the suffering of homosexuals through the centuries. It was necessary to show how homosexuals were an oppressed minority that needed to fight for social equality. Today, in a somewhat more positive social climate, we have begun to recognize the danger of reading gay history simply as a series of persecutions, "from one burning stake to the next." There have been moments of tolerance in the past at least as important as—and in some cases even more important than—the moments of persecution. We must also look at these periods of tolerance for a proper understanding of our history.

With this I aim to introduce one of the most intriguing periods of relative tolerance for homosexuals in Italian history: the intellectual current known as libertinism. Libertinism marks the high point of a generally permissive attitude towards homosexuality that began in the fifteenth century, triumphed in certain sectors of society in the first half of the sixteenth, survived the Counter Reformation through a couple generations and, in those few cities where it was most entrenched (Venice and, surprisingly, Rome), was still thriving beyond the middle of the seventeenth.[2] The importance of libertinism for homosexuality is clear.

Whenever we come across positive attitudes towards homosexuality in the sixteenth and seventeenth centuries or simply attitudes that reject persecution and hysteria, there too without exception we find libertine thinkers. In France and England as well, when we look closely at the times and places where homosexuality was tolerated, we discover the diffusion of Italian libertine thought, which had moved beyond Italian borders to escape repression at home.[3] Later, when Enlightenment thinkers struggle to form an opinion on homosexuality, they turn to libertinism for answers and plunder libertine thought for ideas, sometimes quite blatantly.

Some Characteristics of Libertine Thought

Let us first try to define more precisely this important social and cultural phenomenon. Libertinism is grounded in ancient philosophy, particularly the radical skepticism of Pyrrho of Elis (d. 275 B.C.), and a materialist approach to reality. But as has been apparent for some time now, late medieval Jewish, Christian, and Islamic thought (including heretical strains of Aristotelianism) all contributed to its formation.[4] Even a superficial examination of libertinism reveals a relatively heterogeneous assembly of beliefs, philosophies broadly construed, and moral systems. This heterogeneity is not a coincidence but rather reflects the fundamental tenet of libertine thought, which is skepticism towards all commonly held beliefs. Indeed, no central core of philosophical doctrines can obtain for a movement whose only real dogma is antidogmatism.

Thus any effort to come to terms with libertinism must clearly recognize that it is not a school of thought so much as *a mental attitude toward reality*, a mode of thought. This explains on the one hand libertinism's extreme complexity, even to the point of contradiction; and on the other its extreme adaptability and flexibility, even to the point of sometimes espousing mainstream morality out of mere convenience. Despite this heterogeneity, however, libertinism ultimately remains consistent inasmuch as central to every libertine expression is one of the movement's characteristic elements: belief in the mortality of the soul, a theory of religion as fraud, skepticism, and moral relativism. This last component brings with it a positive attitude toward sexuality in all of its expressions.

Libertinism's extreme pliability is dramatically confirmed by the appearance of libertine attitudes in sixteenth- and seventeenth-century religious debates, particularly as various Christian sects pointed the finger at one another and cried "impostor!".[5] This does not necessarily make the libertine an atheist: Often the libertine is a deist on the grounds that anything is possible or in some cases a genuine believer, Catholic or

Protestant, who is suspicious of external religious practice.[6] Nonetheless, libertinism's skeptical stance toward religion inspired in opposition a vast Christian propaganda campaign both Catholic and Protestant. The current use of the word "libertine" as a synonym for "an immoral and dissolute character" is nothing but the result of these slanderous campaigns.[7]

As we have seen, one typical libertine thesis states that all religion is the work of astute impostors who take advantage of simple people's credulity to terrorize them with fables and myths and thus gain power over them. Thus no moral code can claim to be absolute as the product of divine revelation like Christianity. The only nonarbitrary moral code is the one the learned individual can build using Reason in search of Truth and Virtue,[8] which will eventually lead him to discover and follow the "law of Nature."[9] As such, the libertine flatly rejects any behavioral prohibition based solely on laws "revealed" by "sacred scripture." Only Reason can legitimately prohibit certain behaviors deemed unjust or inhuman. Libertine ethics are thus exquisitely rational and secular. Moral imperatives come not from religion, rather from an understanding that certain regulations are necessary to maintain order and justice in civil life. Add to this the widespread libertine belief in the mortality of the soul as an animating principle destined to disappear with the body it had animated, and we have grasped the roots of libertine sexual morality.[10]

Nature and Against Nature

Libertine sexual morality is extremely open when it comes to homosexuality, which—while not necessarily condoned—was not condemned either. We might consider paradigmatic the attitude of one French libertine who, upon surprising his friend in bed with another man, declared: "Often we arrive at the same destination by taking different paths. I for one don't condemn your choices at all. Every man finds salvation in his own peculiar way. But of course I won't be getting to heaven by quite the same path you have chosen."[11]

As the libertines saw it, Mother Nature was affectionate and benevolent, not cruel, and she provided humans with sexual organs for them to use. Man wasn't born to suffer, rather to enjoy the pleasures he could find without harming his brethren. As we only have this one life on earth, there is no reason to suffer now in exchange for pleasure in the next life, which doesn't exist in any case.[12] For these reasons, the libertine cannot help but consider sexuality in positive terms, including manifestations of homosexual behavior.[13] From a moral perspective, homosexual relationships are as dignified, or—perhaps more precisely—as irrelevant, as heterosexual relationships. For the "strong of spirit" (as libertines defined themselves in opposition to the "weak of spirit," i.e., victims of superstition), the biblical condemnation of sodomy is merely another in a long line of impostures. In reality, there can be nothing wrong with using the genital organs for a pleasure that Nature herself made possible. The famous declaration attributed to Christopher Marlowe (1564–1593)—"All thei that love not tobacco and boyes are fooles"—nicely captures the libertine attitude: you have to be a fool not to enjoy the pleasures life offers us![14]

The Fable of Jesus the Sodomite

It should be clear from the premises examined above that libertine thought systematically aimed to cut down to human dimension all those things that the "weak in spirit" ascribed to the supernatural. One major obstacle to this effort was the omnipresence of sacred mythology in the society in which the libertines lived. It was difficult to resist the temptation to demythologize the characters of sacred history by bringing them back to human reality—by giving them human defects and human desires, including sexual desires. Thus were born the terrible, picturesque blasphemies that so scandalized the Church in the past.[15]

The extent to which, for the libertine, homosexual behavior was simply a part of human reality is demonstrated by the commonplace libertine notion that Christ and St. John the Evangelist were lovers.[16] We find this idea already in 1550 among the charges in the trial against Francesco Calcagno:

"Interrogato per quali cose gli fosse stato detto che era stato denunciato, risponde: 'El me fu ditto che era [ero] sta' querelato che aveva ditto che Cristo teneva per suo bardassa san Gioanni.' Interrogato su quel che avesse detto al proposito, risponde: 'Io me ricordo che in casa di un Giovanni Antonio da Preselij, . . . una volta, dicendo Messer Lauro di Glisenti da Vestone ch'el non credeva in cosa alcuna, se non quel che se vedeva, io gli disse: "Adoncha se po credere et dir de Cristo tutti li mali del mondo, et ch'el teneva s. Gioanni per suo bardassa." ' "

"When asked what he had been told about why he was accused, he responded: 'They told me I was charged with having said that Christ kept Saint John as his boy.' When asked what he had said about it, he responded: 'I remember that I was in the house of one Giovanni Antonio da Preselij, . . . and one time Mr. Lauro di Glisenti da Vestone said he didn't believe in anything, only what you could see with your eyes, and I said to him, "Well then you can believe or say anything you want about Christ no matter how bad, like that he kept Saint John as his boy." ' "[17]

It shows up again in the formal accusation against Christopher Marlowe, who is reported to have stated "that St. John the Evangelist was bed-fellow to Christe, that he leaned always in his bosom; that he used him as the synners of Sodoma."[18] From subject to king, the story reappears on the lips of James I (1566–1626) as he defends his love for Lord Buckingham: "I am neither god nor angel—angels we know are sexless—but a man like any other. I love the Earl of Buckingham more than any other. Christ had his John and I have my Stenie."[19] From Protestant to Catholic lands, libertinism manages to leap even religious divides. In Lisbon in 1618, the twenty-four-year-old sodomite Michel Figuereido is accused of having said that "Christ was very attached to St. John because they used to sleep together."[20] And from one continent to another: In 1685 the best-known poet of colonial Brazil, Gregório de Matos e Guerra, a cleric, is accused of having said that "our Lord Jesus Christ was 'nefando,' except that he used another word, more vile and heinous." "Nefando" was a common euphemism for "sodomite" in the seventeenth century.[21]

From one century to the next, this commonplace demonstrates the continuity between libertine and Enlightenment thought. In his 1766 *Essai sur la peinture*, Denis Diderot (1713–1784), discussing the hypocrisy inherent in paintings that represent the beauty of the human body, states: "[I]f the Magdalen had had an erotic adventure with Christ; if, at the wedding at Cana, a slightly unorthodox Christ, a bit drunk, had caressed the throat of one of the female guests as well as Saint John's buttocks, unsure whether or not to remain faithful to the apostle of the down-dusted chin: then you'd see what our painters, poets, and sculptors could do."[22] If such a blasphemous anecdote managed to survive two centuries of Inquisitorial persecution, how many other libertine notions survived, swirled about in the caldron of Enlightenment thought to trickle down to the present?[23] The list demonstrates that what may appear at first to be a disparate series of off-hand comments by select individuals in fact coheres—across epochs, social classes, nations, and religions—to reveal an underlying mode of thought: in a word, libertinism.

Libertinism and Society

Of course it would be absurd to think that society, object of these blasphemous libertine broadsides, did not react in defense. Antilibertine propaganda was both widespread and strategically focused. The adversaries of libertinism took particular advantage of the unconventional sexual morality of many libertines to characterize them all as depraved, lust-crazed beasts who would go to any length to satisfy their carnal urges. In reality, the typical libertine respected the law to the extent possible. Particularly in its early stages, libertinism was primarily a middle- and upper-class urban phenomenon; libertines had a strong sense of belonging to an élite and restricted circle of enlightened individuals in a world where ignorance and stupidity reigned. Such "strong-spirited" individuals were not interested in creating scandal among the ignorant masses, who could in any case never comprehend the reasons for their behavior. As such, libertinism is an inherently conservative attitude inasmuch as it insists that the ignorant masses are incapable of using Reason to control their base animal instincts and thus need the curb of religion and superstition. It is no mere coincidence that Antonio Rocco, author of the celebrated *Alcibiade fanciullo a scola* (*Alcibiades Schoolboy*), was among Galileo's most ruthless adversaries.[24] For this reason, we might describe the libertine attitude towards religion as amused indulgence or at most irreverent (blasphemous!) play, but not open and programmatic opposition. For all that superstition is evil, it is a necessary evil. It also became necessary for some to make a purely superficial show of religious devotion, not so much out of hypocrisy as, often, out of a simple desire not to upset the small-minded and "weak in spirit."

A Case Study: Antonio Rocco (1586–1652)

Now that we have examined the basic libertine attitudes towards sexuality, let us turn to one concrete illustration. I have chosen the rather well-known, if little studied, example of Antonio Rocco's *L'Alcibiade fanciullo a scola*, a text written around 1631 and published in 1651, which now enjoys a modern edition after having been something of a bibliographical rarity for centuries.[25] That Rocco, a priest, was also an impenitent libertine there can be little doubt: The Venetian Inquisition assembled a series of charges against him between 1635–1652 without ever managing to arrest him due to the protection he enjoyed "in high places."[26] One entry from 1635 contains a denunciation of Rocco by "an individual of true Christian zeal" who reported that, during a meeting of the Accademia degli Incogniti (of which Rocco was a member), the priest

> "nel suo discorso portando la scrittura di S. Paolo che si lamentava del stimolo della carne, al qual essendoli risposto 'sufficit tibi gratia mea,' espose e interpretò che detta gratia del Signore era la delettation carnale che l'huomo riceve nell'atto venereo, della qual esposition fù ponto e ripreso altamente all'hora da un Padre di S. Francesco ivi presente, che fù sentito da tutti gl'Accademici et auditori."

"cited the writings of Saint Paul where he complains about the incitements of the flesh and where God responds 'sufficit tibi gratia mea' [my grace is all you need]. He said that this grace of our Lord was the carnal pleasure you receive in the act of love-making. At the time, he was severely rebuked for such an interpretation by a Franciscan father who was present. And this was heard by all the members of the Academy and those in attendance."[27]

In 1648 one Enrico Palladio, on his sickbed and hoping to clear his conscience, confessed to having spent time with Rocco: "'[S]ignor Rocco spesso ci domandava quanto tempo era che havevamo usato carnalmente ò naturalmente ò contra natura, e noi gli dicevamo alle volte di si, et egli soggiungeva, havete fatto bene, perché quello instrumento è stato fatto dalla natura, perché noi ne habbiamo i nostri gusti e diletti.'" ("[M]ister Rocco used to ask us how long it had been since we'd had carnal relations, either naturally or against nature, and sometimes we would tell him yes, and he would say "good job!," because that tool was made by nature so that we could use it as we pleased.")[28] More to the point is the declaration of one "vilissima pecorella, anima christiana" (most humble little lamb, a Christian soul), dated 1652: "'[I]l Rocco non crede niente'" ("Rocco doesn't believe in anything").[29] For this individual who appears in the last of the accusations against Rocco, there can be no doubt: He is a promulgator of antireligious doctrines, even though "'sapendo tutti che lui non dice Messa e vive come atheista non puòl far tant'impressione'" ("it doesn't have much effect because everyone knows that he doesn't say Mass and he lives like an atheist").[30]

L'Alcibiade fanciullo a scola

As we move from private denunciations to the text of the *Alcibiade* we see that the underlying mentality is exactly the same. The book describes the schoolmaster Filotimo's successful efforts to convince young Alcibiades to give in to his desires. It is an important work for the history of homosexuality thinly disguised as "libretto da Carnevale." Rocco starts with a topic that is difficult and intentionally unpalatable for many, but he manages to get sexual (in this case homosexual) behavior out from under the dictates of conventional social morality by creating a space of individual conscience in harmony with Nature. Some of Rocco's arguments can be characterized as burlesque parody, as when he explains that sodomy is only "against" or "opposed to nature" (contro natura) in the sense that sodomites use their "natura"—to this day a synonym for the genital organs in Tuscan dialect—on the opposite side.[31]

Other arguments come directly out of libertine thought. The master affirms:

"Sono naturali quelle opere a cui la natura ci inclina, de' quali pretende il fine e l'effetto. Se adunque è natural inclinazione veder de' bei fanciulli, come sète voi contra natura? . . . Stimate voi la natura così improvida? È forse ìnvida al nostro bene? Impoverisce ella nelle delizie nostre? Gli si rubba cosa ch'ella non voglia? Se il tutto ha fatto per noi, il tutto a sua gloria è ragionevole che si goda da noi. Chi non si serve de' suoi doni la dispreggia; chi non mette in esecuzione le sue invenzioni si disnatura e gli diventa ribelle, onde merita d'esser tolto di vita; ella ne somministra il piacere, perché godendo noi la celebriamo per cara, provvida, ricca e cortesissima madre."

"Those acts to which we are inclined by nature are natural, and she has seen to their end and their effects. So if it is your natural inclination to look at beautiful young boys, how can you be 'against nature'? . . . Do you think nature to be so utterly lacking in foresight? Do you think she's not looking out for our welfare? Is she somehow diminished when we enjoy pleasure? Are we stealing something from her against her will? If she created everything for us, it's only reasonable that we enjoy these things to bring her glory. Those who don't make use of her gifts cast scorn upon her. Those who refuse to put her inventions to use de-nature themselves and rebel against her, for which they deserve to be taken from this life. She bestows pleasure upon us so that by enjoying her pleasures we celebrate her as our dear, provident, rich and most honorable mother."[32]

When Alcibiades objects that such thinking loses sight of procreation, his master replies: " 'Ma che? Forse sempre si prendono o devono prender i piaceri amorosi per generare? S'averà d'aver tanti figlioli quanti diletti carnali? Son follie lontane dal vero sentimento e dal giusto.' " ("What are you talking about? As if every time we enjoyed lovemaking were in order to procreate. So that we should have precisely as many children as carnal pleasures? These are ridiculous notions that have nothing to do with what is true or what is right.") Not to mention that there are plenty of people around " 'che più a loro [le donne] che a' fanciulli inclinano' " ("who prefer [women] to boys").[33]

When Alcibiades takes recourse in the law, the master seducer remains unperturbed:

"Che le leggi d'alcuni popoli lo vietano, non è che in se stesso non sia buono. Aggiustano costoro le leggi a' suoi interessi; non sottomettono gl'interessi al giusto. . . . Hanno così fatto ordeni riguardi piuttosto agl'interessi di stato e di politica, che a dittami della ragione, all'inclinazione della natura; anzi, sopra questa maledetta ragion di stato gran parte delle umane leggi e le religiose stesse si fondano, talché alcune di loro esecrabili sono dal sciocco volgo stimate venerabili e sacrosante."

"Just because the laws of certain nations prohibit it doesn't mean that it isn't good, per se. Those nations tailor their laws to serve their own interests; they don't submit their interests to what is right. . . . They have made their laws according to the interests of the state and politics, not according to the dictates of reason or the inclinations of nature. As a matter of fact, most human and even religious laws are based on these accursed political rationales, so that even those laws that are truly hateful are held by the ignorant masses to be honorable and sacrosanct."[34]

In other words, the law follows the reasons of the state and results from the opportunism of those in power, not from the pursuit of justice. And yet people lay down their honor and their lives for these laws and religions, which are often arbitrary and cruel. In conclusion, Filotimo asks his student:

" 'Vi paiono elle giuste?' 'Anzi, irragionevoli e pazze' rispose il fanciullo Alcibiade. 'Nondimeno—ripigliò il maestro—canonizzate dall'uso, stabilite dal timore e autenticate per vere non meno dalla simplicità de' creduli che dalla severità di chi regge, sono per giustissime mantenute.' "

" 'Do they seem just to you?' 'On the contrary,' the boy Alcibiades answered, 'they seem irrational and crazy.' 'Nevertheless,' the master responded, 'enshrined in custom, entrenched by fear, authenticated as true by the simplicity of the credulous and the brutality of those in power, they are held to be most just.' "[35]

Alcibiades has but one weapon left in his arsenal: divine law. But that too is quickly done away with by his implacable master, who shows him how "divine law" is nothing but a convenient label applied by those in power to the laws they promulgate in order to get people to obey them:

"Coloro a' quali, per loro privati interessi, è parso vietare questo diletto, stimando che li giudiziosi s'opponessero al vero, che le sue leggi fossero a ragione neglette, il caduco delle lor posizioni hanno cercato fulcire nel immutabile dell'apparente auttorità di Dio. Ove è manco di vero, ivi s'apportano più giuramenti, e per far credibile il falso si meschiano le cose profane con le sacre. Si vince la mente pura con l'attrocità delle opere delle pene e de' tormenti."

"Those who have taken it upon themselves, for their own personal interests, to outlaw this pleasure—anticipating that judicious men might oppose the truth, that their laws might rightfully be neglected—have tried to

strengthen their position by appealing to the apparently immutable author-
ity of God. Where truth is wanting, there will you find many sacred oaths.
To make what is false credible, the sacred is often mixed with the profane.
The pure mind is overcome by the atrocities of punishment and torment."[36]

As for the story of Sodom, Rocco comes up with an explanation
that might be considered laughable were it not so in vogue these days in
gay Christian circles. Filotimo explains that the story of Sodom and
Gomorrah and the Biblical prohibition on homosexuality were thought
up in order to encourage procreation among the Jews, who were struggling to survive in tiny numbers. But "l'auttor di questa invenzione"
(the author of this fable), who attributed to God the prohibition against
loving boys, ended up contradicting himself, because:

> "parendogli esser troppo rigore di porre in precetto quel che aveva inven-
> tato per amplificazione e per terrore nelle sue leggi scritte, non dice che per
> l'uso simplice de' fanciulli fossero le predette città sommerse, ma perché
> erano impie, crudeli, avare, rapaci, violente; e che l'ultimo della loro ruina
> fu la violenza che vollero usare agl'angeli. E così mancò poco che non ritrat-
> tasse con questa limitazione quel che pareva di voler vietare del tutto:
> fu dunque castigata la violenza, non il piacere; la crudeltà, non l'amore;
> l'inumanità, non gl'amplessi."

> "it seemed too severe even to him to set down as a written commandment
> what he had invented out of mere rhetorical flourish to incite terror. So he
> doesn't actually say that the infamous cities were destroyed because of the
> simple love of boys, rather because they were unholy, cruel, avaricious, rapa-
> cious, and violent. The real cause of their ruin was their violent treatment
> of the angels. And so with this qualification, he almost ends up taking back
> precisely what he at first appeared to want to prohibit: for it was violence
> that was punished, not pleasure; cruelty, not love; inhumanity, not loving
> carnal embrace."[37]

Natural Law and Moral Responsibility

Such is Rocco's critique of laws human and divine. But does that mean
that we must live without laws? Is the libertine nothing but a lust-crazed
animal who stops at nothing in his quest for pleasure? By no means.
Libertines obey the law of Nature, the only law they consider true and just.
And what is this? Alcibiades's master explains:

> "Chiamo leggi di natura . . . quelle che dal lume dell'intelletto sono a
> ciascuno degl'uomini, di qualsivoglia setta o nazione, naturalmente, senza
> artificio, sino dalla culla inserte; e approvate con universal consenso da tutti,

e da' più savii e da' più giusti. In due parti principali si dividono: l'una concerne l'onor di Dio, l'altra la benevolenza ed equità del prossimo."

"I call laws of Nature . . . those laws infused naturally, without artifice, by the light of reason into all men of all tribes and nations, from the moment they are born. They are approved by universal consent, and among the wisest and most just. They fall into two main categories: those that honor God, and those that espouse goodwill and equity in treating their fellow man."[38]

Homosexual relationships do not violate the laws of nature.

"Si è qui offeso il prossimo? Chi direbbe queste pazzie? e se dal libero albitrio, dono regale di Dio, dipende il volere e poter far ciò che piace del suo, perché non si può di questo? . . . Chi è tiranno sì empio che donando la libertà ad un suo servo gli proibisca l'uso? Ci averà dunque fatti liberi Dio perché siamo schiavi delle nostre passioni e dell'eccesso sregolato di esse? Egli dunque, nella tempra che ha data al nostro frale, vedrà languire le cagioni, riprenderà quel ch'è suo? O forse ha pena del nostro bene? Invidia il nostro diletto?"

"Do they somehow harm our fellow man? Who could maintain such folly? And if wanting and being able to do what we wish with what is ours is a condition of free will, God's supreme gift, why is it not so in this case as well? . . . What sort of tyrant would be so wicked as to grant his servant liberty while at the same time forbidding him to enjoy it? Could God have made us free just for us to be enslaved by the unregulated excesses of passion? Did he create our mortal bodies just to see them weaken so he could take back what is his? Or perhaps our happiness causes Him suffering? Could He be envious of our pleasure?"[39]

This then is the key to the libertine's code. His behavior must be regulated not by external laws, rather by the natural laws that he carries within himself. These laws tell him to avoid not homosexual love, rather the tyranny imposed by "unregulated excesses of passion"—including sexual passion.

Alcibiades's master then turns to the "scientific" thinking of the era that classified sperm as a form of "super-refined blood," "distilled" from the human organism. Harkening back to the theory of corporeal humors so dear to ancient medicine, Filotimo explains that:

"Il cazzo deve esser moderato, perché l'eccesso, privandoci della più pura e spiritosa sostanza, ci estenua, ci dissecca e consuma. E ben spesso in loco di seme si manda fuori sangue vivo, si distilla il cervello, si dischiano i spiriti: onde si cangia figura e colore, e s'accellera [sic] velocissimamente la morte, perché la natura, intenta più alla conservazione della specie che del individuo, mette ogni sforzo a preparar materia per la generazione, sì che dato fuori il seme ne apparecchia subito dell'altro, e ne toglie la materia dal sangue più puro, onde ne rende vuote le vene e le parti più principale e più vitali."

"The cock must be used with moderation. Excess use deprives us of our most pure essential substance and thus weakens, dehydrates, and generally consumes us. Oftentimes in place of seed real living blood spurts forth, depleting the brain and dissipating the vital spirits. This causes us to change form and color and hastens the arrival of death, because Nature—more intent on the survival of the species than the individual—spares no effort in preparing the material necessary for procreation. No sooner has one seed been emitted than She sets about preparing another, taking her material from that purest blood, all of which drains away the most important and vital elements of our being."[40]

This is a curious thesis that sets theology aside and finds in biology a rationale for sexual temperance. Curious, perhaps, but not unsuccessful, if we consider that secular moralists well into the eighteenth and nineteenth centuries will continue to find a basis for their sexual proscriptions in human physiology. Consider a figure like the famous eighteenth-century antimasturbation crusader Simon-André Tissot (1728–1797). In light of Rocco's statements, he no longer seems to be the precursor of Western bourgeois morals, as scholars argued some time ago; instead we might now see him as the epigone of the kind of morality promoted by the libertines.[41] Here is yet another reason to take an interest in libertine thought.

Indeed, our interest cannot help but grow when we recognize that Rocco did not stop at merely presenting the arguments libertinism could muster against moral and religious strictures. He went further by appealing to the right of every individual to live according to his own innate "inclinations" (today we might say "tendencies"), a move that strikes us as very modern and much in line with our hopes and desires even today.

"Se l'orologio ha il moto dalle ruote e dalli contrapesi che gl'ha dati l'artefice, sarà difettoso d'esso orologio che batta l'ore a questo tempo o in un altro? Le inclinazioni sono contrapesi datici dalla natura e da Dio, chi segue quelli non s'allontana dai propri principii, non fa contro l'istitutore."

"If a clock has a certain motion because of the gears and counterweights that the clockmaker gave it, would it be considered a defect if it happens to strike the hour at this time as opposed to that? Just so, our 'inclinations' are like the counterweights given to us by Nature and by God: whosoever follows these cannot possibly stray from his origins nor act in opposition to his Creator."[42]

Rocco concludes that, since we did not choose our innate tendencies, we cannot possibly act against Nature or God, who created us with those very tendencies. Perhaps others will think of the homosexual as a clock that strikes the hour at the "wrong" time. Even so, since God and Nature constructed him to tick that way, how could he possibly have any guilt in the matter? Needless to say, a philosophy capable of these sorts of reflections created significant space for explaining and accepting homosexuality.[43] Historians have begun to ask whether in some cases the prevalence of libertine thought did not intervene to save "sodomites" from persecution.[44]

The Fate of Libertinism

Although it started out strong in sixteenth- and seventeenth-century Italy, libertinism was ruthlessly persecuted by Counter Reformation society and reduced to a clandestine, underground movement, at least in its most visible manifestations. This transformation of Italian libertinism by no means signaled the movement's end. Before being cut down, the "evil stalk" managed to spread its seeds in France and England, where it blossomed again in the seventeenth century to give life to the "classic" libertinism of the eighteenth that we all know and love. The real decline began in the seventeenth century, when western thought evolved through Galileo, Descartes, and Hume away from a scientific speculation mired in Aristotelianism towards a more productive materialism. This proved a blessing in disguise, for it brought to the fore what had always been libertinism's strong suit: ethical reflection.

Libertinism thus remained productive through the advent of the Enlightenment, which it anticipated and by which it was replaced. Typical libertine arguments and attitudes reemerge, as we have seen, in the writings of Enlightenment thinkers. Well into the eighteenth century we find a thoroughly libertine attitude in the writings of the Marquis de Sade. And yet it is precisely Sade that signals the end of libertinism, which in his hands becomes exactly what its enemies had always accused it of being: a pursuit of pleasure, reserved for the élite, that stops at nothing, not even another's suffering. This is a far cry from the demand for balance and *urbanitas* that characterized libertinism's earlier manifestations. Nor can Sade's version be reconciled with the "laws of nature" that libertinism had always pursued, laws the French Revolution would before long struggle to embody. With Sade, what had been born of the desire to maximize enjoyment of the only life we are given—thus of a positive, joyful attitude toward life—becomes a single-minded pursuit of pleasure that might even lead to suffering and death, as in *The 120 Days of Sodom*. Having reached this point of no return, libertine thought could only be condemned to extinction. In the end, the French Revolution destroyed once and for all the aristocratic social fabric that held libertinism's few remaining threads.

Popular Libertinism

The above review of the major tenets of libertine thought does not take into consideration the movement's importance as a social phenomenon. Libertines were by definition "cultivated" individuals, which at that time meant they were either wealthy or clergymen. It does not necessarily follow, however, that libertine ideas and lifestyles never moved beyond a privileged few, in part because the lifestyles of the élite remained a continual source of fascination for the rest of the population, in part because some of the most important libertine ideas managed to become "common sense" before the Counter Reformation took the upper hand. Nor should we underestimate the effect of the religious wars that pitted church against church, each convinced of its own righteousness and ready to condemn all others as impostors.[45] In such a climate, it is not difficult to understand how many, even among the "lower classes," decided that all religions without exception were the result of imposture. They were thus forced to consider other, more or less libertine belief systems, however crude or lacking in the refined philosophical garb so vaunted by libertine *philosophes.*

For these and other reasons, libertinism became something of a "popular" movement in Italy, or at least more popular than in France or England. Alongside the "philosophical" form of libertinism cultivated by those who had studied ancient Greek thought (and this is the only form that has interested scholars to date), there existed another, if you will, "vernacular" libertinism that found expression above all in the derision of religious authorities and the respect they demanded, adherence to a secular and open-minded morality, and—of greatest interest—a joyous view of life and its pleasures. In this view, sexuality becomes a positive aspect of living, not simply a road to perdition. This rather overlooked manifestation of libertinism enjoyed common currency in countless little acts of mockery against religion (from elaborate parodies to the desecration of sacred images), but is most evident in the impunity and ease with which libertines were able to parade their ideas in public, not to mention their unorthodox sexual proclivities. The trial of Francesco Calcagno mentioned above offers one striking example of this freedom.[46]

Conclusion

Needless to say, the above represents a first, very general consideration of the influence of libertine thought on the morality and sexual behavior of our ancestors. Several pieces of the puzzle are still missing. Scholarly interest in libertinism generally is relatively recent (only the last half century or so), and there has been relatively little interest in the erotic aspect of libertine thought.[47] Too many scholars have taken for granted that we already know all there is to know about libertine sexual morality (which is to say that it was, of course, "libertine") or that it offers nothing of real interest, just a pretext for self-indulgent debauchery.[48]

On the contrary, even a superficial investigation like ours reveals that libertine attitudes were more nuanced and balanced than one might expect. While the enemies of libertinism lost the war against "free thinkers," they did manage to win the all-important image battle by convincing the world that libertines were nothing but dissolute hedonists interested only in their own egotistical pleasures. This image has prevented us from seeing libertinism as a pioneering first attempt at a secular ethics as well: an attempt to discover within our own humanity the bases for respect towards other human beings. I am not trying to cast libertinism as the precursor to "modern man." It was not. Many libertines espoused an attitude of frank hypocrisy or "nicodemismo": They conformed externally to the prevailing morality while inside still cultivating their heterodox beliefs. In the final analysis, most libertines were perfectly content with the society they so ridiculed. We cannot make revolutionaries of them. The priest Francesco Calcagno constantly parodied the Church and its beliefs while continuing to celebrate mass, even though he no longer had the legal right to do so. Equally inappropriate, however, is the attempt by historians like Spini to dismiss libertinism as the unruly stepchild of the Catholic Counter Reformation, particularly since libertinism, despite its many contradictions, managed to find its way to tolerance for homosexuals and others outside the mainstream. Libertinism influenced western thought by softening its anti-gay attitude. This may not constitute a Revolution in the true Marxist sense, but it's a lot more than many gays would settle for even today. And that's no small accomplishment.

Giovanni Dall'Orto is an independent journalist and historian living in Milan. He is a pioneer of lesbian and gay studies in Italy who has been publishing on the entire scope of queer Italian history for more than 20 years. A regular contributor to the Italian periodicals *Babilonia* and *Sodoma*, he is currently editor-in-chief of *Pride*. Many of his dozens of articles have been translated for international journals. In English, his work has appeared in *The Journal of Homosexuality*,

The *Encyclopedia of Homosexuality* (Garland, 1990), and *The History of Homosexuality in Europe and America* (Garland, 1992). You can visit his website, *La gaya scienza*, at http://digilander.libero.it/giovannidallorto.

Notes

* I'd like to thank Guiseppe Panella and Walter Lupi for their help on this essay, which it sometimes seemed I'd never complete. They kindly helped me sort out my ideas on libertinism and this essay incorporates some of their suggestions. Responsibility for the assertions made here, and particularly for any errors, remains entirely my own. This essay was originally published in an earlier version in Italian: " 'La natura è madre dolcisima.' L'accettazione dell'omosessualità nel libertinismo italiano dei secoli XVI e XVII," *Sodoma* 5 (Spring–Summer 1993), pp. 27–41. The English translation here is by Cestaro. On this same topic, see Giovanni Dall'Orto, "Il trionfo di Sodoma. Poesie erotiche inedite dei secoli XVI–XVII," *La fenice di Babilonia* 2 (1997), pp. 37–69.

1. Mario Mieli, *Elementi di critica omosessuale*, (Turin: Einaudi, 1977), translated into English as *Homosexuality and Liberation: Elements of a Gay Critique*, trans. David Fernbach (London: Gay Men's Press, 1980). See the title of chapter two, "Come gli omosessuali, di rogo in rogo, divennero gay," which Fernbach rendered as "Fire and Brimstone, or How Homosexuals Became Gay." Mieli's treatise has recently been reissued: *Elementi di critica omosessuale*, ed. Gianni Rossi Barilli and Paola Mieli (Milan: Feltrinelli, 2002).

2. René Pintard, *Le libertinage érudit dans la première moitié du XVII siècle* (Paris, 1943; rpr. Geneva and Paris: Slatkine, 1983).

3. See Pintard and Alan Bray, *Homosexuality in Renaissance England* (London: Gay Men's Press, 1982). I would add that it is amusing to see how scholars of sixteenth/seventeenth-century Italian libertinism and scholars of seventeenth/eighteenth-century French libertinism struggle to discern continuity between the two main periods of the movement. See, for instance, the attempt to synthesize the disparate definitions of libertinism circulating today made by James Turner, "The Properties of Libertinism," *Unauthorized Sexual Behavior During the Enlightenment*, ed. Robert Maccubin, *Eighteenth-Century Life* 9 (1985), pp. 75–87. Among other things, this essay notes that some scholars place "the first major flourishing" of libertinism too early . . . around 1650! Which is to say no less than a full century *after* its first real flourishing in Italy; by 1650 it was already fading away.

4. Giorgio Spini, *Ricerca dei libertini* (Florence: La Nuova Italia, 1983; 2nd edition).

5. See Giorgio Spini, "Alcuni appunti sui libertini italiani" in: *Il libertinismo in Europa*, ed. Sergio Bertelli (Milan and Naples: Ricciardi, 1980), pp. 117–24. Protestant scholar Spini accuses Catholics of having used "a godless theory of religion as imposture . . . for a positive end, that is to defend Catholicism." He goes on: "Nor is it at all beyond the realm of possibility that this type of polemic contributed to the growth and diffusion of libertine ideology" (p. 121; all English translations Cestaro unless otherwise indicated). In the same volume

an amazing example of the use of libertine arguments in religious polemics is studied by Valerio Marchetti, "Nelle fabbriche dell'immaginazione anti-libertina: Andrea Cardoini," pp. 169–80, which deals with a critique of Calvin that ends up turning the "heretic" leader into a diabolical and libertine-style "impostor." On the other side of the fence, the use of libertine thematics to combat "Catholic superstition" is examined by Giancarlo Carabelli, "Libertinismo e deismo in Inghilterra" in: *Ricerche su letteratura libertina e letteratura clandestina nel Seicento*, ed. Tullio Gregory et al. (Florence: La Nuova Italia, 1981), pp. 407–16.

6. Of particular interest on this question is the insightful essay by Ornella Pompeo Faracovi, "L'antropologia della religione nel libertinismo francese del Seicento" in Gregory, pp. 119–42.

7. On this question see Dino Pastine, "L'immagine del libertino nell'apologetica cattolica del XVII secolo" in Gregory, pp. 143–73 and in particular p. 153.

8. As Tullio Gregory emphasizes in "Il libertinismo della prima metà del Seicento" in Gregory, pp. 3–47, libertinism finds natural causes for miracles "and lays the foundations for a secular ethics free from religious myth; at base lies a detached and skeptical relativism that renounces all metaphysics and totalizing visions, refuses dogmatism and religious polemic, and valorizes the use of reason in human affairs; . . . in all things . . . a progressive distancing from the sacred, its exclusion from history, a reduction of religious myths and rites to the practical or political sphere of external behavior" (p. 6).

9. See below, "Natural Law and Moral Behavior."

10. The doctrine that the soul died with the body was even taught with impunity at the University of Padua, one of the capitals of Italian libertinism, by Cesare Cremonini (1510–1631) following the lead of Pietro Pomponazzi (1462–1525).

11. "Souvent on arrive à même fin par différentes voies; pour moi, je ne con-damne point vos manières, chacun se sauve à sa guise, mais je n'irai point à la béatitude par le chemin que vous tenez." Roger de Bussy Rabutin (1618–1693), *Histoire amoureuse des Gaules* (Paris: Garnier, 1868; first edition 1665), vol. 2, p. 151.

12. Such morals were shared by at least certain parts of society beyond the bounds of libertinism strictly speaking. See Armando Marchi's foreward to Ferrante Pallavicino, *Il corriero svaligiato* (Parma: University of Parma, 1984), p. xxvii; Marchi points out that even Giovan Battista Marino (1569–1625) alludes to such thinking in his *Adone* (1623) where he writes: "e chi s'astien da quel piacer giocondo / nega a Natura il suo devuto dritto" (XX.429) [whosoever abstains from such joyful pleasure / denies to Nature what is rightly hers]; see also XII.243: "Fallo non è, poi che d'Amor t'accendi / furto non è, se quanto dài prendi" (It isn't a crime just because Love sets you aflame / nor is it theft when you take as good as you give).

13. On the whole, libertinism was a philosophical attitude positively disposed towards sexuality in all its manifestations. Thanks to its influence, the Italy of three or four centuries ago was much less ascetic than it seems to us today. Though difficult to see today, this is also due to the battle waged by the

Counter Reformation against the widespread opinion that "simple fornication" (that is to say simple sexual relations not accompanied by crimes such
as incest, rape, corruption of minors, sodomy, and the like) was not a sin. This
opinion was described and treated as heretical, which discouraged our fore-
bears from writing or speaking about it. Nonetheless, the idea remained fixed
in popular thinking for some time judging by the tirades of Catholic preachers. See, for instance, a 1424 sermon of Bernardino da Siena (1380–1444),
according to which some people "dicono che la fornicazione e l'andare alle
meretrici non è peccato, perché l'atto sessuale è naturale e ad esso ci inclina la
natura" (claim that fornication and visiting prostitutes is not a mortal sin,
since the sexual act is natural and Nature herself inclines us toward it);
Le prediche volgari, ed. Pietro Bargellini (Milan: Rizzoli, 1936), p. 413.

14. Bray, pp. 63–64.

15. An excellent study of the logic underlying blasphemy in the Church over the
centuries can be found in Luiz Mott, "Maria, Virgem ou nâo? Quatro séculos
de contestaçâo no Brasil" in: *Sexo Proibido: Virgens, Gays e Escravos nas garras
da Inquisiçâo* (Campinas Editora Papirus, 1989), pp. 131–90. The libertine
"matrix" for many of the blasphemous opinions described in this article is
most evident, especially when the accused are Italian.

16. While insisting on its spiritual purity, Saint Aelred of Rievaulx (1110–1167)
in the middle ages had defined the relationship between Jesus and John as a
"marriage"; see John Boswell, *Christianity, Social Tolerance, and Homosexuality:
Gay People in Western Europe from the Beginning of the Christian Era to the
Fourteenth Century* (Chicago and London: The University of Chicago Press,
1980), pp. 225–26.

17. For the transcript of the Calcagno trial, see Dall'Orto, " 'Adora più presto un
bel putto, che Domenedio': il processo a un libertino omosessuale: Francesco
Calcagno (1550)," *Sodoma* 5 (Spring–Summer 1993), pp. 43–55. On Calcagno,
see also P. Labalme, "Sodomy and Venetian Justice in the Renaissance," *Legal
History Review* 52 (1984), p. 241. Spini, p. 156, also mentions the case of
Tommaso Campanella's cellmate, Dionisio Ponzio, by whom "Cristo . . . viene
accusato di avere coltivato vizi nefandi" (Christ is accused of having cultivated
wicked vices). It is important to point out that of the six passages I cite here
on Christ's homosexuality, four are from individuals who either clearly prefer
sex with men or (like Marlowe) are accused of preferring it. As a result, it
should be clear that this libertine "blasphemy" is not just an attempt to insult
what is sacred. If this were so, the four sodomites—far from justifying themselves with such a story—would surely have condemned themselves. It is
instead more like a strategy that aims to bring the sacred back into the realm
of the human, the realm from which—libertines are convinced—the sacred
derives in any event. "Jesus was a man and he had human desires, just like me"
is the message conveyed by the libertine blasphemy. This runs directly counter
to one of the principal objectives of the Counter Reformation, which was to
minimize the human aspects of Christ and the saints. We should note that in
the centuries before the Counter Reformation discussions of Christ's sexual

nature—proof of the reality of his humanity—were not uncommon. See Leo Steinberg, *The Sexuality of Christ in Renaissance Art and in Modern Oblivion* (Chicago: University of Chicago Press, 1996; 2nd edition), a fascinating discussion even for those unwilling to accept its more extreme analyses.

18. Bray, pp. 63–64.

19. Cited by Jim Kepner, *Becoming a People* (Hollywood: National Gay Archives, 1983), p. 19.

20. "O Cristo era afeiçoado a Sâo Joâo porque dormiam ambos." The witness adds that Michel had said: " 'Se Sâo Paulo falou tanto nas molicies, é que alguma cousa obrara nelas,' dando a entender que S. Paulo cometera o pecado de molicies." ("If Saint Paul spent so much time talking about *mollities* it's because he must have had some experience in the area," suggesting that St. Paul had commited the sin of *mollities*), *Arquivio Nacional da Torre do Tombo*, Lisbon. "Inquisiçao de Lisboa," n. 10093. I would like to thank Professor Luiz Mott of Bahia (Brazil; http://luizmott.cjb.net/) for this citation, as well as the one in the note following. On the Latin term *mollities* ("softness," often referring to masturbation in medieval theological discussions), see Mark D. Jordan, *The Invention of Sodomy in Christian Theology* (Chicago: University of Chicago Press, 1997), especially pp. 102–06, 168–69.

21. "Nosso senhor Jesus Cristo era nefando, disse por outra palavra mais torpe e execranda." *Arquivio Nacional da Torre do Tombo*, Lisbon. "Caderno do Promotor," n. 56. From the Latin "ne-fari" (not to be spoken about, unmentionable), "nefando" was a common synonym for "sodomite" in sixteenth- and seventeenth-century Spanish, Portuguese, and Italian. Indeed, the verb "nefandar" was coined for "to bugger, sodomize." See the Archivio di Stato di Roma, "Tribunale del governatore," processi 1505–1599, vol. 290, 28/6/1595, foll. 6r–v: " 'Non già dico che io habbia visto *nefandasse* tali ragazzi, ma solo dico che per publica voce et fama sempre si è detto che per la pratica che teneva con loro, che li *nefandasse*.' " ("I'm not saying that I actually saw him bugger those boys, I'm just saying it's what people have always said about him, that he's got a reputation for that kind of behaviour with them, that he buggers them.") The records of the Inquisition in Lisbon that deal with sodomites are called "Repertorios do Nefando"; see Arlindo Camilo Monteiro, "Il peccato nefando in Portogallo ed il tribunale dell'Inquisizione," *Rassegna di studi sessuali* 6 (1926), pp. 161–76, 265–89, and 7 (1927), pp. 1–28, 162.

22. "Si la Madeleine avait eu quelque aventure galante avec le Christ; si, aux noces de Cana, le Christ entre deux vins, un peu non-conformiste, eût parcourou la gorge d'une des filles de noce et les fesses de Saint Jean, incertain, s'il resterait fidèle ou non à l'apôtre au menton ombragé d'un duvet léger: vous verriez ce qu'il en serait de nos peintres, de nos poètes." *Oeuvres esthétiques* (Paris: Garnier, 1959), pp. 706–07. For English translation, see *Diderot on Art*, 2 volumes, ed. and trans. John Goodman (New Haven, CT and London: Yale University Press, 1995), vol. I, p. 217.

23. See Ira Wade, *The Intellectual Origins of the French Enlightenment* (Princeton, NJ: Princeton University Press, 1972).

24. See Tullio Gregory's remarks on French moralist Pierre Charron (1541–1603) in "Il libertinismo della prima metà del Seicento," Gregory et al., p. 15: "In opposition to a slave ethic linked to fear of the afterlife, Charron affirms the value of behavior founded on nature and reason. This is the ideal that the enlightened man has given up on conveying to the masses because desire to persuade others is typical of dogmatism . . . but mostly because the enlightened man acknowledges the invincible force of *coustume* (habit, custom), a second nature that has definitively corrupted the great mass of *esprits foibles* (the weak in spirit), who are in need of the bridles of 'religion, law, custom, science, precepts, threats, promises mortal and immortal.' If the enlightened man wants to 'keep his conscience out of the gutter,' as Charron so effectively puts it, he should just 'let the world be, there where it is.' "

25. For Antonio Rocco, see also my "Antonio Rocco and the Background of his 'L'Alcibiade fanciullo a scola' (1652)" in: *Among Men, Among Women*, Conference at the University of Amsterdam, 22–26 June 1983 (Amsterdam: Universiteit van Amsterdam, 1993), pp. 224–32, 571–72 (much of this has been incorporated into the present essay). For those interested in the tortuous tale of how the book came to be attributed to Rocco, see Laura Coci, "L'Alcibiade fanciullo a scola: nota biobibliografica," *Studi secenteschi* 26 (1985), pp. 301–29 and pp. 95–98 of Coci's edition, *L'Alcibiade fanciullo a scola* (Rome: Salerno, 1988). Although difficult to obtain, an English translation now exists: *Alcibiades the Schoolboy*, trans. J. C. Rawnsley (Amsterdam: Entimos, 2000). On the literary and cultural context, see Claudio Varese, "Momenti e implicazioni del romanzo libertino nel Seicento italiano" in: Bertelli, pp. 239–69 and Albert N. Mancini, "La narrativa libertina degli Incogniti: tipologie e forme," *Forum italicum* 16 (Winter 1982), pp. 203–29. Armando Marchi, "Il Seicento *en enfer:* la narrazione libertina del Seciento italiano," *Rivista di letteratura italiana* 2 (1984), pp. 351–67, provides valuable insights on seventeenth-century Italian intellectuals and libertines. More recently, see Armando Maggi, "The Discourse of Sodom in a Seventeenth-Century Venetian Text" in: *Reclaiming the Sacred: The Bible in Gay and Lesbian Culture* (New York: Haworth, 1997), pp. 25–43. A German translation with a reprint of the Italian text was published by Wolfram Setz as: *Antonio Rocco, Die Schüler Alkibiades. Ein philosophisch-erotischer Dialog* (Hamburg: MännerschwarmSkript Verlag, 2002). This edition proposes ancient texts relevant to Rocco and the *Alcibiade*, plus a "Nachwort" by Wolfram Setz, *Wär ich einem Tag und eine Nacht Alkibiades. Geschichten um ein kleines Buch*, pp. 199–255.

26. Venetian State Archive (VSA) "Santo Uffizio." *Processi*. Busta 103, 'pezza' n. 3. Partially published in Spini, pp. 163–64, 166–67.

27. VSA as cited above and Spini, p. 163.

28. Ibid., p. 164.

29. Ibid.

30. Ibid., pp. 167–68.

31. Rocco, p. 51. These burlesque passages continue the tradition of works like the *Cazzarìa* by Antonio Vignali de' Buonagiunti, written between ca. 1525, which

includes a similarly burlesque paragraph that explains, "perché si chiami fottere contro natura il fottere le donne dietro" (why fucking women from behind is called fucking against nature); see pp. 66–67 of Antonio Vignali, *La cazzarìa*, ed. P. Stoppelli (Rome: Edizioni dell'elefante, 1984) and *The Book of the Prick*, trans. Ian Frederick Moulton (New York: Routledge, 2003). Not by chance we will find this work again in the hands of Francesco Calcagno, whose trial we mentioned above. On *La Cazzarìa*, see also Rocke, pp. 93 and 284, n. 31.

32. Rocco, pp. 51–52.
33. Ibid., p. 53.
34. Ibid., p. 56.
35. Ibid., p. 57.
36. Ibid., p. 58.
37. Ibid., p. 61. For modern gay scholarly readings of Sodom, see Boswell and Jordan.
38. Rocco, p. 62.
39. Ibid., p. 63.
40. Ibid., p. 74.
41. Jean-Paul Aron and Roger Kempf. *Le pénis et la démoralisation de l'Occident* (Paris: B. Grasset, 1978).
42. Rocco, p. 59. One might compare the Marquis de Sade, *La philosophie dans le boudoir* (from the first dialogue, *Oeuvrès complètes*, ed. Le Brun and Pauvert (Evreux: Pauvert, 1986), vol. III, p. 385) a century and a half later: "l'homme est-il le maître de ses goûts? Il faut plaindre ceux qui en ont de singuliers, mais ne les insulter jamais: leur tort est celui de la nature; ils n'étaient pas plus les maîtres d'arriver au monde avec des goûts différents que nous ne le sommes de naître ou bancal ou bien fait." (Is man the master of his tastes? We might lament the fact that certain individuals have some very peculiar ones, but we must never insult them. Their fault is Nature's fault. They were no more in control of arriving in the world with peculiar tastes than we are of being born lame or sound of limb.) I would also like to emphasize that while it is certainly correct to read Sade in the wake of Rocco's ideas, we should not read Rocco through Sade in the opposite direction, which is what usually happens. Even Laura Coci, who reads Rocco "in light of Sade's thought" (Rocco, p. 26), indulges in subjective psychoanalytic forays. Coci feels, for instance, that "hatred of women projects the *Alcibiade* towards Sade's universe" (Rocco, p. 23).

I also find unacceptable the attempt to read Rocco through Sade, who is in turn read through Klossowski (Rocco, p. 27), which can only result in a mystifying, third-hand account. I tend to agree with Nino Borsellino's position in the Introduction to Antonio Vignali's *Cazzarìa* (cited above, pp. 26–27): "in order to align Vignali's philosophy and sodomitic practice with Sade, it would be necessary to magnify exponentially the hedonism of the Intronati, turn it into an all-powerful entity, Vice, and completely reverse the meaning they gave to Nature, from Good to Evil. If anything, Vignali's academic libertinism professed harmony with the designs of Nature."

43. Eighteenth-century libertinism develops a notable tolerance for homosexuality that leads progressively towards acceptance and finally decriminalization, which begins in the last decades of the century and triumphs in the Napoleonic Code.

44. See, for instance, Gabriele Martini, *Il 'vitio nefando' nella Venezia del Seicento* (Rome: Jouvence, 1988), p. 111. Despite Martini's annoying moralistic tone (which leads hims to invoke "moral weakness" among Venice's ruling class in order to account for the decline in death sentences for sodomites in the seventeenth century), he confirms that in seicento Venice "paradoxically a 'culture of deviance' was able to take root within the very social group delegated to defend institutional values, a group unable to muster the forces needed to react to such phenomena [*sic*]. Setting aside some objective judicial motives, then, one has to wonder if the qualitative and quantitative decline in repressive action against sodomy might not be explained by the particular moral and cultural climate that held sway among the ruling classes."

45. See the texts cited above in note 5.

46. See note 17.

47. See, however, the collection of essays edited by Catherine Cusset, *Libertinage and Modernity* (New Haven, CT and London: Yale University Press, 1998), which includes an essay by Philippe Roger on "The role of female homosexuality in Casanova's memoirs." See also Randy P. L. Conner, "Burning Desire: Claude Le Petit, Libertine Poet," *Papers on French Seventeenth Century Literature* 27, 53 (2000), pp. 421–33, and James Grantham Turner, *Schooling Sex: Libertine Literature and Erotic Education in Italy, France, and England 1534–1685* (Oxford: Oxford University Press, 2003).

48. One excellent example of how Italian scholars simply cannot escape a moralistic approach to the question is Giorgio Spini in the above-cited volume, *Ricerca dei libertini*. His tone ranges from the scandalized to the scornful: On p. 126, for instance, he says of Dionisio Ponzio, who refused to hide his homosexuality, "he bragged as a homosexual about his filthy behavior." But even Laura Coci, who is well aware of libertinism's effort "to provide an alternative morality" (Rocco, p. 18), invokes Satan on p. 12 of her introduction, an allusion to the "demonic" eloquence of the libertine Casanova, as well as a desire to adhere to Sade's concept of evil. In his investigation of Cremonini, Gabriele Martini (p. 105) declares in no uncertain terms that "libertine doctrine contained the philosophical bases for a practical and theoretical immorality widely diffused among the Venetian upper classes in the seventeenth century." Spini's prudishness, the fire and brimstone evoked by Coci, and Martini's facile equation of libertinism and immorality leave no room for an objective, level-headed approach to the subject, which was never a cult of evil or Satan inasmuch as it aimed to escape evil and suffering and it parodied the devil just as it did Jesus. Nor was libertinism immoral simply because it aimed to define an alternative morality. Perhaps it never quite succeeded in this quest (that remains an open question), but it in any case merits the respect of historians, just as any other topic of research.

6

Tra(ns)vesting Gender and Genre in Flaminio Scala's *Il (finto) marito*

Rosalind Kerr

The *commedia dell'arte* occupies a central if underestimated place in early modern Italian culture, spanning almost two hundred years from its emergence in the 1540s until its transformations into the fantastic folktale operas of Gozzi and the early bourgeois realist drama of Goldoni in the 1700s. The name *commedia dell'arte* referred to both the professional status and the improvised performance style of the first commercial theater companies that appeared in all the major centers in the north of Italy in the mid-sixteenth century. It also institutionalized the presence of the actress on the Western stage, a phenomenal change for early modern theater, especially since these performers not only became outstanding members of the companies but also introduced female transvestite roles to the public stage.[1]

In 1611 Flaminio Scala (1552–1624), one of the most gifted of the first generation of actor/company directors of the *commedia dell'arte*, published a collection of 50 of the *scenari* that had been performed over the past 30 or so years by such distinguished companies as I Gelosi (*The Zealous*).[2] Entitled *Il teatro delle favole rappresentative*, it offers somewhat elongated versions of the very brief *canovacci* (plot outlines) that were hung up on the backstage curtain before a show and was published, according to Scala, to halt further theft of his work.[3] Scala's preoccupation with capturing his art form in print is further attested to by his very unusual 1618 publication of *Il finto marito* (*The False Husband*), which takes one of the 1611 *scenari*, *Il marito* (*The Husband*) and extends it into a full-length play.[4]

During the early part of the *seicento*, when several *commedia dell'arte* troupes had distinguished themselves for the brilliance and erudition of their performances with the courts, the more famous performer-authors among them sought to claim legitimacy for the *arte* alongside the official *commedia erudita*, or learned scripted comedy, practiced by aristocratic amateurs.[5] It is arguable that Flaminio Scala's publications of the *scenari* in 1611 was part of a campaign to leave some written records of the *arte* in the hopes of showcasing the accomplishments of its greatest companies as well as raising its status as a respectable theatrical form.[6] In the case of the 1611 publication, 40 of the *scenari* were typical although very diverse comedies, while the other ten represented such different genres as tragedy, heroic operas, pastorals, and romances. More than simply a collection, they were selected to serve as "*modelli* che costituiscono la base dell'arte dello spettacolo" (*models* that make up the foundations of the art of the spectacle) as well as examples of the limits to which knowable theater could be taken.[7]

When *The False Husband* came out seven years later, it seemed to corroborate the evidence that the aging Scala was continuing his project of promoting the *commedia dell'arte*, especially since it included two prologues, one addressed to readers and one to audiences, in which he outlined the basic tenets of a new theater aesthetics that had been developed by the actors as they improvised their performances.[8] Laura Falavolti, editor of a modern edition of *The False Husband*, describes the publication with the dialogue written out as an act of particular importance:

> [U]n'altra delle pietre della costruzione ideologica a cui i Comici-autori stavano lavorando, per la chiarificazione, ed affermazione della propria arte; nella specifica ottica scaliana, questa commedia rappresenta il testamento spirituale di una generazione di Comici.

> [A]nother of the foundation stones in the ideological framework that Actor-Playwrights were laboring to establish in order to clarify and legitimize their own special art form; from Scala's perspective this comedy served as a spiritual testimonial for an entire generation of comedic performers.[9]

Exactly what Scala was trying to legitimize has become a source of serious contention among scholars. For Marotti, Scala should have stopped with the first publication of the *scenari* or should have brought out the promised second volume, because the full comedy fails to capture the essential theatrical quality so much in evidence in the *scenari*. Molinari goes further, insisting that Scala's "cattivo sviluppo verbale" (poor development of the dialogue) ruined the excellent subject matter of the original.[10] For some, the 1618 publication of *Il finto marito* is regarded as a watershed date in the history of the *commedia* because it marked the genre's failure to win legitimation as high culture.[11]

But rather than insisting that the literary merits of *commedia dell'arte*, readable in the full text, were comparable to those of the *erudita*, Scala seems to be making the case that the *commedia dell'arte*'s value originated in its performative qualities; that is, its primary focus was on presenting the acting body rather than the speaking body.[12] Thus in the first prologue, the Comico (the Player) makes this defense to his critic, the Forestiero (the Stranger):[13]

Comico: E che sia il vero che gl'affetti si muovono più agevolmente da' gesti che dalle parole, ciascuno che ha intelletto, e anco gli animali bruti, sempre faran più caso e moverannosi più a chi alza il bastone, che a chi alza la voce, perché, dice il bergamsco, "'dal dech al fach gh'è un gran trach." E ciò avviene ancora in ogni altra cosa al senso sottoposta.

[T]he Player: That feelings are aroused more by gestures than words is obvious, for intelligent men, and even brute beasts, will always better attend and obey those who use a stick than those who rely on words—for as the Bergamask says, "There's a great gulf between asking and doing." And this is the case with everything that bears on the senses.[14]

In fact, I would like to propose that the Comico's remarks referring to the enormous gulf between saying something and putting it into action are part of his larger defense of the *arte*'s merits. The action-based *arte* made a point of travestying—and we should recall here the Italian etymology *travestire* ("to dress up; to wear the clothes of the opposite sex")—the pretensions of the word-based *erudita*.[15] It is no wonder that the *commedia* found it impossible to earn an esteemed place for itself in Baroque culture.

Perhaps it is more fruitful to examine Scala's treatises and works as examples of a new satiric theatrical form rather than as failed high art. In support of Scala's arguments, Tim Fitzpatrick compares Scala's *scenario* with the full play text and demonstrates that the text was not composed in accordance with literary rules but was exactly what Scala claimed it to be: a full extension of the *scenario*, a writing-out at length of the script that emerged when the formulae for improvising were put into effect.[16] Fitzpatrick's painstaking scene-by-scene comparison proves that physical action, including the *lazzi* (comic turns)—often considered extraneous— always remained the springboard on which all the dialogue, including heightened rhetoric, was built. In writing out the full text, Scala simply includes the dialogue that would have been developed during the course of performance. These extensions grew out of the devices that *commedia* employed to stretch even the smallest units of the prepatterned routines used in the oral tradition in which it was rooted. These are repetition, contrast, elaboration, parallelism, delay, all of which were essential to advance the plot structures physically, verbally, and thematically.[17] Viewed in this light, Scala's defense of his art as arising from a "logica naturale" (natural logic) that bases its performance on everyday practice rather than rules becomes less of a boast and more of a statement of theatrical praxis.[18]

In the more colloquial second prologue, when the Forestiero refers to the *commedia dell'arte* as "cenciaie" (rag bag of tricks), the Comico turns it back on him, asking him how he can apply such a label to "lo specchio della vita umana" (the mirror of human nature).[19] It is precisely this mirror that offends the Stranger, who repeats the standard charge that the *arte* causes social disorder and immorality:

> Forestiero: Così chiamo un'azzione la quale insegna alle giovane oneste il modo di divenir vagabonde, solleva i giovani a ingannare i padri con l'esempio, per scapestrarsi e scapigliarsi, et avvezza i servitori a metter in mezzo i padroni, e le serve a far la ruffiana. Ma, deh!, lasciatemene andare.

> [T]he Stranger: That's what I call an action that teaches honest young girls how to become runaways, sets out examples for young men to swindle their fathers, to throw off the reins and run wild, leads servants to trick their masters, and maids to become procuresses. But enough, let me go.[20]

In fact, almost every deviant behavior is mentioned with the exception of same-sex attractions, although they may be implied. However, the Player insists that the *commedia* is only representing "le cose umane sottoposte a gl'oppositi et a' contrarii, e non è biasimevole né lodevole per se stessa" (human behavior in all its vagaries and contradictions, and is not deserving of blame or praise for itself).[21] He argues that merely representing human nature in action is not the cause of the immorality that may follow but the way that evil humans choose to react. A man who is predisposed to goodness "cava i veri precetti del ben vivere dal veder chi mal vive" (draw[s] the true precepts for the good life by seeing who lives badly).[22]

But when we look at the subject matter of *The False Husband* as a demonstration of *commedia*'s avowed purpose to "giovare con l'esempio" (instruct by example),[23] we may wonder whether Scala really believed that only bad people would fail to draw the correct moral lessons. There can be no doubt as to the explicit sexual content of the script that had been developed from what is probably the most transgressive *scenario* in Scala's earlier collection. Although 13 of the 50 *scenari* feature female transvestite performances, it is usually the *innamorata* (beloved; first lady) who impersonates the well-positioned young male, whereas here it is the maid who plays the false husband of the title. Crossing over gender lines has now been made doubly subversive because the masquerading maid pushes the fantasy to the limits by usurping a higher-class position.[24] Before the play begins, she has engineered an elaborate ruse to protect her mistress, who has been forbidden to marry the one she loves. The maid fakes her own death, returns in the *persona* of a rich *signor*, and succeeds in marrying her mistress, all before the play begins. Their love relationship becomes the thematic and theatrical focus of the action as other characters turn up to challenge their subterfuge.

The examples of bad behaviors that Scala purports to be drawing from real life experiences were made even more explicit by the presence of female performers in the female roles. Claims of "naturalness" that were used by *commedia* apologists to defend the novel presence of real women fed into the debate that Scala was advancing about the greater realism his art form was able to achieve.[25] This new performative genre created in opposition to the literary-based drama raised very different questions about gender representation. Derrida's observations about the ways in which gender issues overlap with genre in creating definitions of both can be fruitfully examined here.[26] Since the official *commedia erudita* maintained the convention of using boys to represent women, the *commedia dell'arte* could play back and forth across these generic/gendered restrictions.

Indeed it seems that Scala's choice of this *scenario* to promote the artistry of *commedia* indicates that he was aware of the enormous impact that the subversive female performers had on enhancing both its commercial and critical success. For one, *commedia* allowed for the homoeroticism of the traditional male transvestite theatrical traditions to expand to include the possibility of same-sex attractions between women. Hence the transvested maid's role, especially if played by a female, suggested the possibility of a lesbian relationship.[27] Ultimately, in *Il finto marito* the *innamorata* and her maid are the characters in control of the subterfuge and take on the task of convincingly portraying themselves as long-term lovers for almost the entire length of the *scenario*—until, that is, they choose to be revealed.

Highlighting scenes from the full text reveals that the sustained trope of the lesbian husband remains in effect until every other possible subversive combination that could arise from such a threatening situation has been played out. When we compare the very short *scenario* outline and the full text, it becomes obvious that although the names are changed, the characters and plot line are very much the same, with the three-act skeletal *scenario* expanded to five acts in the play.[28] The lesbian marriage between Porzia and Licinio (Brigida), accomplished before the play begins, is the hidden but central issue driving the action since it is their acceptance into the community as a typical heterosexual couple that allows all the other subplots to emerge. The young lover, Lepido, who had been banished by his father, Demetrio, to stop him from marrying Porzia is back to see if he can break up her marriage with the proverbially jealous Licinio (Brigida). Demetrio is trying to forward his own interests again by marrying off his ward, Giulia, to his old crony, Gervasio—but only if he can arrange to have the first night with her himself. Although Giulia, who is in love with Flavio, doesn't know this final little twist, she is well aware that marrying her off to Gervasio is the equivalent of marrying her to an incestuous father-figure. She protests to Demetrio:

> Giulia: Che volete voi, ch'io vi risponda, messere, s'io veggo, che non di marito, ma di padre mi andate provedendo! Fate voi forse questo per la doglia grande ch'io sentii per la perdita del primo, poi che hora volete darmi il secondo? La Fortuna mi providde di voi, che come figliuola mi havete sempre tenuta et allevata, e però dovrebbe bastare à questa pazza, d'havermi pur troppo travagliata, senza volermi dare hora in poter di Gervasio, che più mi si conviene per padre, che per marito.

> Giulia: How can I answer you, Father, when I see you're giving me a father, not a husband? Are you giving me a second one because of the suffering I endured when I lost my own father? Fortune was kind, and gave me you— and you've raised me as your own daughter. But Fortune has already made me suffer enough, without delivering me now to Gervasio, who's certainly more of a father than a husband.[29]

If Licinio (Brigida) is the primary false husband, the play repeats the trope of the false husband in all the subplots since the patriarchs themselves desire to be incestuous (false) husbands.

When we see Porzia and Licinio for the first time, their marriage relationship is portrayed as one ruled by jealousy with Licinio trying to control Porzia's every move. She is so under "his" thumb that we find ourselves drawn into supporting the plan of the wily servant Scaramuccia to cuckold Licinio by sneaking his young master Lepido into Licinio's bed to enjoy Porzia, thus letting him play another "false husband." These plot repetitions continue to proliferate as Scaramuccia has to take care of the two old men as well if he is to get all the rebels into the prohibited beds. In order to do this he uses cross-dressed, cross-gendered disguise in two subversive ways. Since both of the old patriarchs want to consummate their union with Giulia, he dresses both the male servant, Trappola, and the female servant, Ruchetta, in Giulia's clothing and sends them in to Demetrio and Gervasio, respectively. Not even Scaramuccia is clever enough to escape being put into the same situation of risking illicit sexual contact. Porzia forces him to dress in her clothes and take her place in bed with

Licinio while she and Lepido (and Giulia and Flavio) are off consummating their prohibited desires. The seemingly endless proliferation of false husbands of varying sexes and statuses spins dangerously out of control as disempowered sons, women, and servants show us ways to overthrow the social order by violating class, gender, professional, and other taboos that protect upper-bourgeois power and privilege.

In the scene where Porzia forces Scaramuccia to act out his own trick by impersonating her in bed with Licinio, the extended dialogue takes up an entire scene and includes graphic details of all the outcomes that might ensue if Licinio turns to make love to another man. Scaramuccia's apparently horrified reaction to the immorality of this suggestion of homosexual relations is given so much space that his fears of breaking such a terrible taboo become a running gag:

Scaramuccia: L'intervenzione è bella e buona, ma alquanto pericolosa, anzi pericolosissima. Come domine, c'io mi spogli in camiscia, mi metta una cuffia da donna in capo e stia tutta la notte accanto a vostro marito? Questo latino, affé, non me farete voi fare, né me lo insegnò mai il mio maestro! Eh, signora Porzia, dite voi da vero o pur burlate?

Scaramuccia: Well, it's a good plan, a nice plan, but it's a bit dangerous—no it's not, it's very dangerous. Let's see: I strip to my nightshirt, I put a lady's bonnet on my head, and I bed down for the whole night with your husband? You're not going to make me do this sort of homework—I never learnt this sort of conjugation from my Latin teachers. Portia, are you joking or serious?[30]

He continues to outline in graphic detail what might happen in bed only to have Porzia shrug off his fears. His next alternative is to suggest to Porzia that she try a threesome with Licinio on one side and Lepido on the other—so that she can take care of both of them if Licinio wakes up in the mood for love. When she balks at this, Scaramuccia tries another homosexual solution, suggesting that Porzia put Lepido into bed with Licinio and she come to bed with him: "Scaramuccia: Ma aspettate, facciamo un'altra cosa: mettiamo Lepido con vostro marito e voi venitevene a star meco. To' To', che balordo ch'io sono! la pavura mi fa dir di gran cose, perdonatemi." (Scaramuccia: But wait a minute. What if we tried something else: we put Lepido with your husband, and you come and sleep with me—Oh, Scaramuccia, don't be an idiot! I'm sorry, I'm so scared I'm saying stupid things.)[31] Finally, she refuses to have sex with a servant and so forces him back into a homosexual tryst with Licinio. After Scaramuccia so vividly describes the range of possible outcomes that these intimate but dangerous liaisons might affect, nothing remains but to put them all into action. Predictably, the outraged old men flee when they discover that they have been having sex with the wrong person—and wrong sex; Demetrio's indignation is greater because he's been caught out in a same-sex coupling. Scaramuccia is himself tricked for most of his long stint in bed with Licinio—only at the very end does he clue into the fact that he has seen a braid in Licinio's hair and that she is not a man at all but his former wife Brigida. Once the discoveries are made and the threat of violence diminished, all is forgiven, and heterosexual order is reimposed.

But rather than dismiss the subversive behaviors we have witnessed, it is useful to look at the ways in which the improvizational devices typical of *commedia* have been employed to defer, delay and, hence, draw attention to the social structures that need to be in place to serve the dominant order. In the full text, it is very obvious that the central improvizational devices of repetition, contrast, elaboration, and parallelism are being used to their maximum effect. At the same time, it is also significant to note that these devices—central to advancing the plot structures physically, verbally, and thematically—all have the effect of delaying the inevitable return to heteronormalcy and rigid class divisions.[32] Patricia Parker comments that the rhetorical device of delay can be read as part of the Derridean *différance*, which not only defers meanings but also dilates/delays them. She argues that delaying an outcome for the entire length of the play has the effect of making the subversive behaviors so prominent that the threat they pose to the state becomes too serious to deny.[33]

Thus, we have witnessed a typical *commedia* plot that turns on a subversive state of affairs, which proliferates until it creates a situation so out of control that it has to be brought back to order. When Licinio and Porzia admit to each other that it is time to end their masquerade and that "la natura patisce" (nature is suffering),[34] they follow their confessions with an intimate embrace and depart indoors—traditionally a sign that sex is about to occur.[35] This crucial scene falls about two-thirds into the action and may well represent the moment in which they signal their artifice to the spectator, but it still takes the last third of the play and much more chaos before order is reimposed. Even if we interpret "la natura patisce" as a reference to Porzia's desire to have sex with her banished male lover Lepido and, hence, to return to heterosexual normalcy, we still have to recognize that the entire plot hinges on carrying out an act of supreme deception: living in a same-sex/transclass marriage in order to bring about a successful comedic overthrow of dominant patriarchal forces. The figure of the transvestite maid masquerading as successful husband comments on the possibility of both gender and class revolution and is repeated three times in the intrigue in the transvesting of Trappola, Scaramuccia, and Ruchetta. Committing crimes against "nature" may be necessary if social hierarchies are to be challenged. Stories of upstart lesbians make excellent cautionary tales to play on patriarchal fears of usurped marriage beds.[36] In a society where respectable women are not allowed to appear in public places let alone fall in love with one another (unless in a court setting), presenting transgressive women who take on male power offers endless possibilities for the overturning of social conventions on which *commedia* depended. Furthermore, as the play text bears out, we cannot ignore the importance that *commedia* gives to the physical body as a strategic theatrical site, because all the various transvestite bodies are mimetically presented, especially in the scene detailing the illicit combinations that might occur when this many people are sent off to bed each other. In fact, Scala's *scenario* and play enact Judith Butler's argument that, rather than trying to transcend power relations, we must "multiply their various configurations, so that the juridical model of power as oppression and regulation is no longer hegemonic."[37]

To conclude, I hope that these arguments help to show that Scala's *Il marito* and *Il finto marito* are vitally important documents that encapsulate certain processes at work in the *commedia dell'arte* as it transvested itself from marketplace to professional theater. Rather than regarding the publication of *Il finto marito* as a backward step in the history of the *commedia dell'arte*, it should be hailed as a profoundly self-conscious reflection of the subversive workings of an art form that tra(ns)vest(i)ed both gender and genre in its efforts to reveal the oppressive new class and gender structures emerging in the making of the early modern state.

Rosalind Kerr is an Associate Professor of Dramatic Theory and teaches in the Drama Department at the University of Alberta, Edmonton; Alberta, Canada. Her interest in the formation of sexual identities in the early modern period is reflected in a number of conference papers and in the book she is completing, *Improvising Isabella Andreini: Female Transgression and Transvestism on the 16th century Commedia dell' Arte Stage*. Her recent publications include articles on Tasso's sonnet to Isabella Andreini and treatments of the Romeo and Juliet narrative in Shakespeare and Scala.

Notes

1. Ferdinando Taviani and Mirella Schino, *Il segreto della commedia dell'arte* (Florence: La Casa Usher, 1969), pp. 331–44, discusses how the arrival of the actresses revolutionized the stage.

2. Ferruccio Marotti, "Introduzione," in: Flaminio Scala, *Il teatro delle favole rappresentative overo la recreatione comica, boscareccia, e tragica: divisa in cinquanta giornate*, 2 vols., ed. Ferruccio Marotti (Milano: Edizioni Il Polifilo, 1976), vol. 1;

for Scala's biographical details, see pp. xlv–xlvii. Scala had previously published the play *Il postumio* (Lyons, 1601) under the initials I.S. (p. xxii).

3. In an opening letter to his readers, Scala claims that he is publishing to take away the opportunities for others "di appropriarsi le mie fatiche" (to take advantage of my efforts); see *Il teatro delle favole rappresentative*, p. 5. For an English version, see *Scenarios of the Commedia dell'Arte: Flaminio Scala's 'Il teatro delle favole rappresentative,'* trans. and ed. Henry F. Salerno (New York: Limelight Editions, 1989).

4. For the full-length play, see Flaminio Scala, *Il finto marito* in: *Commedie dei Comici dell'Arte*, ed. Laura Falavolti (Turin: Unione Tipografico Editrice Torinese, 1982), pp. 222–365. For the earlier *scenario*, see *Il marito (Giornata IX)* in: *Il teatro delle favole rappresentative*, pp. 101–09; *The Husband* (The Ninth Day) in: Salerno, pp. 66–72.

5. Taviani and Schino, pp. 406–07. Duke Vincenzo Gonzaga of Mantua brought together an all-star troupe drawn from the best companies in northern Italy in 1585; Taviani considers the occasion as evidence that a new theatrical element was coming into existence.

6. Marotti, "Introduzione," pp. xlvi–xlvi, discusses Scala's performance and publishing links with the Andreinis and the ways in which their paths crossed in promoting the *arte*. The early death of Isabella Andreini—the first great diva—in 1604 resulted in the disbanding of the internationally-esteemed *Gelosi* troupe and precipitated the posthumous publication of much of her theatrical work along with that of her actor/company-director husband, Francesco Andreini. With the help of Scala, Francesco published Isabella's letters and other miscellaneous collections of her staged pieces, as well as his own defense of the profession in *Le bravure del Capitano Spavento*.

7. Marotti, "Introduzione," p. lii.

8. Marotti, "Introduzione," pp. l–lxiii, speculates on Scala's motives for publishing the full-length play.

9. See Laura Falavolti, "Nota al Testo," in: *Il finto marito*, pp. 223–24. Unless otherwise noted English translations are my own.

10. Marotti, "Introduzione," pp. lv–lxiii, insists that *Il finto marito* fails because in following the traditional rules of comedy, it loses the more exciting, more complex transcription into another register of the spectacle, which has been created by the actors that the *scenario* provides. See also Marotti's essay, "La Figura di Flaminio Scala," in: *Alle origini del teatro moderno: la commedia dell'arte* (Rome: Bulzoni Editore, 1980), pp. 21–44; and Cesare Molinari, "*Le favole rappresentative*" *di Flaminio Scala* in: *La commedia dell'arte* (Milan: Mondadori, 1985), pp. 133–50, who is vehement in his attack on Scala (p. 136): "[R]icalca piuttosto le formule letterarie dell'erudita che i modi della drammaturgia dell'arte" ([H]e copies the literary formulae of the *erudita* instead of following the dramaturgical model of the *arte*).

11. Marotti, "Introduzione," p. lxiii.

12. Scala may have been promoting the argument that acting was a theatrical extension of the art of rhetoric and that action and gesture therefore precede

the spoken text. His defense of everyday speech and the use of dialects as more natural also suggest that literariness is not the prime concern. Angelo Ingegneri's *La rappresentazione delle favole sceniche* (1598) stresses the equal importance of gesture and voice; see Marotti, *Lo spettacolo dall'umanesimo al manierismo: teoria e tecnica* (Milan: Feltrinelli, 1974), p. 305. I am indebted to Paul C. Castagno, *The Early Commedia dell'Arte: The Mannerist Context* (New York: Peter Lang, 1994), pp. 111–19, for outlining aspects of the connections between acting and rhetorical practice.

13. "Prologo della comedia del finto marito," in: *Il finto marito*, pp. 229–36; "Prologo per recitare," in: *Il finto marito*, pp. 237–41.

14. *Il finto marito*, p. 234. Falavolti's note 18 explains that "dal dech al fach gh'è un gran trach" (from word to deed there's a big gap) is a Bergamask variation on "*dal dire al fare c'è di mezzo il mare*" (saying it and doing it are oceans apart). English translation is from Kenneth Richards and Laura Richards, *The Commedia dell'Arte: A Documentary History* (Oxford: Basil Blackwell, 1990), p. 200.

15. The *Canadian Oxford Dictionary* (Toronto: Oxford University Press, 1998), *s.v.*, defines "travesty" as "a grotesque misrepresentation or imitation."

16. Tim Fitzpatrick, *The Relationship of Oral and Literate Performance Processes in the Commedia dell'Arte: Beyond the Improvisation/Memorisation Divide* (Lewiston: Edwin Mellen Press, 1995), p. 235.

17. Fitzpatrick, pp. 226–92.

18. See *Il finto marito*, p. 232.

19. Ibid., p. 237.

20. Ibid., pp. 237–38.

21. Ibid., p. 239.

22. Ibid., p. 240.

23. Ibid., p. 240.

24. Marjorie Garber, *Vested Interests: Cross-Dressing and Cultural Anxiety* (New York: Routledge, 1997), p. 36, observes that trangressing both gender and social status creates dual anxieties.

25. See Nicolò Barbieri, "Esser più naturale che le femine rappresentano figliuole da marito che travestire giovanetti da femina" in: *La supplica*, ed. Ferdinando Taviani (Milan: Edizioni Il Polifilo, 1971), liii, pp. 121–23. This text was first published in Venice in 1634.

26. Jacques Derrida, "The Law of Genre" in: *Acts of Literature*, ed. Derek Attridge (London and New York: Routledge, 1992), pp. 221–52. Derrida (p. 227) proposes that "the law of the law of genre . . . is precisely a principle of contamination, a law of impurity, a parasitical economy."

27. The maid's part also continued to be played by men long after the *innamorata* parts were taken over by women. Even so, a manservant playing a woman playing a gentleman's part carries many possibilities for transgressive desires.

28. Fitzpatrick, pp. 234–38, notes the similarities with a few omissions. Most of the examples I have selected are from the full text where the dialogue is written out since these are easiest to follow.

29. *Il finto marito* I.iv (p. 258); English translation Fitzpatrick, p. 413.
30. *Il finto marito* IV.vi (p. 339); English translation Fitzpatrick, p. 410. Here Scaramuccia is playing on the ancient correlation between grammar masters and pedagogical sodomy, where grammar is treated as a parodic metaphor for sex.
31. *Il finto marito* IV.vi (p. 341); English translation Fitzpatrick, p. 421.
32. Fitzpatrick, pp. 226–31.
33. Patricia Parker, "Deferral, Dilation, Différance: Shakespeare, Cervantes, Jonson" in: *Literary Texts/Renaissance Texts*, eds. P. Parker and D. Quint (Baltimore: Johns Hopkins University Press, 1986), pp. 182–209.
34. *Il finto marito* III.vii (p. 318).
35. Typically a *scenario* uses the convention of showing or saying that a man has gone into a woman's private dwelling as evidence that they are going to perform an intimate act. Notice that Lepido must be kept outside when he is courting Porzia in order not to compromise her marriage.
36. Henry Fielding's *The Female Husband* (London: Cooper, 1746), published over a century later, is a good example of such a cautionary but salacious tale.
37. Judith Butler, "Variations on Sex and Gender" in: *Feminism as Critique: On the Politics of Gender*, ed. Seyla Benhabib and Drucilla Cornell (Minneapolis: University of Minnesota Press, 1987), p. 138.

7

Beauty and the Beast: Lesbians in Literature and Sexual Science from the Nineteenth to the Twentieth Centuries

*Daniela Danna**

At the turn of the century and into the 1920s, we find the rather questionable beginnings of a scientific discourse on lesbianism in Italy in the work of sexologists and in studies on masculinity and femininity (considered natural categories). What influence did this discourse have on the portrayal of lesbians in novels of the period? To be sure, the presence of lesbian characters is rather scant, but what is there holds some surprises and offers a fascinating contrast to the deprecating attitudes of positivism, and not just in literature written by women.[1] The fact is that positivist theories of sexual inversion represented a reactionary strain of thought: Internationally, the second half of the nineteenth century witnessed the first gay rights movements inspired by the writings of Ulrichs and Kertbeny in German-speaking countries as well as the organizational activities of Magnus Hirschfeld. In 1897, Hirschfeld founded the Scientific Humanitarian Committee, which worked for the abolition of antisodomy laws and included lesbian women.[2] Hirschfeld, a doctor, theorized the distribution of human sexuality across a natural scale that went from masculinity on one end to femininity on the other and embraced any number of possibilities in between. These intermediate forms took on the popular collective designation of "the third sex." The research journal he founded, *Yearbook for the Sexual Intermediates*, published, among other things, autobiographical accounts by women who loved women.[3]

The medical establishment's reaction was not long in coming, and it hinged on the notion of degeneration: These authorities allowed that the cause of homosexuality can be located in nature, but it is a corrupt and diseased nature. A year after Kertbeny coined the lexical hybrid "homosexual" (1869), the psychiatrist Carl von Westphal began a series of clinical case studies on women.[4] Like Ulrichs, Westphal spoke of "conträre Sexualempfindung," an inverted sexual sensibility that was thought to be hereditary and symptomatic of a neuropathic or psychopathic constitution.

Already in 1878 Arrigo Tamassia, a doctor and expert in medical law, brought German theories of "Conträrsexualität" to Italy with an article entitled "On Sexual Inversion," in which he presented the fourteenth confirmed clinical case of "inversion."[5] Such analyses were extended to women by Guglielmo Cantarano in 1883 with the internationally celebrated case of a twenty-three-year-old woman known as X.[6] What had caught Cantarano's attention were manifestations of an apparently transsexual nature:

> L'inversione dello istinto sessuale comprende quella anomalia psichica ed istintuale, per la quale l'individuo di un dato sesso sente gli attributi intellettuali ed istintivi del sesso opposto, ed è spinto ad amare persone del proprio sesso, avendo ripulsa o indifferenza verso gl'individui di sesso contrario.

> Inversion of the sexual instinct constitutes a psychological and emotional anomaly whereby individuals of one sex feel the intellectual and instinctual attributes of the opposite sex, and thus desire individuals of their own sex while feeling indifference or disgust for those of the opposite sex.[7]

In Cantarano's view, such desires are transitory if they occur as one with other manifestations of insanity, but if manifested in individuals who appear otherwise sane, then they are congenital and inherent to the individual's nature. They are a sign of disequilibrium among the various intellectual faculties and undue influence of the emotions; they may also be hereditary:

> Questi non sono i pazzi riconosciuti da tutti, ma neppure sono individui con la giusta armonia necessaria tra tutte le loro facoltà. In essi però la coscienza della propria personalità è conservata, e nasce quindi il tremendo dualismo tra la propria riconosciuta organizzazione e le tendenze sessuali opposte e contraddicenti ad essa.

> These aren't the demented everyone is used to seeing; at the same time, these individuals do not possess a proper and necessary balance among their various faculties. They remain very much aware of their proper personhood.

Thus a terrible conflict arises between knowledge of one's proper sexual orientation and sexual tendencies that oppose and contradict this.[8]

In fact, X responds to the problems posed by this awareness of sexual "inversion" by becoming a man, which is to say cross-dressing as a man (only after she had begun to have lesbian relationships). Cantarano traces other signs of inversion in this woman who is "femminile fisicamente" (physically female) but "dolente di essere nata donna" (unhappy to have been born a woman):

> [T]utti gl'istinti muliebri in lei sono pervertiti o meglio sono invertiti. Non l'attaccamento alla figlia, non la vita casalinga, non il trasporto all'abbiglia-mento donnesco ed ai lavori del suo sesso, non il desiderio di essere ammi-rata e corteggiata dai giovanotti, non il tormentoso pizzicore del matrimonio, non la riservatezza e il pudore della fanciulla. La vita girovaga, la scelta di occupazioni virili, la ripugnanza all'uomo e la tendenza verso il proprio sesso, l'ardire del discolo e l'improntitudine dello scapestratello fanno del suo carattere un'insieme armonizzante interamente col carattere di un giovane, cui si sia allentata la briglia sul collo.
>
> All of the womanly instincts in her have been perverted, or rather inverted. She shows no sign of attachment to her daughter, no interest in domestic life, no joy in wearing women's clothes or performing the tasks of her sex, no desire to be admired and pursued by young men, much less know the tortuous delights of marriage, no sign of the reserve and modesty that becomes a young woman. Instead she prefers a disordered life, virile labors, repugnance towards men and feelings for her own sex. The boldness of a young rascal and the effrontery of a dissolute *bohémien* make for a charac-ter much like a young man—one of those young men on whose neck the bridle has been rather slack.[9]

Cantarano concludes with a statement of principle that clearly demon-strates how the cateogory of "inversion" is based on the researcher's *a priori*, essentialist notions about gender: "[L]'uomo che non si sente mai spinto verso l'affascinante bellezza muliebre, non è un uomo; la donna che non desidera mai essere avvinta tra due maschie più forti braccia, non è una donna." (The man who never feels drawn to the enchanting beauty of women is not a man; the woman who feels no desire to be wrapped in two strong, manly arms is not a woman.)[10]

In 1885, Cesare Lombroso made his first contribution to the definition of lesbianism as degeneration by focussing on the sexual practices of women in asylums, which tended to confirm the genetic nature of their abnormalities.[11] It was Lombroso who oversaw the Italian translation of

Krafft-Ebing's *Psichopatia Sexualis*, which came out in 1889. Lombroso closely follows Krafft-Ebing's ideas. In addition to the hereditary component—numerically not very significant given most women's relative dis-inclination to sex—Lombroso posits a tribadism of occasion caused by "excessive libido" and by the influence of one's surroundings. Such behavior might occur in asylums or prisons, where female criminals end up under the influence of inborn inverts (who are said to be "extremely lascivious" in contrast to normal women), or on any occasion where many women come together, "specie se tra queste vi sieno delle prostitute o delle lascive" (especially if there are prostitutes or loose women among them). Even aging, which inverts many sexual characteristics, can result in a tribadism akin to the feelings of "apatia e lo schifo prodotto dal maschio" (apathy and disgust brought about by men) in prostitutes.[12]

Two novels published towards the end of the nineteenth century at the height of positivism include lesbian characters: the first is Alfredo Oriani's 1889 *Al di là* (*Beyond*),[13] followed by Enrico Butti's 1892 *L'automa* (*The Robot*).[14] Both authors were relatively well-known in their day, mostly as writers for the stage. *Al di là*, Oriani's second novel, enjoyed a fairly large readership. The plot turns on the galant intrigues among four characters, two men in love with two women whom they pursue. But the women always manage to run off together. The openly lesbian Marchesa di Monero's passion for Mimy starts off as a simple spiritual affection (albeit shot through with many a turbulent emotion) but ends up being fully reciprocated in a climactic love scene.

Mimy is struck by Elisa di Monero's androgynous appearance from the moment she first appears: "[N]uotava con la forza del più robusto marinaio" ("[S]he swam with the power of the most robust of sailors").[15] But Elisa's personality turns out to be more complex than a simple mimicking of men. Already passionately in love, she writes in her first letter to Mimy: "Il cuore di una donna è capace di sentimenti di infinita delicatezza, che gli uomini ignorano." (A women's heart is capable of an infinite delicacy of feeling unknown to men.)[16] According to Francesco Meriano, who professes in his introduction that he did not like the book at all, Elisa is simply a "virago che rapisce la moglie dell'avvocato Carlo" (virago who takes advantage of the lawyer Carlo's wife).[17] But for Mimy no aspect of her marriage has been positive; she speaks of her wedding night as a horrid experience: "La vicinanza di lui mi destava un indefinibile ribrezzo." (His proximity awoke in me an indescribable sense of loathing.)[18] Mimy thereby affirms Elisa's theories of female supremacy, which brand all men "inferiori in bellezza e nel sentimento" (inferior in beauty and in feeling):

"e se io dicessi a vostro marito, che è pure un gran giureconsulto: Una donna ama una donna con maggiore passione dell'uomo più sensibile, di

Byron o di Heine, mi risponderebbe: Stravaganza! e avrebbe torto. . . . . Ma
se io ripeto a voi, intelligente quanto bella: il matrimonio è il peggiore fra i
contratti ammessi e proibiti dal codice, la famiglia un ergastolo per la passione, la gioventù senza amore il delitto più insensato contro noi stessi e
la natura: se vi ripeto che noi donne siamo la poesia e dobbiamo essere i
nostri poeti, che Eva amò gli angeli perché soli le somigliavano."

"[A]nd if I were to say to your famous lawyer of a husband, 'women can love
women with a passion far greater than that of the most sensitive man, even
Byron or Heine,' he would react, 'That's insanity!' and he would be wrong. . . .
But to you, as brilliant as you are beautiful, I repeat: of all the contracts both
allowed and prohibited by law, matrimony is the lowest! the family condemns passion to life in prison! youth without love is a senseless crime
against ourselves and against nature! I say to you that we women are poetry
itself and we have to be our own poets, that Eve loved the angels because
only the angels could resemble her!"[19]

And yet the Marchesa also appears in the thoroughly Decadent image of a
room cluttered with objects with a naked black slave woman in shackles at
her feet, while an Arabic slave woman, also naked, waits upon her. Still, she
is a protofeminist who advances arguments that even at that time must
not have seemed entirely unreasonable:

"Si vede che le leggi sono fatte dagli uomini: ci vogliono immacolate nel
matrimonio e, appena contrattolo, ci si rivelano nella più ributtante ani-
malità: prima il morso, poi gli speroni. Le donne vi assentono; alcune, le più
volgari, vantano perfino la vita di famiglia. Partorire figli, essere idropica
nove mesi dell'anno e gli altri tre convalescente, diventare brutta dieci volte
prima di essere vecchia, baloccarsi coi piaceri della nonna avendo intorno
una torma di bambini . . . ecco tutto."

"It seems obvious that the laws are made by men: they want us immaculate
in marriage, but as soon as the deal is signed they reveal the repugnant brutality of their true natures. First the bit, then the spurs. And women just go
along with it. Some of the most vulgar even brag about the joys of family
life. And having children! Bloated nine months out of the year and in recovery the other three, you loose your looks while still young, forced to pass the
time like a grandmother with a bunch of little kids running around—that's
all there is."[20]

In this dialogue, Mimy timidly objects that if all women felt this way
the world would never survive. But the Marchesa responds by expressing
her disdain for the world, by which she means the multitude who accept
degradation, particularly the most common women. She does not stop
here: " 'Una volta vidi una tigre domata lambire la mano a un facchino, e ne
patii: ecco la donna e il marito. Ci battano, ma non ne siamo innamorate.

La tigre non deve amare che la tigre; la tigre è più bella dell'uomo.' "
("Once I saw a tamed tigress licking the hand of the man who kept her
cage, and I felt a profound sympathy: here is the picture of a woman and
her husband. They may beat us down, but we must not love them for it. A
tigress can only love another tigress. She is more beautiful than any
man.")[21] Mimy notes: "Così parlando gli occhi le lanciavano fiamme, e il
viso le si era colorato. Bella e superba! Ma che discorsi! eppure ha ragione.
Io tacevo, non sapevo che fare o dire: la sua audacia mi spaventava." (As
she said these things her eyes shot forth flames and her face
was aglow with color. Beautiful and proud! What kind of talk is this!
And yet, she's right. I kept quiet. I didn't know what to do or say. Her
audacity frightened me.)[22] The exchange ends with a kiss between the two
women.

Butti's first novel, *L'automa*, is less marked by the Decandent influence
evident in Oriani's work. Instead it shows signs of a crisis in positivist
thought and aspirations toward a new spiritualism. As a first novel, it met
with little success. It numbers among its protagonists Lavinia Casàuri,
"l'androgina dagli sfrenati desideri" (an androgyne whose desire knows no
limits), a chanteuse, and of course aristocrat by marriage (this time she's a
princess), not pretty but enchanting in the eyes of Attilio Valda, the true
protagonist and embodiment of bourgeois idleness. When they first meet,
Lavinia "lo fissava con quelle sue pupille dilatate, febbricitanti, e sorrideva
impercettibilmente inclinando in basso gli angoli delle labbra esangui"
(set upon him with those feverish, dilated pupils of hers, barely allowing a
smile to escape the down-turned corners of her bloodless lips) and he
found her repulsive, but before long his repulsion is transformed into a
kind of nightmarish adoration.[23] This is a clear case of what Lombroso
had categorized as excess libido: "Un'indole come quella era indomabile
e definitiva: Lavinia era affetta d'una delinquenza innata, d'una aber-
razione fisiologica e psicologica, ribelle a ogni cura e a ogni rimedio."
(A character such as hers was permanent and could not be tamed: Lavinia
suffered from an innate delinquency, a physiological and psychological
aberration that rebelled against any and all attempted cures.)[24] Not only
had Lavinia taken many lovers and driven her lovesick, abandoned husband to suicide: She makes her first appearance on the arm of her girlfriend, the singer Ghizzi. Attilio reacts badly: "Sopra tutto l'idea
ripugnante de' suoi amori lesbici con quell'ambigua figura della Ghizzi,
nel cui corpo, nei modi, perfino negli abiti, si scorgeva fremere l'androgine
dagli sfrenati desiderii, lo faceva rifuggire, quasi inorridito, dall'ipotesi
ch'ella potesse divenire un giorno la sua amante." (More than anything else
it was the repugnant image of her making love to that strangely ambiguous Ghizzi—whose very body and mannerisms and even clothes bespoke

the classic lust-crazed androgyne—that repulsed him, horrified at the possibility that she might one day be his lover.)[25]

Ghizzi soon disappears altogether from the plot as Attilio begins to court Lavinia. Lavinia doesn't even mention her name when she thinks back over her past loves in the second part of the novel. Ghizzi is a kind of lesbian vampire who shows physical signs of her depravation and "infamia."[26] She is the classic invert:

> La Ghizzi vestiva un abito chiaro, assai semplice, aperto sul petto a guisa d'una giacchetta da uomo, per modo da lasciare scoperta la rigida camicia inamidata, a bollicine rosee: il volto suo pallidissimo, dai fini lineamenti e dagli occhi umidi cerchiati d'estese lividure, s'ergeva su l'alto solino a punte, con un piglio audace e spavaldo.

> Ghizzi wore a light suit, very simple, jacket unbuttoned just like a man's to reveal a crisp starched shirt with a pale pink print. Her face was beyond pale with delicate features and moist deep-set eyes surrounded by dark circles. It stood erect—brazen and bold—upon a high, pointed collar.[27]

Unexpectedly, she redeems herself in Attilio's eyes because she has a daughter. The man's astonishment is great: "[S]'era offerta anche lei al desiderio di un maschio, come tutte le donne? Quella scoperta inattesa gli produsse l'effetto subitaneo d'un dolce calmante su i sentimenti ostili fino allora nudriti verso la Ghizzi." ([S]o she too had submitted to a man's desire, just like all women. That sudden, surprise discovery cast a sweet calm over Attilio's nerves and the hostility he had felt towards her.)[28]

In 1908 an unidentified individual (perhaps a woman) under the pseudonym Fede ventured into the ancient genre of lesbian pornography with the publication of *L'eredità di Saffo* (*Sappho's Legacy*), which s/he attributes in part to one "Franz."[29] The various sections of this "viaggio nei bassifondi del vizio" (voyage into the depths of turpitude) place lesbianism along with simple schoolgirl friendships in a disgusting light, which is inspired—as the writings themselves declare—by contemporary theorists of sexual pathology.[30] The turn of the century brought authentic lesbian voices writing in first person onto the French literary scene: Natalie Clifford Barney, the poet Renée Vivien (who withheld her real name at the beginning of her career), and Liane de Pougy (although not a lesbian, de Pougy wrote about her Platonic love for Barney in the 1901 *Idylle saphique*).[31] In Germany 1901 saw the publication of *Sind es Frauen?* by Aimée Duc, the penname of Minna Wettstein-Adelt, a journalist from Alsace who worked in women's publishing.[32] *Are They Women? A Novel on the Third Sex* was a popular book intended for a large audience that offers a relatively friendly portrait of a group of feminist and "uraniste" women at the University of Geneva. The book was a success and sold about ten thousand copies.

It didn't take long for a lesbian-themed novel to appear in Italy: *Il passaggio* (*The Passage*, 1919) by Sibilla Aleramo, author of *Una donna* (*A Woman*, 1906).[33] Aleramo had become the very emblem of Italian feminism after having left behind a son and a husband she did not love— a man who suspected she was cheating on him and who threatened to kill her, a man she was forced to marry after he had raped her. These painful experiences provided the courageous narrative of *Una donna*, which was more powerful than any essay in denouncing the condition of women at the turn of the century. Sibilla corresponded with Natalie Barney and used to visit her in Paris. It was from Barney that she got hold of a book by Renée Vivien. In terms of literature, Sibilla was mostly interested in poetry, but concrete political action occupied a great deal of her time. In a very lyrical passage of *Il passaggio*, she dedicates the section entitled "La favola" ("The Fairy Tale") to a young girl with golden eyes: "La favola era bionda. Un color caldo si moveva su tutte le cose. Qualcuno giungendo ogni giorno mi riempiva di fiori il grembo, diceva: 'Vieni,' mi conduceva correndo all'argine vivo e silenzioso del fiume. Cantava. Due punti d'oro negli occhi, una piega violenta e luminosa nei capelli." (The fairy tale was blond. A warm hue spread out across each and every thing. She filled me with flowers, a few more every day, and said "Follow me." She led me to the riverbank, silent and alive. She sang. Two points of gold in her eyes. A violent, luminous wave in her hair.)[34]

This "blond fairy tale" was Cordula—known as "Lina"—Poletti. Sibilla had met Poletti at the 1908 Women's Congress, which was called by the Congresso Nazionale delle Donne with the support of Elena di Savoia and attended by some 1,400 women. Lina was born in 1885 and was nine years younger than Sibilla. She was still a student while Sibilla was one of the big names of the Congress, already well known as a writer and an activist in the Unione Femminile Nazionale (National Women's Union). About 100 of Sibilla's letters, along with a few of Lina's, are all that remain of their correspondence, which began in the spring of 1909.[35] In *Il passaggio*, Sibilla characterizes Lina's strength of spirit:

> Ella supponeva a se stessa un maschio cuore; e foggiata s'era veramente a strana ambiguità, sul nativo indizio forse del timbro di voce, forse della tagliente sagoma. S'era foggiata ed agiva. Con volontà d'uomo o di angelo ribelle, con forza quasi di dannato—ma io, nessuno potrà mai giudicare se più demente o più veggente, ero toccata invece da ciò che in lei permaneva d'identico alla mia sostanza.
>
> She assumed for herself a man's heart. She had fashioned herself to reflect this curious ambiguity, taking the lead from certain inborn traits—that

peculiar tone of voice, or perhaps her sharp, angular profile. She was her own creation and so she acted. With the will of a man or rebellious angel, and the power of a demon. But I—it's impossible to say whether insightful or just demented—had been touched by whatever it was in her that was identical to my very being.[36]

A few years later we find a curious text whose allegedly female author is given as "una tribade."[37] *Tribadismo, saffismo, clitorismo* is a collection of clinical cases by sexologists and psychiatrists, excerpts from novels, and lesbian pseudo-history. There can be no doubt that it was written by a man: Despite the attribution on the cover, he assumes a completely detached tone and makes no attempt to keep up the pretense of autobiographical narrative.

On a more positive note, we find a passionate description of love and eroticism in a novel by Mura, a woman writer well-known in her day. Mura's 1919 *Perfidie* contains a section dedicated to the relationship between its two female protagonists, Sibilla and Nicla, proudly entitled "Perfetto Amore" ("Perfect Love").[38] Mura was the pseudonym of Maria Volpi Nannipieri, and *Perfidie* was only one of the many novels, short stories, and advice columns she wrote that enjoyed huge popularity among women after the First World War. Indeed, it was *Perfidie* that first made her a popular success. According to Antonietta Drago, Mura "set in motion with her agile pen a craze for serial romances around 1920 (before the advent of cartoon photo romances), romances destined to quench the thirst for love stories of Italy's day-dreaming seamstresses, typists and schoolmarms."[39] As for the plot of *Perfidie*, at least we can say that it is unusual. Sibilla takes her place among her woman friends as if in a nest of brilliant vipers; she makes plain her true feelings from the very start of the novel: "Amo le donne. Mi appassionano. M'interessano. Sono il più bell' esempio di semplicità attraverso una rete complicata di stati d'animo." (I love women. They enflame me with passion. They fascinate me. They present the perfect picture of simplicity through a complex network of thought and emotion.)[40] And in the end she will be seduced by Nicla, by the "fascino supremo della sua nudità" (supreme enchantment of her naked body) as she senses that something mysterious and unknown is about to happen, "forse qualche cosa come una perfezione di bellezza. . . . [L]o sentiamo e un po' ne tremiamo e un po' ne soffriamo." (perhaps something like a perfection of beauty. . . . [W]e feel it and tremble slightly in its presence and suffer a little bit too.)[41] Sibilla longs for a caress that only Nicla can provide, that will allow her to know truly perfect love:

Vivendo così intimamente con la mia piccola Nicla io sono una coraggiosa: perché ho creato un nuovo mondo in mezzo al vecchio mondo, perché ho

creata una nuova esistenza in mezzo alla vecchia decrepita esistenza. E strin-gendo fra le braccia questa piccola creatura che a volte si spaurisce per la mia foga appassionata, mi sento un po' la padrona di questo nuovo mondo, di questa nuova esistenza.
Un mondo imperniato su due sole persone che si amano. Su due donne.
Un mondo che è quasi una perfezione assoluta di bellezza, d'arte e di vita.

I am brave and bold in my intimacy with little Nicla: because I have created a new world in the middle of the old, because I have created a new existence in the middle of the old, decrepit existence. And when I squeeze this little creature in my embrace and sometimes startle her with my passion, I feel somehow that I am ruler of this new world, this new existence.
A world built entirely on two people who love each other. Two women.
A world that is, as it were, the absolute perfection of beauty, art and life.[42]

The novel celebrates the beauty, refinement, and elegance of their union, but ultimately Sibilla's love is shown to be overly possessive, the last, dying flame of her adolescence: Her adulthood will begin in earnest—this is how the novel ends—only when she meets and accepts the love of a man.

But let us return to the realm of sexual science. Only in the 1920s did the ideas of the first homosexual rights movement in Germany find their way to Italy. We discover them in the *Rassegna di studi sessuali, demografia ed eugenetica* (*Review of Sexual Studies, Demography and Eugenics*), a peri-odical under the direction of Aldo Mieli, the great Italian advocate for the "third sex."[43] Founded in 1921, the journal served as mouthpiece for the Società Italiana per lo Studio delle Questioni Sessuali (Italian Society for the Study of Sexual Matters), the Lega Italiana Contro il Pericolo Venereo (Italian League Against Venereal Risk), and the Società Italiana di Genetica ed Eugenetica (Italian Society of Genetics and Eugenics). But a crackdown in the cultural politics of the fascist regime in 1931 brought about a change in title (*Genesis*) and contents. In fact, only the early years of the *Rassegna di studi sessuali, demografia ed eugenetica* included translations of articles by Hirschfeld and Carpenter, as well as articles by "Proteus" (who was probably Aldo Mieli himself or the endocrinologist Nicola Pende), which refuted that "homosexual nature" was pathological.[44] Mieli ended up in exile in Argentina.

During the heyday of fascism in 1927, a text offering equally positive images of lesbianism (without recourse to theories of a "third sex") appeared on the literary scene. *Lesbiche* was written by the humorist Guido Stacchini and inspired by the celebratory verses on love between women by French poet Pierre Louys, who had set his idylls in the age of Sappho.[45] Indeed, Stacchini's book is a partial translation. Just like Louys,

Stacchini expresses adoration for lesbians. For him, they represent the quintessential female and the perfection of love: "Il desiderio di una donna per un'altra donna è una reciproca offerta ed un'equilibrata brama del corpo e dello spirito." (The desire of one woman for another woman is a reciprocal and perfectly balanced longing of body and spirit.)[46] For Stacchini, Sappho was the first self-aware feminist who rebelled against the submission of women in family life. This must not be confused— he warns—with a false feminism whose objective is the aesthetically unappealing identification of women with men.

There are few other references to lesbianism in Italian literature of this period. One finds occasional allusions in the erotic novels of Pittigrilli (pseudonym of Dino Segre), such as *Cocaina*.[47] There is also an amusing incident in Guido da Verona's 1930 parody of Alessandro Manzoni's classic nineteenth-century novel, *I promessi sposi*.[48] Verona's book was banned in stores and burned by "hordes of irate Manzonians."[49] Among many irreverent passages, Verona writes that Manzoni had become immortal for a story in which "una contadinotta per nome Lucia non riusciva mai a congiungersi in giuste nozze con un suo beneamato biforco dei laghi lombardi, Renzo Tramaglino" (a simple peasant girl named Lucia who somehow never manages to hook up properly with the stablehand from the lake region she's sweet on, Renzo Tramaglino) because the Church keeps getting in the way. Verona alludes to the peculiarly strong interest that the Monaca di Monza (the Nun from Monza—a cloistered nun featured prominently in Manzoni's novel) seems to have taken in Lucia:

D'altronde la Signora spesso la chiamava in un suo parlatorio privato, avvolto in mezze luci, foderato di morbidi cuscini. La tratteneva a lungo, coprendole di lente carezze gli occhi, i capelli, le mani, indugiandosi a lodare e tastare la bellezza delle sue forme, poi facendole certi ambigui discorsi intorno alla non assoluta indispensabilità del sesso forte, e dandole infine da leggere certi libri clandestini d'iniziazione agli amori più perfetti che lasciavano la bella montanara con gli occhi pieni di sogno e la fantasia fortemente colpita.

What is more, the holy woman would often summon Lucia to her private parlour where she would detain her at some length. Wrapped in dim lights and surrounded by soft pillows, she would lavish slow caresses upon Lucia's eyes, her hair and hands, lingering to praise and touch the beauty of her members. She would speak to her with rather puzzling, ambiguous words suggesting that the 'stronger sex' was, after all, not absolutely indispensable. And she would lend her certain clandestine books of initiation into the most perfect forms of love. These had a profound effect on the phantasies of the peasant girl and left her with a dream-like quality in her eyes.[50]

Finally, we should mention that 1930 saw the Italian translation of Radclyffe Hall's *The Well of Loneliness* (1928), often defined as "the first lesbian novel" and considered by many as a kind of bible for gay women.[51] The book's enduring, quasi-canonical status is a mystery that cannot be explained by its nonexistent literary value. We have seen that by 1928 there were already many other books on the international scene that offered more positive visions of lesbianism than Hall's invert Stephen Gordon. Direct from the pages of Havelock Ellis—the author of *Sexual Inversion* (1897), which considered homosexuality a congenital (but not degenerative) trait—Stephen is the classic male *manqué* who is forced to renounce her abnormal love in the end to join the unhappy plight of her fellows in the third sex.

In the years after the war, many other titles appeared, including *Der Skorpion* by Anna Elisabet Weirauch, which was published in two parts (1919 and 1921) and translated into English in 1932.[52] Unlike Stephen in *The Well of Loneliness, The Scorpion*'s lesbian protagonist Mette Rudloff comes to discover that love between women is a viable alternative.[53] Nor can the difference in fortune between the two novels be explained by the legal persecution of *The Well of Loneliness*, since *The Scorpion* met a similar fate: In 1926 there was an attempt to have it banned on charges that it corrupted youth. Might it be the simple fact that Hall wrote in English? Still, sexual relations between women had already been dealt with in English fiction. Earlier in 1928 (the same year *The Well of Loneliness* appeared), Compton Mackenzie had published *Extraordinary Women*, a satirical novel that portrays the lesbian dolce vita on the isle of Capri, whose main character, Rosalba Donsante, is based on the baroness Mimì Franchetti, a friend of Mackenzie.[54]

But in Italy fascist presses had in store a fate even more dreadful than *The Well of Loneliness*. 1933 saw the Italian translation of a German book lucid in its madness, E. F. W. Eberhard's *Femminismo: decadenza. Gli aspetti sessuali della lotta per l'emancipazione femminile* (*Feminism and Decadence: Sexual Aspects of the Fight for Female Emancipation*).[55] "Cinque anni di illimitata emancipazione femminile sono ormai sufficienti per redigere un primo bilancio" (Five years of unchecked female emancipation will suffice for an initial assessment) begins the hasty premise of what will turn out to be a veritable anthology of misogynist commonplaces: Hundreds upon hundreds of mean-spirited and reactionary pages that denounce women's social progress. For Eberhard, "il progresso del genere umano è possibile solo se ogni sesso continua a occupare il posto assegnatogli da Madre natura" (the human race can progress only if each sex continues to play the role assigned to it by Mother Nature), which is to say that men shall occupy positions of power while women see to it that their tired little warriors get enough rest and relaxation. In this logic, the masculine woman represents a total "degenerazione dei naturali caratteri sessuali" (degeneration of the natural sex traits); the increasingly common presence of such women in a society is a sure sign of its decadence. Eberhard devotes an entire chapter to the relationship between lesbianism and feminism entitled "Tribadia ed emancipazione." The sad fact is that in fascist Italy—with its complete lack of social progress—such a violent reaction was hardly necessary. This is clear in the Italian editor's self-satisfied introduction to the book:

> Non vi è dubbio che se E. F. W. Eberhard vivesse in Italia, gli sarebbero mancate le condizioni di ambiente per poter scrivere un libro così veemente. . . . [I]n Italia questi pericoli non esistono, o non rivestono il carattere di gravità che hanno assunto in altri Paesi. Vi è una fondamentale sanità della donna italiana che non può soffrire lesioni per mancanza di mode o contagio di esempi.
>
> There can be no doubt that if E. F. W. Eberhard lived in Italy, he would not have found the social conditions necessary to write such a vehement book. . . . [T]hese dangers simply do not exist in Italy, or at least they are not as serious a problem as they seem to be in other countries. There is a basic wholesomeness to Italian women that cannot be compromised by the latest trend or infected by foreign example.[56]

Eberhard's anonymous editor affirms that there were few "beasts" in the Italian social panorama at the time: The masculine inverts studied by the positivists remained something of a scientific rarity to be hunted out and examined under the microscope. But despite all the "scientific" attempts to pathologize love between women and brand them "beasts," more often (and with much greater verve) the literature of the period offers exalted portraits of passionate women. Certainly more beauty than beast.

Daniela Danna is a fellow and researcher in sociology at the University of Milan. She has published *Amiche, compagne, amanti: Storia dell'amore tra donne* (Milan: Mondadori, 1994) on love between women in history, *Matrimonio omosessuale* (Pomezia/Rome: Erre Emme, 1997) on gay marriage and the recognition of same-sex couples, and *Io ho una bella figlia: le madri lesbiche raccontano* (Forlì: Zoe, 1998) on lesbian motherhood in Italy. In English, her articles have appeared in *The Advocate* and in the volume *Lesbian Motherhood in Europe*, ed. Kate Griffin and Lisa A. Mulholland (London and Washington: Cassell, 1997). Her most recent publication in English is "Italy: The Never-Ending Debate" in *The Politics of Prostitution: Women's Movements, Democratic States, and the Globalisation of Sex Commerce*, ed. Joyce Outshoorn (Cambridge University Press, 2004), pp. 165–84." You can visit her website at www.danieladanna.it.

Notes

*   "La bella e la bestia: Lesbiche nella sessuologia e nella letteratura tra Otto e Novecento," trans. Cestaro.

1. Most of the relevant bibliography has already been set down thanks to the invaluable work of Giovanni Dall'Orto, *Leggere omosessuale* (Turin: Edizioni Gruppo Abele, 1984).

2. For a synthesis of the studies of the period, see Magnus Hirschfeld, *Die Homosexualität des Mannes und des Weibes* (Berlin: Louis Marcus, 1914). *The Homosexuality of Men and Women*, trans. Michael A. Lombardi-Nash; intro. Vern L. Bullough (Amherst, NY: Prometheus Books, 2000).

3. See Frau M. F., "Wie ich es sehe" in: Ilse Kokula, *Weibliche Homosexualität um 1900 in zeigenössische Dokumenten* (Munich: Frauenoffensive, 1981), pp. 177–78; rpr. in *Jahrbuch für sexuelle Zwischenstufen* 3 (1901), pp. 308–12. In the same collection, see E. Krause, "Die Wahrheit über mich," p. 181; rpr. in *Jahrbuch für sexuelle Zwischenstufen* 3 (1901), pp. 292–307.

4. Carl Westphal, "Die conträre Sexualempfindung, Symptom eines neuropathischen (psychopatischen) Zustandes" in: *Archiv für Psychiatrie und Nervenkrankheiten* 2,1 (1870), p. 75.

5. Arrigo Tamassia, "Sull'inversione sessuale," *Rivista sperimentale di freniatria e medicina legale* 4 (1878), pp. 97–117.

6. Guglielmo Cantarano, "Contribuzione alla casuistica della inversione dell'istinto sessuale," *La psichiatria, la neuropatologia e le scienze affini* 1,3 (1883), pp. 201–16. Again in 1892 Sighele emphasized the rarity of such cases. He wrote that relationships between women, a monstrous parody of real love, "represent the strangest, most depraved, and fortunately rarest type of relationship that two people can have"; he also spoke about Ulrichs, but only as filtered through Krafft-Ebing; see Scipio Sighele, "La coppia delinquente," *Archivio di psichiatria, scienze penali ed antropologia criminale per servire allo studio dell'uomo alienato e delinquente* 13 (1892), p. 530. For a review of other such studies, see Nerina Milletti, "Analoghe sconcezze," *DWF, Donnawomanfemme* 4 (1994), pp. 50–122.

7. Cantarano, p. 201.

8. Ibid., p. 209.

9. Ibid., p. 216.

10. Ibid., p. 216.

11. Cesare Lombroso, "Del tribadismo nei manicomi," *Archivio di psichiatria, scienze penali ed antropologia criminale per servire allo studio dell'uomo alienato e delinquente* 6 (1885), pp. 218–21.

12. Cesare Lombroso and Guglielmo Ferrero, *La donna delinquente* (Turin: Fratelli Bocca, 1927). See in particular the chapter on "Sensibilità sessuale (tribadismo, psicopatie sessuali)," pp. 251–70.

13. Alfredo Oriani, *Al di là* in: *Tutte le opere*, 2 vols., ed. Benito Mussolini (Bologna: Cappelli, 1926–1934) vol. 1, p. iv.

14. Enrico Butti, *L'automa. L'incantesimo*, ed. Giuliano Manacorda (Cappelli: Bologna, 1968).

15. Oriani, p. 97.
16. Ibid., pp. 101–02.
17. Francesco Meriano, "Prefazione," in: Oriani, p. vi.
18. Oriani, p. 88.
19. Ibid., p. 106.
20. Ibid., pp. 103–04.
21. Ibid., p. 104.
22. Ibid., p. 104.
23. Butti, p. 181.
24. Ibid., p. 206.
25. Ibid., p. 163.
26. Ibid., p. 153.
27. Ibid., p. 161.
28. Ibid., p. 164.
29. Fede, *L'eredità di Saffo* (Rome: Lux, 1908).
30. Fede, p. 80: "Le mie compagne vivono accoppiate come fidanzati; e ogni coppia vorrebbe essere un'anima sola; ma dov'è l'anima in tutto ciò?" (My friends all live as couples and every couple wishes it were one, single spirit. But what could possibly be spiritual about that sort of thing?).
31. Liane de Pougy, *Idylle saphique* (Paris: Librarie de La Plume, 1901).
32. Aimée Duc, *Sind es Frauen? Roman über das dritte Geschlecht* (Berlin: Eckstein Nache, 1901).
33. Sibilla Aleramo, *Il passaggio*, ed. Bruna Conti (Milan: Serra e Riva, 1985; 1st ed. 1919). *Una donna* (Milano: Feltrinelli 1999; 1st ed. 1906). *A Woman*, trans. Rosalind Delmar (Berkeley: University of California Press, 1980). For a recent assessment in English, see Anna Grimaldi Morosoff, *Transfigurations: the autobiographical novels of Sibilla Aleramo* (New York: Peter Lang, 1999).
34. *Il passaggio*, pp. 71–72. These words come after the invocation "che mi serbino il loro bene, le donne dolci e pure che ho sulla terra" (so that they reserve for me all that is good in them, the sweet and pure women I have on earth).
35. Sibilla Aleramo, *Lettere d'amore a Lina*, ed. Alessandra Cenni (Milan: Savelli, 1982).
36. Aleramo, *Il passaggio*, pp. 73–74.
37. *Una tribade: Triadismo, saffismo, clitorismo* (Florence: Il pensiero, 1914).
38. Mura, *Perfidie* (Milan: Sonzogno, 1919). The jacket cover features an elegantly-dressed woman in black with a long, drawn-out face who pierces the heart of a man-puppet with her hairpin.
39. Antonietta Drago, *Dizionario delle italiane per bene e per male* (Milan: La tartaruga, 1983), p. 182: "diede con agile penna l'avvio intorno al 1920 al romanzo da rotocalco destinato, prima del fumetto, alle sognanti sartine, dattilografe e maestre d'Italia assetate di romantiche trame."
40. Mura, p. 11.
41. Ibid., p. 180.
42. Ibid., p. 193.

43. On Aldo Mieli (1879–1950), see Giovanni Dall'Orto, "Aldo Mieli," *Babilonia* 57 (June 1988), pp. 52–54, as well as the biography at Dall'Orto's website, http://digilander.liberto.it/giovannidallorto.

44. See also Carola Susani, "Una critica della norma nell'Italia del fascismo," in: *Le parole e la storia: richerche su omosessualità e cultura*, ed. Enrico Venturelli (Bologna: Il cassero, 1991) [*Quaderni di critica omosessuale* 9].

45. Guido Stacchini, *Lesbiche (libera versione da Pierre Louys)* (Milan: Morreale, 1927).

46. Ibid., p. 31.

47. Pitigrilli, *Cocaina* (Milan: Bompiani, 1999; 1st ed. 1921).

48. Guido da Verona, *I promessi sposi* (Modena: La vela, 1976). The definitive edition of the original *I promessi sposi* by Alessandro Manzoni was published in 1840. It is the best-known nineteenth-century Italian novel and a canonical text in Italian middle schools and high schools. For a modern English edition, see: *The Betrothed*, trans. B. Penman (Harmondsworth: Penguin Classics, 1983).

49. Alberto Piromalli, "Guido da Verona" in: *Novecento. I contemporanei. Gli scrittori e la cultura letteraria nella società italiana*, ed. Gianni Grane (Milan: Marzorati, 1979), vol. 1, pp. 681–86.

50. Verona, p. 99.

51. Radclyffe Hall, *Il pozzo della solitudine*, trans. Annie Lami (Milan: Dall'Oglio, 1930).

52. See Anna Elisabet Weirauch, *Der Skorpion: ein Roman* (Berlin: Askanischer Verlag, 1919 and 1921); and the more recent edition from Maroldsweisach: Feministischer Buchverlag, 1992–1993. There exist various English editions of *The Scorpion* (trans. Whittaker Chambers) and its sequel *The Outcast* (trans. S. Guy Endore). Originally published by Greenberg (New York, 1932–1933), they were reissued in 1975 by Avon Press (New York). In 1958, Fawcett Publications (Greenwich, CT) reissued *The Scorpion* under the title *Of Love Forbidden*.

53. For more on this novel, see Claudia Schoppmann, *"Der Skorpion": Frauenliebe in der Weimarer Republik* (Hamburg: Frühling Erwachen, 1985).

54. Mackenzie admits this in his memoirs, *My Life and Times*, quoted in *Capri 1905/1940; Frammenti Postumi*, ed. Lea Vergine (Milano: Feltrinelli, 1983).

55. Ehrhardt F. W. Eberhard, *Femminismo: decadenza. Gli aspetti sessuali della lotta per l'emancipazione femminile*, ed. Drs. A. V. and P. T. (Milan: Universum, 1933); originally *Die Frauenemanzipation und ihre erotischen Grundlagen* (Vienna: W. Braumüller, 1924); second edition as *Feminismus und Kulturuntergang: die erotischen Grundlagen der Frauenemanzipation* (Vienna: W. Braumüller, 1929).

56. Editor's introduction to Eberhard, pp. vi–vii.

8

Desire and Disavowal in Liliana Cavani's "German Trilogy"

Áine O'Healy

In a recent essay on the films of Liliana Cavani, Chantal Nadeau makes a brief, undocumented reference to the director's reputation "as a radical lesbian."[1] Focusing on the contractual structure of the sado-masochist scenarios in Cavani's work as a potential model for lesbian eroticism, this is the only essay in a substantial critical bibliography that makes an overt allusion to her sexuality. It is hardly surprising that Nadeau fails to cite any references for the reputation she invokes. Generally wary of the constraints of ideological affiliations or identity politics, Cavani would almost certainly resist being categorized as a "radical lesbian." I note this not to discount anecdotal reports suggesting that she may be a lesbian, but rather to assert that the issue of her sexual identity, orientation, or politics is more complicated than Nadeau suggests.[2] In opposition to Nadeau's assumption that Cavani's sexuality is readily manifest in her work, I will argue that a specifically "lesbian" signature does not manifest itself here in any direct or unequivocal way. Focusing on three of Cavani's best known films, where we find a recurrence of "gay" and "lesbian" configurations (and, even here, the application of these terms is already problematic), I will examine the director's complex engagement with the discourses of gender and sexuality and her provocative destabilization of identity categories. In all three films we find an array of textual displacements, substitutions, and oscillations, not unlike the type that Eve Kosofsky Sedgwick has associated with the apparatus of the closet.[3] Yet, while the closet is not entirely absent in the films I will discuss, the deployment of patterns of indeterminacy and vacillation in this body of work serves mainly to problematize conceptions of sexual identity, embodiment, and object choice.

Over a period of 11 years, Cavani directed *The Night Porter* (1974), *Beyond Good and Evil* (1978), and *The Berlin Affair* (1985), which she conceptualized collectively as "the German trilogy."[4] Based on screenplays that she wrote in collaboration with other writers, these films, which unfold mainly in German or Austrian settings, offer a series of striking psychosexual scenarios articulated against a backdrop of crucial moments in modern German history (the consolidation of Bismarckian nationalism in the late nineteenth century, the tightening grip of Nazi terrorism in the 1930s, and the horror of the concentration camp system in the 1940s). At the heart of Cavani's work is a concern with the connections among sex, politics, power, and knowledge, a preoccupation developed in each film of the trilogy through the exploration of a central erotic relationship, which is intertwined with other, equally complex relationships and played out against a backdrop of political repression.

Since *The Night Porter* is the only one among Cavani's films to have received broad international distribution, it is unsurprising that several studies have been dedicated to this work in a general attempt to interpret the "scandalous" heterosexual relationship at the center of its narrative unfolding. The more limited circulation of *Beyond Good and Evil* and *The Berlin Affair* may account for both the comparative scarcity of critical analyses of these films and the absence of critical commentary on the representation of queer desire throughout the films of the trilogy.[5] Cavani's own pronouncements on her work have undoubtedly contributed to this critical blind spot. Although she has frequently acknowledged the symbolic importance of the erotic scenarios in *The Night Porter* and *Beyond Good and Evil* and has elaborated in interviews and other public statements her interest in the politics of power relations, her comments fail to address the preponderance of homoerotic discourses that sets the German trilogy apart from her other work.

In the course of its initial distribution in 1974, *The Night Porter* met with a clamorous response from critics and audiences alike. Although reactions were sharply divided, many found the film's central premise unthinkable.[6] Focusing on the erotic bond between Max (Dirk Bogarde), a former SS officer, and Lucia (Charlotte Rampling), his onetime victim, the film shifts back and forth between scenes set in Vienna in the 1950s (where, following a chance reunion, the two embark on a consensual reenactment of their earlier relationship) and flashbacks to the concentration camp (where Lucia was imprisoned as a teenager and where she was first subjected to the officer's sexual fascination with her). The sadomasochistic rituals depicted in *The Night Porter* proved particularly controversial.

These were construed by many viewers to suggest a mutuality of desire on the part of victim and victimizer. More scandalous still was the fact that Max, the protagonist, is not coded as unequivocally evil and reprehensible but is presented at various junctures as quietly appealing and seductive. In response to the challenges presented by this film, feminist critic Kaja Silverman embarked on the first major examination of the Italian filmmaker's work in English, ultimately isolating the trope of phallic divestiture as the most consistent feature of Cavani's authorial signature.[7] Arguing from a psychoanalytic framework, Silverman asserts that the director's male protagonists are characteristically configured as men who cast off the privilege of hegemonic masculinity in order to embrace marginalization, renunciation, or defeat. According to the logic of this reading, it is not the Nazi officer's lust for power and domination that motivates his relationship with Lucia in *The Night Porter*, but his identification with her helplessness. By acknowledging his own "castration," Max ultimately assumes "a subject-position that is more classically 'feminine' than masculine"[8] and becomes willing to die alongside Lucia at the hands of his former Nazi colleagues. Silverman further argues that the strategies used in the construction of the characters in this and other films by Cavani serve "to erase the boundaries separating male from female subjectivity, positing highly transversal and unstable heterosexual relationships."[9]

According to Silverman, Cavani's entire body of work is marked by a strong phantasmatic identification between the director and her male protagonists. She supports this assertion through textual analysis as well as extracinematic information, citing among other references the director's startling observation that the actors embodying her principal male characters bear a physical resemblance to herself.[10] Attempting to identify the desire that finds expression through Cavani's insistent preoccupation with male subjectivity, Silverman suggests that the libidinal investment at the core of the filmmaker's inspiration might best be characterized as a "dream of androgyny"[11] and argues that Cavani's fascination with scenarios of male masochism presents a clear challenge to classical constructions of sexual difference.[12] Yet, even as she demonstrates the fluidity of the sexual relationships and gender positions constructed in Cavani's films and emphasizes the director's cross-gender identification with her marginalized male characters, Silverman does not expand upon the queer implications of these revelations. Rather, she stops at an abstract assertion of the filmmaker's phantasmatic commitment to "androgyny," without expanding on this concept.

If, as Silverman claims, there is a fluidity of gender positions in the relationship between Max and Lucia in *The Night Porter*—wherein the ex-Nazi officer is gradually feminized through the abdication of masculine privilege and the young woman occasionally mimics the codes of masculinity—can it still be said that these textual enactments construct *heterosexuality* (even if qualified as "unstable")? Silverman's use of the term "unstable heterosexual relationships" to characterize the principal intersubjective relations constructed by Cavani's films fails to take into account both the "queer" interconnectedness of these scenarios (i.e., their propensity to intersect with configurations of same-sex desire) and the "queer" signifying operations that subtend their representation.

In an essay that takes issue with Silverman's reading of Cavani's films as realistic psychological narratives, Marguerite Waller has pointed out that the construction of gender positions in *The Night Porter* is so unstable that it is no longer possible simply to describe them as "male" or "female" according to the binary logic of conventional sexual difference."[13] Her essay also argues that, far from transcending sexual categories completely, the film unsettles our expectations about sexual identities, attributes, and desires by reconfiguring and recombining these in a constantly shifting dynamic. To begin with, Max's encounters with Lucia in *The Night Porter* are not the only erotically inflected interactions in the film. As Waller notes, Max also engages in sexually charged transactions with a lascivious ex-Nazi countess and a closeted gay colleague with a passion for ballet dancing. But Waller, like other commentators on this film, does not elaborate on Max's "queer" potential. Yet the queer nuances that adhere to Cavani's male protagonist are blatantly in evidence at several junctures in the narrative and are signaled to the viewer from the beginning through the casting of Dirk Bogarde, an "out" gay actor, in the lead role.

Throughout the postwar sequences of the film, Max's refined physical presence and elegant mannerisms set him apart from the other male characters. In an early scene we see him zipping up the fly of a young male cook in an elevator at the Viennese hotel where both men are employed. The gesture—ostensibly a reproach to an unkempt underling en route to an assignation with the German countess—is shown in close up, and the camera then pans up for a glimpse of Max's expression as he holds the other man's gaze with a sardonic, slightly flirtatious smile. This moment of erotically charged intimacy precedes Lucia's entrance into the mise-en-scène, complicating Max's character with intimations of queerness even before the narrative discloses his relationship with her.

The scene in the elevator also sets the stage for the film's construction of a more explicitly queer scenario—Max's relationship with Bert, the closeted homosexual who, like Max, is part of a tightly knit group of former SS officers living incognito in Vienna. Although Bert's sexuality is purportedly a secret, he flirts with Max in private, and their conversation is laced with erotic innuendo. In a particularly suggestive sequence, having asked for a dose of Luminal, Bert lowers his pants and Max injects him with the sedative. The sexual connotations of this moment are reinforced as the camera lingers on Bert's exposed buttocks and registers the pleasure on his face as Max inserts the needle, facilitating the "little death" of temporary oblivion.

Max also regularly facilitates the other man's desire to be watched as he performs the ballet routine he had danced years earlier for an audience of SS officers. While Max holds a spotlight to illuminate the dancer's movements in the darkened room, he remembers (in flashback) Bert's performance at the concentration camp, where he danced—almost entirely nude—for the entertainment of his assembled colleagues. As he moves Bert is transformed into the athletic, Aryan body of Nazi iconography, whose homoerotic appeal is clearly suggested by the composition and editing of the shots. In the "past" and "present" versions of the scene, Max mediates the spectacle of the dancer's body for the cinema audience, and Bert occupies the position of fetishized object of the gaze, a site usually reserved for the female figure in dominant cinema practice.[14] Bert's body demands to be looked at, both in the legitimized space of official Nazi culture, where his physical form corresponds to a model of idealized masculinity, and in the secret, guarded space of his postwar lodgings, where the foregrounding of his desire for self-display lends to his performance a contrastingly effeminate valence. The unstable sexual meanings that attach themselves to Bert's performance are further compounded by the juxtaposition of this scene with a subsequent flashback sequence, where the waif-like prisoner Lucia, bare-chested and in Nazi drag, performs a torch song for the assembled officers. While these contrasting performances expose and denaturalize the discourses of normative gender and sexuality, Max's participation in each of them is aligned with the controlling power of the gaze.

Control of the gaze, however, is radically revised in the film's concluding moments. Having discovered that he has lost Max to the "little girl," Bert vengefully reverts to the role of loyal Nazi. Thus, from an off-screen space that equates his point of view with the camera's perspective, it is Bert who shoots both Max and Lucia in punishment for Max's refusal to kill her. This murderous gesture may be read literally as the dutiful response of an obedient officer who eliminates a troublesome witness of past atrocities along with a traitorous colleague. Yet it may also be interpreted as the expression of a lover's jealousy. In the shot sequence that precedes the murder, we see Bert following Max and Lucia as they drive towards what is to become the place of their death. Here, instead of isolating the fleeing couple from their pursuer in a classic shot/countershot composition, close-ups of the three characters alternate with each other without a change of angle. This composition creates the momentary impression that Max, Lucia, and Bert occupy a contiguous space and suggests a tense intimacy among the trio, thus resurrecting the queer nuances that have previously adhered to Max at the very moment of his martyrdom in the cause of his relationship with Lucia. The apparently heterosexual victims at the center of the film's concluding violence can thus be perceived, not as a tragic, transgressive couple, but rather as part of an equally transgressive erotic triangle.

The ambivalent sexual discourses I have observed in *The Night Porter* follow a pattern that is articulated more overtly in the other narratives of the trilogy. In each of these films, the initial presentation of a heterosexual encounter or relationship gives way to a scenario of same-sex desire, which is eventually superseded by a scene of phallic divestiture or voluntary self-sacrifice. Yet each film ends with an apparent reassertion of the heterosexual matrix, however ambivalently evoked. Cavani's "now-you-see-it-now-you-don't" approach to the representation of queer desire may suggest a vacillating, if not closeted, attitude vis-à-vis gay sexuality on the filmmaker's part. Yet, at least in *The Night Porter*, the closet is constructed as a reprehensible choice. By emphatically repositioning Bert the ballet dancer—who may previously have elicited some sympathy from the audience—as Nazi murderer in the final moments of the film, the narrative exposes the full horror of his double life. On the most literal level of the film's enunciation, this closeted gay man—who, unlike Max, ultimately refuses to accept the vulnerability of a transgressive, nonphallic subjectivity—is shown to be as brutal as those who would punish homosexuality and other forms of proscribed difference with death.

Beyond Good and Evil, made three years after *The Night Porter*, raises the issue of the closet in more complex and interesting ways. The film offers a fictionalized account of the legendary relationship of Friedrich Nietzsche, Paul Rée, and Lou Andreas-Salomé, who first met in Italy in 1882. In a lavish visual style that alternates realistic sequences with surreal, hallucinatory tableaux, the narrative purports to sketch the course of this triangular friendship from its intense beginnings to its painful aftermath, ending with Nietzsche's decline into madness and Rée's untimely death. Cavani's story begins in Rome, where Paul (Robert Powell) and Fritz (Erland Josephson) meet the twenty-year-old Lou (Dominique Sanda) through a mutual acquaintance.[15] Rejecting the amorous advances of both men, Lou suggests that they establish an intellectual ménage-à-trois, an iconoclastic "trinity" of like minds. Following their attempt to set up residence in Leipzig, however, the rivalry between Fritz and Paul for Lou's attention and Lou's reluctance to commit herself sexually to either man conspire to make the arrangement unlivable, and the ménage is dissolved.

The narrative follows the three characters over the subsequent years, cross-cutting from one to the other as they pursue their increasingly divergent paths and foregrounding the powerful phantasmatic bonds that continue to haunt them. Fritz ultimately succumbs to opium and to the effects of syphilis and is obliged to return in a state of helpless insanity to the care of his bourgeois family. Paul pursues his desire for sex with men and dies of drowning following a violent erotic encounter with a group of rough German youths. Lou alone survives.

When described in summary fashion, the conflicts played out by the characters of *Beyond Good And Evil* may indeed seem sensationalistic or banal. Yet these scenarios are not conceptualized simply as private dramas; rather, they are positioned symbolically within a larger sociohistorical context and resonate with themes articulated in Nietzsche's writings. Although the narrative opens in Rome—a timeless, Dionysian space from the perspective of the German visitors—most of the action is set in Germany in the 1880s, a period marked by the rise of nationalism, xenophobia, and antisemitism, as well as the development of the new science of sexology. It is against the backdrop of these tensions and transformations that the personal struggle of Lou, Paul, and Fritz to transcend social prohibitions—and the conventional polarities of "good" and "evil"—must be understood.

The film presents the encounter between Lou and Paul in the film's opening moments as an instance of spontaneous mutual attraction. It soon becomes clear, however, that this is scarcely a conventional heterosexual coupling. Late at night Lou leads Paul through Rome to watch gay men engage in orgiastic sex among the ancient ruins. Enthralled by what she sees, Lou encourages the more inhibited Paul to share her voyeuristic pleasure. The street through which they approach this spectacle is named, significantly, Via San Sebastiano, evoking the queer connotations that surround the image of this early Christian martyr[16] and foreshadowing Paul's own "martyrdom" at the hands of the German workers. Stylistically, the scene is constructed as an elaborate *tableau vivant*, giving Paul's discovery of his repressed sexual yearnings the connotations of a ritual initiation in which Lou serves as his knowing guide. At the moment of his death he will retrieve this memory and transform it phantasmatically, imagining himself—in a scenario otherwise reminiscent of a crucifixion—at the center of the Roman orgy as the object of eroticized violence. Appearing to equate Paul's acceptance of his desire for men with his self-immolation, the hallucinatory spectacle of his brutal sodomization is disturbing to watch. Further light is cast on this scene, however, when Paul appears to Lou at a séance and utters the poignant message: "Since discovering that I wanted to be a woman and wanted to get fucked, I've been happy."

Urging Lou to tell this to Fritz, he laughs powerfully, and Lou laughs too, even as she weeps. Paul's voluntary embrace of his violent death, through which he is transformed into a desiring, masochistic subject, is thus presented by the film as a victory over the brutal prohibitions of the world he inhabits, and his laughter signals the recognition of a triumphant self-transcendence.

The historical Paul Rée has been described as "a self-hating Jew."[17] Cavani's construction of Paul suggests, by contrast, that it is his long struggle to accept his transgressive desire—and not his Jewishness—that feeds his restlessness and alienation. In the environment depicted by the film, however, Jewishness, "foreignness," homosexuality, and other forms of social deviance (such as a woman's active pursuit of her own pleasure or a man's passive jouissance) are antithetical to the values championed by the dominant ideology and to those nurtured by Fritz's bourgeois family. In the streets of Leipzig we see demonstrators assaulting a group of unassimilated Jews as Paul reacts with indignation, announcing to all that he too is Jewish. At the Nietzsche family residence, Elisabeth, Fritz's sister, virulently attacks Lou, calling her a Jew and a whore. Although Fritz denounces this assault and is shown elsewhere to be in vehement opposition to nationalism and antisemitism, he retains other prejudices characteristic of his era, most notably a disdain for male effeminacy, particularly for the "softness" he discerns in Paul. In a beer hall in Leipzig, Fritz drunkenly taunts Paul for his purported inability to offer sexual satisfaction to a "real" woman. Later, he disparagingly refers to his friend as Lou's "lady in waiting." These outbursts appear to be provoked by sexual jealousy. But who, or what, is the object of this jealousy?

Cavani's characterization of Fritz is overlaid with clues of disavowal and displacement, operations that Sedgwick associates with the discourse of the closet. It may be useful here to consider the film's construction of Fritz in the light of Sedgwick's queer reading of Nietzsche. In her boldly innovative commentary on the sexual discourses embedded in the philosopher's writings, Sedgwick observes at the outset that "many of Nietzsche's most effective intensities of both life and writing were directed toward other men and toward the male body."[18] Yet, as is well known, there is much in the philosopher's work that can be construed as homophobic. Noting that the energy Nietzsche devotes to excoriating male effeminacy indicates how crucial this issue was for him, Sedgwick argues that these repeated condemnations, typical of antisodomitic discourses of the time, coexist in his work with positively charged references to a homoerotic desire that is associated with "the precious virility of Dionysiac initiates or of ancient warrior classes."[19] In this way Nietzsche's rhetoric on male sexuality "charges with new spikes of power some of the most conventional lines of prohibition, even while preserving another space of careful de-definition in which certain objects of this prohibition may arbitrarily be invited to shelter."[20] Tracing the particular modality of disavowal evidenced in the philosopher's work, Sedgwick argues that Nietzsche's assertions of libidinal investment in other men are generally countered by a "confession" of narcissistic displacement. Although Nietzsche affectionately invokes his friend Rée as "my Epicurean garden" in *Human, All Too Human*, Sedgwick notes that later, in *Ecce Homo*, he interprets this effusion as a manifestation of disguised narcissism: "It was not 'one of my friends, the excellent Dr. Paul Rée, whom . . . I bathed in world-historic glory'; that was merely how, 'with my instinctive cunning, I here too avoided the little word 'I.' "[21]

At several junctures in the narrative, Cavani's film raises the possibility of Fritz's closeted queer desire by foregrounding his fascination with the male body (suggested in the hallucinatory ballet sequence performed by two nude dancers, which mimes the agonistic encounter between Dionysus and Christ) as well as his delight in contemplating a Roman fresco that depicts an all-male orgy. At the same time, Fritz's scorn for effeminacy is absolutely unequivocal. In Cavani's narrative the philosopher's quest to overcome his own "unmanliness" (a quest that is perhaps symptomatic of an internalized homophobia) ultimately fails. Far from attaining the model of manhood he endorses, Fritz is progressively feminized. Finally bereft of his phallic status, he regresses to a wordless state, languishing helplessly at his mother's home. Here, in the film's concluding moments, Lou pays an unannounced visit to her mute friend, whose melancholy abjection serves to place her strength and assurance in clear relief.

It has been observed that "in creating the Superman, Nietzsche was merely translating Lou into the masculine."[22] Those who hold the view that the historical Salomé was the inspiration for the Übermensch note that the philosopher published *Thus Spoke Zarathustra*, in which he first articulated this concept, just after his most intense involvement with her. With the concept of the Overman (or "Superman" in some translations), Nietzsche repudiated the belief in the equality of all persons. Claiming that the majority of humans were weak, despicable beings, he proposed the possibility of exceptional individuals rising above the common level of humanity through the transcendence of pain, resentment, and pity.

Cavani's Fritz explicitly invokes the necessity to overcome the emotions that make it impossible for ordinary men to rise above their ordinariness. Rejecting the influence of his bourgeois family, he fashions himself according to his own iconoclastic principles and denounces the weakness and hypocrisy of others. He becomes a tragic character in this narrative to the extent that his struggle for self-transcendence fails. Although he exalts sexual freedom, he clings to conventional constructions of heterosexuality. Although he disdains resentment, jealousy, and dependency, he is shown in the thrall of these emotions and takes refuge in opium. Although he despises his family, he is ultimately restored to the care of his mother and sister. Recognizing that only Lou has the strength of character to abandon the shackles of conventional morality and trite sentiment, Fritz tells Paul: "She is the character I have created, she is my Overman."

In an interview following the release of this film, Cavani stated that in reconstructing the triangular relationship of Salomé, Nietzsche, and Rée, she became fascinated by what she perceived as the "masculine-feminine psychological ambivalence" of all three figures.[23] In a rare moment of self-disclosure, she also suggested that the construction of these psycho-sexually indeterminate characters enabled her to externalize a personal struggle: "[Their ambivalence] was emblematic of some personal anxieties of mine, which, I believe, are everybody's: we all have different faces and yet we feel we have only one."[24] Yet, in the director's identification with the divided subjectivities of these similar-but-different characters, it is her phantasmatic investment in Lou that ultimately prevails. For only Lou, among the three, succeeds in transforming her "masculine-feminine ambivalence" into a triumphant engagement with life.

The construction of Lou's sexuality in *Beyond Good and Evil* is more complex and ultimately less legible than that of Fritz or Paul. In contrast to the subjective fantasies and eroticized hallucinations attributed to Fritz and Paul that unfold within the mise-en-scène, Lou's phantasmatic invest-ments are not visually articulated. The film's vagueness about Lou's inti-mate erotic life is strangely at odds with the suggestive frisson emanating from her participation in many situations that are not specifically erotic (peeing in a flower pot in the presence of Fritz and Lou, climbing into the bathtub with Fritz, or rolling with him in the mud outdoors). Indeed, Lou's spontaneous access to pleasure appears to spring from an untrou-bled, polymorphous perversity that she negotiates within clear contractual boundaries.

Arguing that it is counterproductive to reduce the sexual configura-tions offered in *Beyond Good and Evil* to the binary categories of homo-sexuality and heterosexuality, Félix Guattari suggested in his enthusiastic response to the film that these scenarios be read as manifestations of a "poetic," infantile eroticism.[25] Guattari describes how Cavani's three protagonists engage in sexual practices that lie outside the normalizing, bipolar oppositions imposed by phallocratic sexuality. Elsewhere in his writings—in a passage that resonates with the final statement made by Cavani's Paul—Guattari collectively describes homosexuality, infantile eroticism, psychotic sexuality, and other "deviant" forms of sexual practice as "becoming-woman," that is, as a way of escaping the tyranny of social repression.[26] He emphasizes, however, that "becoming-woman" should not be thought of "as belonging to the woman category." Rather, it indicates a process of change, "a screen for other types of becoming."[27] Associated with a shattering of the social norms, it is an option for both men and women. Guattari's perspective here is strikingly close to Cavani's. Her refusal to endorse conventional categories of sex and gender and her affirmative conceptualization of sexual transgression and play point toward the kind of "shattering" invoked by Guattari here. I must point out however that, while the three principal characters in *Beyond Good and Evil* aspire to similar transformation, only Lou seems capable of pursuing a polymorphous jouissance without succumbing to internalized prohibitions.

Lou's experience of "sex"—beginning with the scene of her transgressive voyeurism among the Roman ruins—is generally constructed as a form of play. The only instance of her participation in an act of adult, heterosexual intimacy occurs early in the narrative when she spontaneously makes love to Paul in the presence of the resentful Fritz. On the three occasions that she is urged to enter into a heterosexual relationship—by Paul, Fritz, and Carl, respectively—she recoils, for she is clearly a woman who chooses her partners rather than allowing them to choose her. Although she finally agrees to marry Carl Andreas, it is on condition that their relationship remain unconsummated, adding a celibate marriage to the list of her unconventional social arrangements. It is worth noting, however, that the one "deviant" practice that is conspicuously denied to Lou in Cavani's film is lesbian sexuality. Nonetheless, in the absence of specific indications of Lou's private fantasies, this possibility is not entirely foreclosed until the film's concluding moments.

Most important among the "lesbian" nuances that hover over this polymorphously perverse figure is the casting of Dominique Sanda as Lou. Since the French actress was already widely known for her role as the seductive, bisexual Anna Quadri in Bernardo Bertolucci's *The Conformist* (1970), this casting choice automatically brought with it intertextual connotations of queer desire. In the mise-en-scène of *Beyond Good and Evil*, Sanda's conventionally "feminine" beauty frequently becomes the object of the camera's lingering gaze, while at other times she is photographed in more classically "butch" attitudes, smoking cigars or cheroots or rolling tomboyishly on the ground. Cavani's construction of Lou vacillates between images of femme fatale and high-spirited tomboy, masculine woman and fag hag (at least in the initial phase of her relationship with Paul). Despite the striking sexual ambiguity that characterizes Lou throughout much of the narrative, however, the concluding sequence seems intent on recuperating her image within a familiar heterosexual matrix.

Here, as she departs from Fritz's somber home in a carriage, a tight close-up of Lou's face—exquisitely lit with soft *chiaroscuro* effects—offers itself as an instance of the director's own desiring gaze. This image is intercut, however, not only with a flashback to memories of Lou's earlier relationship with Fritz but also with a counter-shot of her new, unidentified male companion. The anonymous youth (perhaps intended to represent Rainer Maria Rilke, Salomé's lover in middle age) appears in the mise-en-scène only at this juncture, where his presence recuperates the camera's lingering gaze within a heterosexual scopic regime. The juxtapositions articulated by this scene and its accompanying flashback (where Lou is seen rolling in the mud with Fritz) reaffirm Lou's heterosexual status at the film's conclusion by showing her, not with one male lover but effectively with two, thus implicitly foreclosing the suspended possibility of an "other" desire.

If lesbian sexuality is occluded or disavowed in the first two films of the trilogy, desire between women becomes the ostensible focus of *The Berlin Affair*. Although this is the only one among Cavani's 12 films to offer explicit images of lesbian eroticism, the operations of indeterminacy and disavowal that I have observed in *The Night Porter* and *Beyond Good and Evil* are evidenced here also. At the same time, the difficulties inherent in the representation of lesbian desire are brought into question by problematizing the authority of the narrative voice.

The Berlin Affair was inspired by *Manji*, a novel by Jun'ichiro Tanizaki, first published in Japan in the late 1920s.[28] The novel recounts the story of a married woman who embarks on a passionate affair with another woman and—despite her husband's eventual seduction by her lover—pursues this erotic obsession to the point of participating in a triple suicide attempt. Cavani's retelling of Tanizaki's plot complicates the original situation by shifting the setting to Berlin in the late 1930s, thus adding a provocative political dimension to what might otherwise have been an intimate, erotic melodrama. The film centers on the obsessive love of Louise (Gudrun Landgrebe), the wife of Heinz, a German government official (Kevin McNally), for Mitsuko (Mio Takaki), the daughter of a Japanese diplomat living in Berlin. This relationship unfolds against the tense background of the Nazi "moralization campaign," in which proscribed sexual behaviors, such as homosexuality or sexual relations between Germans and non-Aryan people, are condemned and severely punished. The film thus revisits some of the issues evoked in *The Night Porter*, complicating these with the discourse of racial difference.

The affair between the two women unfolds in an extended flashback, framed in the film's opening sequence by Louise's visit to her former professor to whom she confides her memories. The first image presented by the film is, in fact, a long shot of the professor as he sits at his desk, typing. Due to the strategic position of this shot, the male writer's presence becomes an implicit part of the narrative that follows. The long flashback that corresponds to Louise's narration of her memories is interrupted at several junctures by a return to the initial setting, where we are presented with alternating close-ups of Louise as she tells her tale, and the older man, quietly absorbing her account. The professor's office evokes an atmosphere, at once intimate and formal, that is strongly reminiscent of the psychoanalytic scene.[29] When Louise first enters the room lined with books and works of art, she tells the professor that, although she had tried to record her memory of the events of the previous year in the form of a novel, she had been unable to give words to her experience. Her interlocutor is both an academic and a novelist, notorious for the frank, sexual themes of his fiction and already a target of the moralization campaign. Louise indicates that she desires his help to transform the raw content of her memories into an intelligible narrative. The professor's privileged alignment with the symbolic order (even if complicated by an official intolerance toward his work) is thus established diegetically by Louise, who, in the role of seductive student/daughter/analysand, invokes his ability to "authorize" her voice. In effect, Louise and the professor constitute the first "couple" introduced by the film. The prominence of this male figure in the enunciation of Louise's tale of "lesbian" love might be compared to the figure of the male witness or participant who commonly triangulates the construction of female homosexuality in mainstream or (hetero)pornographic representations.

At the center of the long flashback is the enigmatic figure of Mitsuko. Louise's attraction to the Japanese girl (who is no more than 17 or 18 years old) appears at first to be a phenomenon of aesthetic enthrallment. When Louise first catches sight of her at the art institute where they are both enrolled, she is riveted by her exotic beauty, which stands in sharp contrast to the model of Aryan femininity promoted by the cultural institutions of the regime. Mediated by the admiring gaze of the German protagonist, Mitsuko's elaborate kimono, pale makeup and stiff, ceremonial posture lend her the appearance of a porcelain statue, votary figure or idol. Mitsuko is thus orientalized through Louise's point of view as a fetish-object of rare beauty and is evacuated of all subjectivity.

The erotic encounters between the two women, though highly aestheticized, are presented in sensuous detail. As Louise fetishizes the exotic elements of Mitsuko's self-fashioning, her bondage to the Japanese woman is suggested visually in the scene of their lovemaking through the playful winding and unwinding of Mitsuko's silk sash (the *obi*). Yet the Japanese woman's body is a site of increasingly illegible meanings. Louise's discovery of an intricate tattoo on her buttocks alerts her to the fact that she does not possess exclusive access to Mitsuko's intimate rituals and unveilings. Although Heinz, Louise's husband, and Benno, the art teacher, initially denigrate Mitsuko's foreign appearance, both of them are now shown to be equally in her thrall. Louise thus finds herself implicated in two erotic triangles, with Benno and Mitsuko on the one hand and with her husband and Mitsuko on the other.

At first the relationship between Louise and Mitsuko is presented as a passionate bond of love maintained in the face of great peril. Yet the positive alignment of Louise and Mitsuko, transgressive of both sexual and racial taboos in the face of the negative powers of government influence, is no sooner established than it collapses. Although the culture of the Third Reich functions on a rigid division of self and other, insider and outsider, no clear-cut binary system of good and bad, innocence and guilt, holds up within the economy of intersubjective relationships deployed by *The Berlin Affair*. The apparently vulnerable and childlike Mitsuko proves to be cunning and manipulative and has used her relationship with Louise to hide a heterosexual relationship with her art teacher Benno. At the same time, Louise, despite her declared opposition to the Nazi moralization campaign, passively collaborates with the Berlin police to precipitate the downfall of a closeted homosexual general.

Because of her youth and apparent vulnerability, Mitsuko initially appears to occupy the position of the child in the Oedipal triangle she forms with Louise and Heinz. Yet, while Louise and Heinz desire only Mitsuko, Mitsuko is willing to participate in a relationship with each of them on her own severe terms. As she assumes the role of cruel, phallic mother, the German couple willingly submit themselves to her ritualized demands. Although Louise recognizes the deceptions underlying Mitsuko's behavior, she remains magnetized by her, believing that the Japanese woman provides her with a symbolic refuge from the oppressive environment they inhabit. Ultimately, Heinz too experiences Mitsuko as an all-powerful refuge. Following the pattern of phallic renunciation common to Cavani's male protagonists, he allows himself to be dismissed from his high-ranking position and chooses to participate in the triple suicide pact orchestrated by Mitsuko.

Here, more clearly than elsewhere in Cavani's films, the characteristic scenario of voluntary abjection and self-sacrifice resonates with the affirmative conception of masochism articulated by Gilles Deleuze. In his recuperative reading of Leopold Sacher-Masoch's essay "Venus in Furs,"

Deleuze makes a radical distinction between the symbolic structure of masochism and that of sadism. Linking masochism to a theater of regressive, pre-Oedipal sexuality rather than to the development of the Oedipus complex (where it is located by Freud), he argues that it is a manifestation of the subject's desire to re-merge or identify with the mother by rejecting the internalized father. For Deleuze masochism is contractual and consensual, repetitive and theatrical in a way that sadism is not. Its violence—more emotional than physical—is prompted and controlled by the subject, who ecstatically submits to the mother's cruelty. The male masochist, by denying the mother's "castration" and investing her with infinite power, wishes to destroy all traces of the father and to disavow his own phallic potentiality.[30] Ultimately, this radical rereading of "Venus in Furs" suggests the potential of masochism to destabilize the conventional binary oppositions that subtend the construction of phallic sexuality.

Deleuze's formulation of the masochist has particular resonance in Cavani's characterization of both Heinz and Louise. In their desire to merge with the socially vulnerable though highly manipulative Mitsuko, whom they invest, through a process of fetishistic disavowal, with absolute power, the German couple radically negates the Father, as embodied in the infernal machine of Nazi law (here, as elsewhere in the German trilogy, the Father is equated with a repressive political system). Embracing the death pact offered by the cherished (m)other, they thus renounce their privilege as Aryan citizens of a brutal, phallic regime.

The development of a bisexual, masochistic triangle in the second half of *The Berlin Affair* dramatically eclipses the earlier configuration of a lesbian love story. In the phantasmatic economy of Cavani's narrative, Louise and Heinz are "gendered" female in relation to Mitsuko, as both of them expose their castration by voluntarily submitting to her (purported) phallic power. Following the triple suicide attempt, however, Louise discovers that she has mysteriously survived, that only Heinz has been "chosen" to accompany Mitsuko in death.

The Berlin Affair seems at first to invite spectator identification through the figure of Louise, who reappears from time to time in the framing sequence as she tells her story. Yet, as we have seen, her ability to speak is cast into doubt from the beginning, for she admits that she needs the professor's help to give expression to her experience. As her memories unfold in flashback, they take on a detached, theatrical quality, as though relegated to another space—a space simultaneously contemplated by her male interlocutor. At the conclusion of her account, a richly suggestive detail serves to problematize further the issue of narrative voice.

As Louise's visit draws to a close, the professor, realizing that the police are about to enter his office to arrest him, hastily entrusts her with his most recent manuscript, which he conceals in a chocolate box. Clutching the circular box, which happens to be the same shape and about the same size as a film can, Louise leaves his office in the film's final shot. We might ask what figurative relation this concealed text bears to the narrative we have been watching. Does the manuscript in some sense constitute Louise's story? Or is it one of the professor's stories, which will now be "recycled" by Louise? The container's circular shape certainly points to the possibility of a film adaptation. If Louise, as narrator within the text of the film, stands in an analogous relationship to Cavani as the storyteller outside the film, her final gesture may evoke the filmmaker's appropriation of a story of "lesbian" love from the pages of a provocative male writer from Japan famous for his narratives of erotic obsession.

With the Freudian figure of the patriarchal professor on the one hand and the quivering ghost of Jun'ichiro Tanizaki on the other, *The Berlin Affair* ultimately draws attention to the fact that this purportedly "lesbian" tale is part of a narrative tradition deeply implicated in the apparatuses of a masculine, heterosexual imaginary. In seductively redeploying some of the most clichéd elements of "Japaneseness" (the "inscrutable" oriental, the seductive geisha, the ritualized suicide, and so on) and of "lesbianism" (in the guise of the heterosexual male fantasy of a triangulated erotic configuration), Cavani simultaneously takes her distance from these images through the articulation of the frame story in which the figure of a white, (presumably) heterosexual, male writer is prominently positioned.

Nonetheless, in *The Berlin Affair*, as in the earlier films of the trilogy, the director also raises the possibility—however obliquely and provisionally—of alternative, nonphallic discourses and sexualities, of pleasures that elude the controlling, binary logic of the dominant tradition. Here, too, the director draws attention to the subversive power of outlawed sexual practices and suggests the paradoxical strength of a contractual masochism by implicitly valorizing the divestiture of power and privilege. It is worth noting, in conclusion, that the ideas on sexuality and embodiment that emerge from these films stand in sharp contrast to the perspective being formulated by Italian feminist theorists in the late 1970s and early 1980s under the rubric of sexual difference, where the focus of attention was on the specificity of lived, female, bodily experience. The director's acknowledged fascination with masculinity and her emphasis on a fluidity of gender identifications and object choices seem similarly incompatible with the position of many Italian lesbians who during the same period had begun to formulate a radical separatism. Ultimately, however, as the result of its oscillations, displacements, and ambivalences, Cavani's work refuses to place itself in a clearly legible relation to lesbian identity, politics, or desire.

Áine O'Healy is Professor of Modern Languages and Literatures at Loyola Marymount University in Los Angeles. She is the author of *Cesare Pavese* (Boston: Twayne Publishers, 1988) and of numerous chapters in critical anthologies. Her publications also include several articles in *Screen, Cinefocus, Spectator, Annali d'Italianistica, Italian Culture, Romance Languages Annual, Italica,* and *Women's Studies Review.* In addition, she is the translator (or cotranslator) of a number of critical studies, including Marco De Marinis's *The Semiotics of Performance* (Bloomington: Indiana University Press, 1993) and Adriana Cavarero's *In Spite of Plato: A Feminist Rewriting of Ancient Philosophy* (New York: Routledge, 1995). O'Healy is currently completing a volume on contemporary Italian cinema.

Notes

1. Chantal Nadeau, "Girls on a Wired Screen: Cavani's Cinema and Lesbian S/M" in: *Sexy Bodies: The Strange Carnalities of Feminism,* ed. Elizabeth Grosz and Elspeth Probyn (New York: Routledge, 1995), p. 213.

2. Cavani is not generally classified as a "lesbian filmmaker." Note, for example, that Richard Dyer's broad-ranging survey of international films containing representations of gay and/or lesbian sexuality made by gay or lesbian directors omits any mention of her name; see Richard Dyer, *Now You See It: Studies on Lesbian and Gay Film* (London: Routledge, 1990).

3. Eve Kosofsky Sedgwick, *Epistemology of the Closet* (Berkeley: University of California Press, 1990).

4. "I wanted to make a German trilogy, or I should say a Mitteleuropean trilogy, because we are all descendents from the same culture. I wanted to pay my debt to Thomas Mann." Cited by Gaetana Marrone in *The Gaze and the Labyrinth: The Cinema of Liliana Cavani* (Princeton, NJ: Princeton University Press, 2000), p. 86.

5. Among the studies on Cavani's work published in English, the only detailed examination of the three films of the trilogy is found in Marrone's *The Gaze and the Labyrinth.* Nadeau's essay, which discusses in some detail the erotic scenarios in *The Berlin Affair* and *Beyond Good and Evil,* has little to say about *The Night Porter.*

6. Among the dismissive critiques of the film were those written by Holocaust survivors Bruno Bettelheim and Primo Levi; see Bruno Bettelheim, "Reflections: Surviving," *The New Yorker* (August 2, 1976), pp. 31–52 and Primo Levi, *The Drowned and the Saved,* trans. Raymond Rosenthal (New York: Summit, 1988).

7. Silverman's first essay on Cavani's work was a short article dedicated entirely to *The Night Porter;* see Kaja Silverman, "Masochism and Subjectivity," *Framework* 12 (1979), pp. 2–9. She later applied the central insight that emerged in this

essay to a reading of Cavani's work as a whole; see Silverman, *The Acoustic Mirror: The Female Voice in Psychoanalysis and Cinema* (Bloomington: Indiana University Press, 1988), pp. 141–234.

8. Silverman, *The Acoustic Mirror*, p. 219.

9. Ibid., p. 224.

10. Ibid., p. 220.

11. Ibid., p. 224.

12. Ibid., p. 233.

13. Marguerite Waller, "Signifying the Holocaust" in: *Feminisms in the Cinema*, ed. Laura Pietropaolo and Ada Testaferri (Bloomington: Indiana University Press, 1995), pp. 206–19.

14. For a discussion of the gendering of the cinematic gaze, see the seminal essay by Laura Mulvey, which—though criticized for its purportedly universalizing assumptions, subsequently addressed in another of Mulvey's essays—remains an important point of reference in critical considerations of cinema's signifying operations. Laura Mulvey, "Visual Pleasure and Narrative Cinema," *Screen* 16,3 (Autumn 1975), pp. 6–18.

15. For the sake of distinguishing the film's fictional constructions from the historical figures they represent, I will refer to Cavani's characters by their first names only—Lou, Paul, and Fritz—as they are designated in the script.

16. For a discussion of the fetishizing constructions of the wounded body of St. Sebastian in queer art and culture, see Richard A. Kaye, "Losing His Religion" in: *Outlooks: Lesbian and Gay Sexualities in Visual Culture*, ed. Peter Horne and Reina Lewis (New York: Routledge, 1995), pp. 86–105.

17. Robert C. Holub, "Nietzsche and the Jewish Question," *New German Critique* 66 (Fall 1995), p. 99.

18. Sedgwick, p. 133.

19. Ibid., p. 134.

20. Ibid., pp. 134–35.

21. Cited in Sedgwick, p. 162.

22. Angela Livingstone, *Lou Andreas-Salomé: Her Life and Work* (Mount Kisko, NY: Moyer Bell, 1984), p. 57.

23. Cited in Marrone, p. 120.

24. Marrone, p. 120.

25. See Liliana Cavani and Félix Guattari, "Una conversazione" in: Liliana Cavani, Franco Arcalli, and Italo Moscati, *Al di là del bene e del male* (Turin: Einaudi, 1977), pp. 173–80.

26. Félix Guattari, "Becoming-Woman," trans. Rachel McComas and Stamos Metzidakis in: *Soft Subversions*, ed. Sylvère Lotringer (New York: Semiotext(e), 1993), p. 42. Guattari's articulation of "becoming-woman" in this essay differs slightly from the formulation of the same term in Gilles Deleuze and Félix Guattari's *A Thousand Plateaus*, trans. Brian Massumi (Minneapolis: University of Minnesota Press, 1987), pp. 275–79.

27. Guattari, p. 41.

28. *Manji* was translated into Italian as *La croce buddista* (*The Buddhist Cross*), the title cited in the credits of Cavani's film. It has been translated into English by Howard Hibbett as *Quicksand* (New York: Knopf, 1994).

29. I am indebted to Holly Willis, a graduate student in a seminar I taught at USC several years ago, for making this association.

30. See Gilles Deleuze, "Masochism: An Interpretation of Coldness and Cruelty" in: Gilles Deleuze and Leopold Sacher-Masoch, *Masochism*, trans. Jean McNeil (New York: Zone, 1989), pp. 15–96.

9

Adapting to Heterocentricity: The Film Versions of Umberto Saba's *Ernesto* and Giorgio Bassani's *The Gold-Rimmed Spectacles*

William Van Watson

Umberto Saba's *Ernesto* and Giorgio Bassani's *The Gold-Rimmed Spectacles* are two minor classics of modern Italian literature that have been adapted to the cinema. Both tell stories of homosexual relationships between males of different ages and different class backgrounds. In adapting these works to film, directors Salvatore Samperi and Giuliano Montaldo also adapt their homosexual subject matter to a persistent heterocentric filmgoing hegemony. Both directors invent female characters and heterosexual romances to offset or "straighten out" the homosexual affairs central to the original works. Certainly, the change in medium impacts the treatment and presentation of the subject matter, as novels are read individually and in private, while film traditionally addresses a mass audience in a public space. Beyond the simple dichotomy of heterosexual directors approaching homosexual characters lies the issue of acceptance of alterity. Both Saba and Bassani, in distinctly different ways, observe their homosexual characters as an other self. For Saba, Ernesto represents his own alternative life not lived, while for Bassani, Athos Fadigati's homosexuality serves as an objective correlative for the Jewishness of his narrator, as both confront an increasingly rigorous fascist sexual and racial normativity. With their limited use of subjective camera in the treatment of homosexuality, Samperi and Montaldo perpetrate a shift in narrative voice, so that cinematically the homosexual characters appear not as other selves but as others. As Samperi and Montaldo adapt to heterocentricity, empathy (con)descends to sympathy.

Saba, Samperi, and the Importance of Being Ernesto

In his play *Calderòn*, Pier Paolo Pasolini diagnosed the sort of self-alienation suffered by homosexuals condemned by a homophobic society to lead a falsely heterosexual existence: "I continue to run along a track parallel to that along which my life should have run."[1] Umberto Saba led just such a self-alienated parallel existence. In the novella, Ernesto's object of affection is named Ilio; Saba wrote to his daughter, Lina: "Quando sarai a Trieste ricordami che ti faccia vedere la casa dove abitava Ilio. . . . Forse anche ci andremo; chi sa che non ci sia ancora e che mi aspetti." (When you come to Trieste remind me to show you where Ilio lived. . . . Maybe we'll go there together, and who knows whether or not he might not still be waiting for me.)[2] Thus Ilio was not merely a fictional character, and Saba's substitution of the pronoun "me" for Ernesto indicates that he and his protagonist are one and the same. Saba's use of free indirect discourse in the novella frequently blurs his voice with that of his youthful alter ego. *Ernesto* represents the life lived in earnest that Saba discarded for a parallel life, as the title and name of the protagonist suggest. As such, the novel indicts the homophobia of a society that Saba accepted in life. Saba had contemplated entitling the novel *Intimacy* (*Intimità* in Italian), which—like earnestness—was lacking in his life. Despite his decades-long career as a poet, Saba repeatedly referred to *Ernesto* as "la più bella cosa che abbia scritto" (the most beautiful thing I have written).[3] Lina describes her father as being "in a state of ecstasy" during the novel's composition, as having "never been so inspired," as "writing like one transfigured, in a state of grace."[4]

Saba lived his martyrdom to heterocentricity in a state of perpetual depression and chronic neurosis, which calls to mind Freud's theories of neurosis as deriving from surplus repression. Of his alter ego Ernesto, Saba wrote that "non aveva inibizioni, o poche poche" (he had no inhibitions, or very few).[5] In direct contrast, the perennially neurotic Saba was plagued by so many inhibitions, repressions, and defense mechanisms that he considered the Villa Elettra mental health clinic on Monte Mario in Rome a home away from home.[6] He experienced the same sort of nervous crises that a homosexual writer like Tennessee Williams deflected into his faux female characters. For Saba, the writing of *Ernesto* functioned as a similar therapeutic experience. He described its composition in terms of a release from surplus repression "as if a dike in me burst, everything flowing out spontaneously."[7] Saba's claim that he could only have written the novel while in the Monte Mario clinic confirms its therapeutic nature.[8] Even after completion of his novella, Saba continued to compose letters in the liberating guise of the Ernesto persona. Some of these discuss Saba himself in the third person in a dizzying mise-en-abîme of alter egos. Saba also wrote a series of letters in the first person to Ernesto, projecting onto the young aspiring violinist his own life story and identity as a poet. Saba repeatedly and disingenuously declared that the novel was unpublishable not because of its content but because of its language, even though the narrative is in formal Italian along with many of the dialogues. Other dialogues are in Triestino dialect, which Saba renders easily decipherable through simple transpositions of sounds and spelling. He avoided publication of the novel during his lifetime, preferring instead to share the work in private readings with a few close friends and dwelling on their emotional responses. Lina explains his behavior: "He was afraid the book would be misunderstood, that it would give birth to a scandal. I had a copy of the manuscript and Carlo Levi had another. Every so often he would send us a telegram telling us to destroy it. We would assure him we had, but he never believed us because he would always send us new telegrams asking us to destroy it again. It became a game we played."[9] As part of this game, Saba intermittently addresses the reader directly throughout the novel. At times, he even uses the plural pronoun "we" to include the reader as an observer of Ernesto's life. From its inception, despite the internalized homophobia of its author, the book was conceived as having a readership.

Salvatore Samperi's film version (1979)of the book was originally heralded for its frank portrayal of a homosexual relationship, especially when compared with other films of the period. Such frankness is less impressive, however, when viewed within the context of Samperi's overall work as director. From the titillating *Malizia* (1972) to the lurid *La Bonne* (1986), his films verge on soft porn. Within this context, one Italian critic claimed that in *Ernesto* Samperi "tells a scandalous story with castigated images."[10] This comment contrasts directly with the novelist Elsa Morante's observation that, in writing *Ernesto*, Saba "non castiga nessuna parola" (Saba does not castigate a single word).[11] Saba's Ernesto first experiences homosexual desire when he "sentiva che la mano poggiata sulla sua tremava" (felt the trembling hand [of the worker] on his own).[12] While Samperi's heterosexually themed films proliferate with exposed breasts and vaginas, he uses this passage both as a point of departure and as an excuse for conveniently deflecting a truly explicit depiction of gay male sexuality into the more neutral expressivity of hands. In the first sexual encounter between Ernesto and the worker, Samperi begins with their torsos. Ernesto's facial expression conveys the moment of anal penetration. As the worker continues to sodomize him, however, Samperi's uncharacteristically demure camera retreats to an extreme close-up on their interlocked hands flexing, squeezing, and writhing as castigated synecdoche for their entire bodies.

Samperi deploys hands throughout his film as part of his visually discreet lexicon for conveying illicit, and usually gay male, sexuality. As in Saba's novella, Samperi's worker first intimates his desire for Ernesto with his hands, stroking the youth's shoulders, forehead, and face. The worker furtively touches Ernesto's hand with his own, quickly pulling it away only to have Ernesto retrieve it in affirmative response. Prior to their first sexual encounter, a potential mouth-to-mouth kiss becomes displaced to their clenched hands, centered in the frame as they gaze into one another's eyes in an oddly poetic moment. Their second liaison displaces sexuality into the hand even more literally, as the worker masturbates an unsatisfied Ernesto. This time a chastened Samperi keeps the hand outside the frame, although its alluded activity remains clear. A later scene involving a riding crop also deflects the overtly sexual into the hand: The worker intended to give Ernesto a whipping on his rear, but Ernesto ends up whipping him on his outstretched palm.

Samperi employs hands synecdochally in Ernesto's relationships with Ilio and Rachele as well. When Ernesto first meets Ilio, he holds up his hand to examine it between them in the center of the frame. Their shared study of the violin provides a classic opportunity for hands as conveyors of intimacy, as Ernesto instructs Ilio in his fingering and bowing. An extreme close-up of their hands, one atop the other, recalls Ernesto's first encounter with the worker. Here the evasive intimacy of hands can at last lead to the pervasive intimacy of a kiss, but only because Samperi has cast the actress Lara Wendel as both Ilio and Rachele. This casting recuperates the explicit homosexual intimacy of the narrative moment with the heterosexual iconicity of performers. As critic Umberto Silva has noted, "[T]he spectator, knowing that a girl is interpreting the role, can reassure himself with her female sexuality."[13] Adapting to heterocentricity, Samperi supplants the closing handshake of Ilio and Ernesto from the novella with the apparition of Ilio's sister Rachele, who grabs Ernesto's hand to assert her claim to him. Instead of allowing the story of Ernesto to function as Saba's discarded "earnest" life on a parallel track, Samperi pollutes it with the biography of another Triestino writer, the novelist Italo Svevo. Tullio Kezich notes Samperi's "attempt to align the destiny of Ernesto-Saba with that of Svevo: marriage to a high society girl and entrance into a great family, but with a malignant accentuation on the economic opportunism of the future husband."[14]

Samperi invents this high-society girl from a solitary reference in Saba that Ilio has "una sorella, un anno più giovane di lui, che gli assomigliava come una goccia d'acqua ad un'altra." (a sister a year younger who resembles him like one drop of water resembled another.)[15] He uses this character, named Luigia in Saba's novella and Rachele in his own film, to construct an entirely new ending to Ernesto's story. Samperi himself justified his changes: "In modifying the ending we came upon a scheme Saba would have definitely approved. Ernesto is an egotist and his story certainly could not have ended with a handshake."[16] Samperi's remarks are odd given the keen awareness of the metaphorical expressivity of hands demonstrated in his film. Saba pointedly underscores the real symbolic magnitude of the seemingly insignificant closing gesture between Ilio and Ernesto: "sarebbe parso, a chiunque l'avesse osservato, un fatto banale della vita d'ogni ora. Invece . . . era . . . un avvenimento raro, quale può prodursi, sì e no, una volta sola in un secolo e in un solo paese." (The holding of hands would have appeared as a banal everyday occurrence to anyone who witnessed it. Instead . . . it was a unique and rare event, and one which happens maybe once in a century in any given country.)[17] The sexuality of Saba's Ernesto thus begins and concludes with the touching of a hand, the worker's and Ilio's, respectively.

Samperi asserted, "You don't have to be a homosexual in order to direct a film about homosexuality . . . [A] feminine component always lies within us."[18] This statement is extremely revealing in that, while Samperi attempts to lay claim to the pansexuality of a Freudian polymorphous perversity, he actually collapses into a heterocentric and homophobic position by conflating homosexuality with the feminine. This patriarchal strategy demeans both the feminine and the constructed "effeminate" homosexual for their imagined and projected passivity. Saba's Ernesto moves away from an initial Freudian polymorphous perversity. A creature of instinct, Ernesto's "preferenze gli erano dettate unicamente dalla sensualità del momento" (preferences were dictated solely by the sensuality of the moment).[19] Such libidinal impulsiveness prompts him to visit a prostitute on a whim. Samperi extends Ernesto's polymorphous vacillation between the homosexuality of the worker and the heterosexuality of the prostitute to his relationships with Ilio and Rachele. He makes the brother and sister not merely resemble each other but presents them as genetically impossible identical twins of different sexes. Before exchanging Ernesto, Ilio and Rachele exchange clothes, and ostensibly gender, as Rachele cuts her hair to match Ilio's and Ilio applies make-up to match Rachele. Each lay claim to fixing Ernesto's desire upon him or herself, but Rachele's assertion that "the game is over" heralds the acquiescence of Ernesto's polymorphously perverse pansexuality into a heterocentrist conformity. He becomes engaged.

Rather than being "out," Ernesto is clearly "in" as he can only look out at us, the audience, as he gazes directly into the camera, a shot unique in the entirety of the film. Gay critic Vito Russo interprets this shot optimistically: "The final shot of Ernesto's winking face at the wedding is meant to indicate that neither marriage nor time will subdue the rebel in him."[20] However, Ernesto does not so much wink as he shrugs his shoulders in resignation. Samperi himself has conceded that the story of his cinematic Ernesto is one of defeat.[21] The unique freeze frame on the closing shot further fixes him in this impasse of heterosexuality. Moravia justly characterizes Saba's novella in a way Saba himself did not: "Ernesto is the story of an initiation after which the author clearly indicates that Ernesto has become homosexual forever."[22] Moravia's observation that Samperi's film "works in the opposite direction" from Saba's novella proves largely accurate despite Rachele's residual unease that she alone may not be "enough" for Ernesto.

While Saba's Ernesto serves as an alternative subject of his own homosexual life not lived, Samperi's protagonist functions more as an object of cinematic investigation. For Samperi, Ernesto's libido appears as an otherness to which his camera responds with a balance of wariness and fascination. He comforts his cinematic gaze with the impediment of Ernesto's social cage, extending Ernesto's habit of keeping birds into a metaphor for the character's own sense of entrapment. For example, in the workplace Samperi shoots Ernesto through the cage of the railing of the banister. More important, however, Samperi deploys this strategy for scenes involving his protagonist as an object of sexual desire, such as when the prostitute spies upon Ernesto passing on the street below from behind her blinds. More noticeably, during Ernesto's encounter with the worker, Samperi's camera withdraws from a relatively empathetic treatment of the worker's advances to a chink in the wall that emphasizes third-person voyeurism. The cautious camera twice retreats behind some cages stacked in the grain storeroom during this sequence.

Ernesto's association with birds provokes his disgust at the thought of eating the old pet chicken Camilla. (In real life Saba ironically referred to his wife as "the old hen.") Ernesto's mother renders his identification with his birds explicit when she calls him by the name of one of his blackbirds. Ernesto's violin playing most fully links him with his pets. He plays specifically for them, prompting their singing. The violin binds him not only to his birds but also to Ilio. Saba writes: "La notte, verso l'alba, avevo sognato di volare . . . e dicevo ad Ilio . . . che si provasse anche lui a volare. Infatti, poco dopo, egli si sollevava dal suo letto, che si trovava, nel sogno, nella mia stessa stanzetta; e subito volavamo tutti e due, uno vicino all'altro. . . . [V]olare in sogno ha un significato preciso." (Late in the evening around nightfall I dreamt I was flying . . . and I told this story to Ilio . . . that he also should fly. And in fact, after a little while, he began to levitate above his bed and tried flying himself. In my dream, there in my little room we both soon were flying together each beside the other. . . . [T]he desire to fly in a dream has a precise meaning.)[23] As a lifelong psychiatric patient Saba was well rehearsed in the basic Freudian paradigms. Here he coyly alludes to Freud's concept that the desire to fly in dreams encodes the transcendence of the physical law of gravity as a metaphor for the desire to transcend libidinal laws and maintain orgasm. Ernesto's tendency to turn his bedroom into a miniature aviary should be read in such symbolic terms. His ambition to raise his stature through artistic accomplishment as a concert violinist bespeaks this desire for transcendence on an aesthetic and social level, especially as his violin playing is associated with both his birds and Ilio. Aware of his protagonist's defeat, Samperi creates an interesting and pivotal moment in his film when Ernesto frees one of his birds to give it flight. The Italian word for bird *uccello* serves as commonplace slang for the penis. In liberating the bird Ernesto metaphorically frees his own sexuality from the cage of patriarchal heterocentricity. This wistful gesture constitutes a Pyrrhic victory, occurring just prior to his departure for his engagement party where Wilder pointedly informs him: "There'll be no more violin." The formality of the occasion, the formality of the guests who encircle him, the formality of their respective toasts on his engagement, and the formality of Samperi's shooting style during this sequence argue for Ernesto's entrapment in a heterocentric cage from which he can only look out.

The phallocentric Samperi has bluntly dubbed the penis "the most important organ."[24] Given his simple-minded Freudianism, he not surprisingly litters his film with an array of phallic symbols not found in Saba's novel. Many of these, such as Ernesto's pocket watch, prominent at crotch level in his sex scenes with the worker and the prostitute, function as class markers as well. During the opening of the film, Ernesto's cane renders him an assessor of masculinity and strength, as he invests it with phallic potency to tap and choose the workers. Using the idiom of tobacco smoking, Samperi creates a virtual class hierarchy of phallic symbols, ranging from the worker's cigarettes to Wilder's cigars to Ilio's pipe. When Wilder chokes on his cigars, he symbolically chokes on his own patriarchal privilege, prompting him to give lip service to both quitting his habit and leaving his exploitative business. He subsequently exposes his own pretense of abdication of such privilege when he displays the abundance of cigar boxes hidden in his desk. In accordance with his professed interest in the polymorphous perversity of his protagonist, Samperi makes such phallic symbols as interchangeable and transferable as he would have Ernesto's desire. In a gesture of socialist largesse, Ernesto conveys a box of Wilder's cigars to the worker. Wilder's prestigious silver-plated walking stick changes hands between Wilder and Ernesto three times. Upon first receiving it, Ernesto embraces his employer at crotch level in a display of gratitude, emphasizing the phallicism of the exchange. In turn, Ernesto uses the stick to connect with Ilio by tapping his shoulder as they leave the concert. Conversely, he fumbles and drops it when he meets Ilio's father, Signor Luzzati, whose superior wealth and patriarchal social standing disempower him.

Ernesto's final interaction with the worker also occurs on the level of phallic transference. The worker approaches Ernesto with a riding crop, which Ernesto quickly demands be given over to him. Samperi's camera reaffirms Ernesto's assertion of power by switching its position to his point of view, presenting the worker as object. As in the novel, Ernesto administers the precise number of whippings the worker had intended for him. In Saba, Ernesto then sheds this whip, disposing of the phallic economy of power and difference altogether. Samperi's film violates the spirit of Saba's novella not merely in discarding its homosexual specificity for a heterocentric conclusion, but more profoundly because Saba's text presents a protagonist who discards a relationship based upon difference for one based upon sameness and potential egalitarianism. In ancient Rome difference in same-sex relationships was manifested primarily through class, while in ancient Greece difference was a matter of age, as the adult *erastes* took an adolescent lover or *eromenos*.[25] The distinct roles in the relationship were physically symbolized by the beard of the older male and the beardlessness of the youth. The worker's concept of homosexuality continues within the framework of this ancient Mediterranean tradition. In contrast, Brian Pronger notes that "reciprocal fucking represents the ideal of . . . liberation; it is an attempt to change the myths of gender."[26] When Ernesto requests reciprocity in anal penetration, the worker responds: " 'No xe bel far con un omo. Xe robe che se ghe fa solo ai gioveneti, prima ancora che ghe cressi la barba. . . . Che gusto la volessi provar con mi che go, come el vedi, i mustaci?' " ("But it's not nice to do it with a man. It's stuff you do with boys before they grow a beard and before they go with women. What fun would it be with me who, as you see, already has a moustache?") Ernesto explodes the absurd persistence of this obsolete "myth of gender" by simply asking, " 'Nol pol taiarseli?' " ("Couldn't you shave it?")[27] Samperi emphasizes the symbolic importance of facial hair by giving the worker a few days' growth of beard as well. Both Saba and Samperi prominently feature Ernesto's visit to the barber precisely because it reflects upon this outdated homosexual dynamic. When the barber detects peach fuzz on Ernesto's face, he pronounces him a "man" and lathers him up to shave him. Ernesto abruptly departs, washing off the lather in the laundry to indicate his refusal to participate in an arbitrary sexual power dynamic that obtusely manages to equate facial hair with role-play in anal eroticism.

At the concert hall Samperi places Ernesto in a box high above Ilio, immediately establishing an unequal visual power dynamic between them. When he meets Ilio, Ernesto phallically taps him on the shoulder with his walking stick, exaggerates their nominal age difference, and pretentiously assumes the *erastes* role. Conversely, he projects the *eromenos* role onto an Ilio of inferior talent, casting him in the servile position of page-turner in his fantasy about being a concert violinist. Ilio's looks inspire Ernesto with a desire for object possession, replicating his relationship with the worker. He even repeats to Ilio the lines with which the worker initiated their illicit relationship, "Do you know what it means to be the friend of a man like me?" In contrast to Samperi, Saba's Ernesto imagines Ilio the superior violinist and remains overwhelmed by him in a manner unsuitable to the *erastes* role, "Egli non mi considererrebbe degno . . . nemmeno di rivolgergli la parola." (He wouldn't even consider me . . . worthy of telling him "hello.")[28] Saba places Ilio and Ernesto on the same level of the concert hall, minimizes their age difference, and culminates their relationship in the mutuality of handshake. Sexual historian André Béjin claims that, in contrast to the previous millennia that emphasized difference, the late twentieth century is distinguished by a sort of "democratization of sex."[29] The same-sex sexuality of lesbianism and homosexuality anatomically, if not necessarily psychologically, encourages such sexual democratization. Writing his novel half a century prior to the contemporary period and setting it a full century before, Saba's literary scandal was not merely a matter of gender preference but of discarding a relationship based on difference in favor of one based on reciprocity. His story of Ernesto and Ilio constituted a cultural and sexual revolution of modest proportions from which Samperi constructed a reactionary film.

Montaldo's Cinematic Tarnish on Bassani's
The Gold-Rimmed Spectacles

Giuliano Montaldo's 1987 film version of Giorgio Bassani's novella *The Gold-rimmed Spectacles* opens with a high overhead panning shot above the Po River. As the peasants descend to investigate what has happened, from overhead the camera slowly pulls to a tight close-up of Athos Fadigati's gold-rimmed eyeglasses barely distinguishable against the muddy riverbank. The sequence seems to suggest that superiority of position does not necessarily imply omniscience. Certain things are perceived only in close proximity. In his study of Bassani's novella, Douglas Radcliffe-Umstead notes that "[s]pace in Bassani's world shields people . . . and intimate contact bears with it the danger of betrayal."[30] As the mediating consciousness in the story of the middle-aged physician Athos Fadigati and the young boxer Eraldo Deliliers, Bassani's fictive narrator provides a balance between the ostensible omniscience of third-person hindsight and the insight made possible only through the dangerous intimacy of direct interaction. Radcliffe-Umstead has characterized "the narrator . . . as both observer and experiential center for filtering the hero's movement."[31] In film the camera provides this filter, this balance between omniscience and subjectivity that renders Bassani's fictive narrator narratively, if not thematically, redundant. To compensate, Montaldo and fellow screenwriters Nicola Badalucco and Antonella Grassi invented a life for Bassani's narrator that far exceeds his cerebral ruminations in the novella. By dubbing the narrator "Davide," Montaldo individualizes him, abdicating the omniscience inherent in the narrator's anonymity and replacing it with the ostensible anonymity and potential omniscience of his camera. The film can thus contain a number of scenes between Fadigati and Deliliers in which the narrator is not present. By doing this Montaldo can effectively enter the closet of this transgressive relationship.

But Montaldo does not take full advantage of this opportunity. In fact, this rather pedestrian film participates in the same complacent conformity that Bassani attacks in his work. Critical reviews of the film praising its "tact," "discretion," and "delicacy" mark this film as a cinema of evasion, at least as far as homosexuality is concerned.[32] Other critics faulted the film's "sumptuous televisual cadences" and "its concessions to the less than lofty demands of the marketplace."[33] Like television, Montaldo's film accommodated broad demographics, a sort of tyranny of the heterocentric masses. As cinema of evasion, Montaldo's film avoids the obsessive subjectification that characterized Luchino Visconti's psychological study of Aschenbach's pursuit of Tadzio in *Death in Venice*. Instead, Montaldo gravitates toward a more neutral and neutered visual treatment of Fadigati's relationship with Eraldo. Espousing an attitude of "full respect and attention as regards the love story," Montaldo reduces the entire physical relationship between doctor and boxer to a close-up of Fadigati's finger gently grazing Eraldo's hand as they picnic by the water.[34] The moment recreates Michelangelo's *Creation of Adam*, an image whose elevated spiritual connotations risk evacuating its homoerotic content, unless the painter's own sexual history is taken into consideration. After this inhibited moment, Montaldo redeems the heterocentrist sensibility of his film by cutting to Carlotta as she accosts a sleeping Davide on the beach with a playful embrace.

Montaldo asserted, "There are no sex scenes, not because of a sense of shame, but because there was no need for them."[35] This statement is disingenuous. In a film based upon a story about a homosexual relationship,

Montaldo includes a three-minute long, explicitly nude love scene between stars Valeria Golino and Rupert Everett. Shot in the heated red chiaroscuro of a fireplace that throws their intertwined bodies into high relief, this scene contains the most extensive shared close-up and shot-countershot close-up sequences in the film. As such, the scene constitutes a blatant heterocentrist attempt to compensate for the original narrative's homosexual subject matter. Beginning with an intimate shared close-up of his stars, Montaldo teasingly pans their writhing torsos. He then foregrounds Golino's breasts as Everett (ironically a gay icon in his own right) kisses them, culminating in a shot of Golino's face in ecstasy. The placement of this scene within the overall structure of the screenplay proves particularly symptomatic, situated between a scene wherein Fadigati sees Eraldo naked in the shower and another wherein the boxer drives an Alfa Romeo convertible, a gift from the doctor. The screenplay thus deflects the nascent homosexual relationship between Fadigati and Eraldo into a heterosexual love scene between Davide and his invented girlfriend, Nora.

The cinematic addition of Nora to Bassani's original narrative does provide thematic benefits, however, as it highlights the function of the closet and the politics of passing. In one scene the Jewish Nora contemplates the foresight of her father in not naming her "Sara or Judith or Esther." Examining her features in the distorted reflection of a platter, she notes, "You couldn't exactly say I have an Aryan profile." Upon the death of her father, Nora forsakes both Davide and her Jewish heritage, marrying a local fascist dignitary, ingratiating herself into Ferrarese society, and even converting to Catholicism, all in an effort to "pass" for Aryan. She confronts Davide with her imminent baptism on a cold, dark night in an isolated piazza before a church. The ominous mise-en-scène foreshadows the failure of her attempt to pass, as Montaldo's closing titles inform us that Nora died in childbirth, as her Jewish womb refused to nurture the fascist Aryan seed. Nora's effort to closet her Jewish heritage reverses the process of Fadigati's own tentative steps outside the closet. Both characters must negotiate this issue of closeting the self or passing as other. The self-negation of Nora's baptism finds its corollary in Fadigati's own suicide in the river.

The closet constitutes a patriarchal strategy of containment of limited permissiveness. Radcliffe-Umstead assesses Fadigati's closeted existence in the displacement of the doctor's sexual drives into a diluted hedonism. Taste, sound, and smell attempt to compensate for the deprivation of the sense of touch so integral in actual participatory sexual experience:

> Dr. Fadigati longs to construct a private enclosure for powerful aesthetic and sensual stimulation in life. His profession as a medical specialist for the

ear, nose and throat indicates his concern for those parts of the body most responsible for sense stimulation. . . . An individual attempting to mask homosexual inclinations has to find other outlets for his passionate receptivity to physical stimulation. Thus, the repressed Fadigati responds with a Gidean disponibilité to . . . olfactory experiences. . . . Music more than any other art arouses the physician's hyperrefined sensitivity to beauty.[36]

In stark contrast to Visconti's use of Mahler in *Death in Venice*, Montaldo fails to exploit his protagonist's affinity for music in either the film's score or its subject matter. Fadigati listens to an opera recording in only one scene, describing the soaring soprano voice as "sublime," a telling word given its function in sublimating his repressed sexuality. Wayne Koestenbaum has assessed the appeal of opera to the repressed homosexual, noting that "[opera] portrays masochisms, abjections and fulfillments that sober art won't risk."[37] The locus of his sexual repression, opera constitutes a sort of masochism for Fadigati. In Bassani's novella the doctor characterizes a Florentine production of Wagner's *Tristan and Isolde* as "un lungo lamento d'amore" (a long lament of love) leading to an inevitable "notte . . . eterna" (eternal night) of death.[38] As an ear, nose, and throat specialist, Fadigati attends to those parts of the anatomy involved in creating the masochistic sublimations of opera. Koestenbaum illuminates yet another provocative dimension to the repressed sexuality inherent in Fadigati's profession: "The throat, for gay men, is problematized: zone of fellatio, alterior eroticism, nongenitality."[39] In Bassani's novella Deliliers asks the throat doctor to accompany him to the toilet on the train to examine his crotch, an explicit allusion to fellatio made in the presence of the other students. As both physician and homosexual, Montaldo's Fadigati confides to Davide that he thinks of cigarettes primarily in terms of the damage that they cause the throat. When Fadigati first smokes at Eraldo's insistence, he breaks out into a hoarse cough.

For Fadigati the closet entails not only sublimation but also invisibility, the very "hiding of one's self" that Nora advises Davide to pursue. In the novella, Fadigati hides himself among the riffraff of the platea at movie theatres rather than sitting with his own class in the gallery. The narrator speaks of the Ferrarese looking for "il tipico luccichio che i suoi occhiali d'oro mandavano ogni tanto attraverso il fumo e l'oscurità" (the particular glimmer that his eyeglasses gave off every so often through the smoke and darkness).[40] The gold-rimmed eyeglasses serve as Fadigati's synecdochal marker, revealing his presence even as he attempts to remain invisible during his nocturnal escapades. As the standard-bearer of Ferrarese petty bourgeois bigotry, Signora Lavezzoli claims to fault not Fadigati's homosexuality but its exhibitionism. In "Visual Pleasure and Narrative

Cinema" Laura Mulvey asserts, "[T]he male figure cannot bear the burden of sexual objectification. Man is reluctant to gaze at his exhibitionist like."[41] Despite Mulvey's heterocentrist conclusion, the politics of the gaze among men proves fully operational in a film with a homosexual narrative. When Eraldo is first seen in the gym, it is as an object of desire from Fadigati's point of view. The voyeuristic alienation of the moment is emphasized by Montaldo's use of the long shot—Montaldo repeatedly avoids more empathetic psychological close up shots—and by the window panes separating Fadigati from the world of male bonding in the gym. The last time Eraldo appears in the film, it is again as object of the gaze from Fadigati's point of view and again through a window, the window of a café, with Fadigati once more out in the cold. Throughout the film Eraldo, played by an Adonis-like Nicola Farron, functions as object of the gaze. He recurrently appears dishabillé—shirtless in bed, in boxing shorts at the gym—but always from a "discreet" distance. More comfortable with his exhibitionism than Montaldo's camera is with its voyeurism, Eraldo defies Mulvey and tells Davide bluntly, "I like to be watched."

While Fadigati displaces sexuality into the sound, smell, and taste of the ear, nose, and throat, Eraldo's exhibitionism displaces his sexuality into the politics of vision and his avocation as boxer allows him to revel in the direct physical contact of the sense of touch. Eraldo thus functions as Fadigati's complement since sight and touch are the two senses that the doctor's occupation does not address. Montaldo's Eraldo describes boxing in subliminally homosexual terms: "It forces men to know each other in a few minutes without talking. . . . They beat each other to pieces without mercy, and then they embrace." This description echoes Pronger's discussion of the easy slippage between orthodoxy and heterodoxy in such physically charged performances of masculinity. Pronger notes: "In both well-matched sports and homoerotic fucking, masculine power meets masculine power; men play with each other's masculinity, paradoxically probing the places where masculinity can be undermined, painstakingly bringing each other to the edge of masculine dissolution . . . competitive athletes are actually erotic accomplices."[42]

Eraldo's school companion uses English to call boxing a "noble art" in a mincing voice accompanied by a limp-wristed gesture. Through its punching and bloodletting, boxing recreates the "bloody wounds" of the imaginary castration of the female, metaphorically vaginalizing the males in the ring. The hypermasculine performance of what Pronger calls the "stylized aggression" of the sport attempts to erase this textual effeminization of the male, but its subtext remains. Male bonding through violence is still male bonding. Inviting Fadigati to watch him box, the exhibitionist Eraldo metaphorically bids the doctor to watch him have sex with his "erotic accomplice," his challenger. Montaldo again fails to exploit the homoerotic potential of the scene, keeping his camera at an uninvolved distance, failing to suture his audience to the subjectivity of either Eraldo or Fadigati. Only when Eraldo is finally declared champion does Montaldo cut to Fadigati's point of view. The doctor again remains separated from his object of desire, this time by the ropes of the boxing ring. Here Montaldo's film recalls Visconti's *Rocco and His Brothers* as Fadigati follows Eraldo downstairs to congratulate him and discovers the boxer at the turn of a corner fully nude in the shower. The moment lacks the invasive proximity Visconti had used in his corresponding scene, but Montaldo's more distant camera does present the integral male nude that Visconti could not show a generation before. The naked Eraldo confirms his exhibitionism by receiving Fadigati's gaze with a smile.

In the film Fadigati naively claims that he and Eraldo "always shared everything," but Montaldo's shooting style says otherwise. The cinematic correlative of such "sharing" is the close two-shot or the shot-countershot formation of the mutual gaze. Such a method of shooting constitutes a sort of visual egalitarianism freed from the alienating power dynamics of classic voyeurism. While the flabby body of Philippe Noiret as Fadigati can hardly function as object of the desiring gaze, greater use of subjective camera and shot-countershots could have increased audience empathy for the twosome.[43] When Fadigati and Eraldo are out upon the water in a rowboat, Montaldo fails to suture his camera to the "languid looks" that Signora Lavezzoli describes between physician and boxer. Instead, he quite literally prefers the fascist point of view, taking his shot instead from Signora Lavezzoli's predatory and policing gaze. The double iris of her binoculars underscores this alienated and alienating third-person subjectivity. The first shot-countershot between Fadigati and Eraldo occurs on the train and stresses oddity over intimacy. Lying down on the luggage rack above Fadigati, Eraldo leans over into a shared gaze, his upside-down face playing upon the Freudian concept of homosexuality as inversion. Fusing a homoerotic tease with the psychosexual demands of hypermasculinity, Eraldo first gets a light for his cigarette, then blows the smoke and its phallic implications in Fadigati's face.

In contrast to the affluent Fadigati, Eraldo's lower class status prevents him from negotiating a place in Ferrarese society. Montaldo's film creates a hierarchy of vehicles, finding Eraldo without a bicycle so that he must catch a ride to the train station from a girl willing to pedal his extra weight. Fadigati passes through this group of youths in a car, foreshadowing his purchase of the Alfa Romeo convertible for Eraldo. The gift catapults Eraldo on the vehicle hierarchy past his bike-owning contemporaries even as his dress propels him from the adolescence of hand-me-down winter

knickers to the adult affluence of designer summer linens. After all, Eraldo
is a student, an alumnus in Latin. The ancient Roman role of alumnus,
to whom "paying court meant naming a figure," rendered services for
material remuneration.[44] This alumnus role places Eraldo in an untenable
subordinate position, subject to his benefactor, surrogate patriarch, and
potential ravisher.

Mario Mieli has claimed that the Italian male prostitute
who murdered Pier Paolo Pasolini "soddisfaceva i suoi bisogni sessuali
facendosi pagare, dando così una giustificazione economica alla sua froci-
aggine" (satisfied his sexual needs by getting paid, thereby economically
rationalizing his own homosexual behavior).[45] Fadigati paradoxically
rescues Eraldo from financial impotence only to implicate him in the symbolic castration of a homosexual relationship. When fiscal compensation
fails Eraldo as phallic compensation, he punches Fadigati in an overdetermined social display of hypermasculinity. Mieli's assessment of the psychosexual dynamics of the murder of film director Pier Paolo Pasolini at
the hands of a male prostitute proves eerily appropriate to the situation in
Bassani. Mieli notes, "Picchiando, punendo Pasolini il ragazzo era con-
vinto inconsciamente di punire e ricacciare indietro la sua omosessualità."
(Hitting his client, the boy remained unconsciously convinced that he was
punishing and chasing away his own homosexuality.)[46] As in the ring, the
fist attempts to phallicize the self by metaphorically vaginalizing and
diminishing the other. In the novella Deliliers "lasciò cadere su Fadigati, di
traverso, un'occhiata di disprezzo" (looked upon Fadigati with disgust)
and "lo guardò come si guarda uno scarafaggio" (scrutinized him as one
would a cockroach).[47]

Sexual historian Paul Veyne notes that traditionally in Mediterranean
societies "the passive homosexual was not judged for his homosexuality,
but for his passivity."[48] In such a configuration the passive male functions
as faux female. Eraldo's recurrent recumbent positions and his financial
impotency as recipient of gifts bespeak a passivity that he must remedy
through a hyperaggressive social display of violence. Still, ironically, it is in
the traditionally feminine role as object of the gaze that his "corpo da
statua greca" (body of a Greek statue)[49] comes to represent the fascist ideal
of "perfected (politicized) erotic power"[50] admired "dalla maggior parte
degli astanti, dagli uomini come dalle donne" (by the majority of those in
attendance, both male and female).[51] As object of the gaze, Eraldo proves
himself neither passive nor controlled but rather active and controlling,
driving the car, rowing the boat, and punching Fadigati. While Eraldo
ascends as power icon, Fadigati becomes the Girardian scapegoat of
Ferrarese repression and intolerance toward alterity. Eraldo renders
Fadigati the sexually "passive" pariah, while the hypermasculine fascist
patriarchy accepts his violence as a substitute for dubious sexual preference.

Opposed to the mutuality of homosexual relations espoused by Fadigati and sought by Saba's Ernesto, Deliliers defends hierarchical difference with a vengeance. Bassani's narrator even defines Delilier and Fadigati as "uno carnefice, l'altro vittima" (executioner and victim).[52] As victor in a fascist gender game whose only morality is power, Eraldo goes unpunished for his crime. Montaldo's dialogue replicates Bassani's text:

Davide: Why don't you report him to the police?
Fadigati: Report him? Do you really think that is possible?[53]

Near the end of the novella Nino receives a letter from Deliliers from a nearby town, where he is now "alle costole di qualche nuovo facoltoso finocchio" (on the arm of another fag).[54] Deliliers' virulent homophobia merely affirms his latency. Such an internal struggle between homosexual and homophobe, self and other, ego and alter ego, personal and public finds its cinematic correlative in the mirror shot. Outside the restaurant Eraldo and Fadigati participate in one of the most visually peculiar moments in the film, standing before an unlikely outdoor mirror. Neither notices his reflection, although both the characters and their reflected images appear in full view. The scene reveals the simultaneity of the ego and alter ego in the public space of an open street, which demands that their more socially conscious personae be in charge. When Eraldo punches Fadigati, he breaks only one lens of the doctor's gold-rimmed eyeglasses, shown in close-up in the film. The two lenses argue for a duality of vision, that of the self and the other, the ego and the alter ego, the open homosexual and the closeted homophobe. When the glasses are broken, the vision of the open homosexual is impaired. From this point on in the film Fadigati sees only through the lens of his internalized homophobia. It is, after all, not his homosexuality but his acquiescence to the fascist Ferrarese value system that condemns him to suicide. He tells the narrator: "Dopo ciò che è accaduto l'estate scorsa non mi riesce più di tollerarmi . . . certe volte non sopporto di farmi la barba davanti allo specchio." (After what happened last summer, I can no longer tolerate myself . . . sometimes I cannot even shave in front of the mirror.)[55] Fadigati can no longer accept the mirror image of his outed homosexuality but neither can he return to the invisibility of the closet. In its virtually invisible treatment of homosexual intimacy, Montaldo's "discreet and delicate" film is impaired by the same suffocating strategy of the closet that Bassani's novella indicts in Ferrara in the death of Fadigati.

Conclusions

Vittorio De Sica's *Umberto D.* (1952) concludes with its isolated protagonist looking for the dog that has been his only point of connection, his only source of affection, throughout the film. This poignant metaphor of loss prompts Gilberto Perez to argue, "No other work so chillingly conveys the mood of suicide."[56] Montaldo's *The Gold-Rimmed Spectacles* visually echoes De Sica's masterpiece when Fadigati searches for the lost dog that once befriended him and has now abandoned him. This intertextual connection with De Sica's work further alludes to Fadigati's own "mood of suicide." Montaldo's film and Bassani's novella thus conform to the heterosexually determined paradigm whereby homosexuality is considered an unlivable condition. Russo even concludes his landmark study *The Celluloid Closet* with a necrology of 39 homosexual characters from major films who die ideologically predictable—but often narratively bizarre—deaths. Fully a third of these commit suicide, and only one survives to die of old age.[57] In essence, in traditional cinema "the only good homosexual is a dead homosexual."

In contrast, Saba's Ernesto refuses to participate in such a homophobic wish-fulfillment fantasy. While he knows early on that his sexual relations with the worker require secrecy, he remains relatively unaware of the acutely transgressive nature of his actions until his uncle Giovanni discusses the scandal of a local member of parliament whose homosexual liaisons were discovered. His uncle asserts the patriarchal imperative: " 'Ad un uomo che abbia fatto di quelle cose, non resta più che spararsi un colpo di revolver.' " ("Nothing remains for a man who had done such things but to shoot himself with a revolver.")[58] Perhaps in part because he has grown up without an actual father, Saba's Ernesto has managed to construct himself an identity somewhat outside patriarchy or maybe he just has more sense. In any case, as Saba informs us, "ad Ernesto piaceva (allora) vivere, e non aveva nessuna voglia di spararsi per così poco." (Ernesto liked living, and had absolutely no desire to shoot himself over so little.)[59]

William Van Watson is a Visiting Assistant Professor of Italian at the University of Arizona, Tucson. He has taught at universities in Italy, Portugal, and the United States and guest-lectured in Ireland and France. His publications include the book *Pier Paolo Pasolini and the Theatre of the Word;* chapters in anthologies on William Shakespeare, Luchino Visconti, and Federico Fellini; and a variety of articles on theater, film, and MTV in such journals as *Romance Languages Annual, Il Veltro, Semicerchio, Theatre Journal, Annali d'Italianistica, Theatre InSight,* and *Literature Film Quarterly.*

Notes

1. Pier Paolo Pasolini, *Calderòn* (Milan: Garzanti, 1973), p. 31. All English translations are my own unless otherwise indicated.

2. Umberto Saba, *Ernesto* (Turin: Einaudi, 1975), p. 151. This edition of the novel contains a selection of letters written by Saba to his friends and daughter about the work.

3. Ibid., p. 142.

4. Costanzo Costantini, "Fra due veggenti," *Il Messaggero*, 4 March 1979. Newspaper reviews cited herein were consulted at the library of the Centro Sperimentale Cinematografico in Rome. While the library diligently collects such reviews, it fails to include their page numbers; thus the page numbers are mostly missing here as well.

5. Saba, p. 145.

6. Saba returned to this clinic repeatedly throughout his life, particularly in his later years. His daughter Lina explained, "In the clinic he felt protected because he could filter his interpersonal relationships"; see Costantini.

7. Saba, p. 141.

8. Ibid., p. 149.

9. Costantini. For more on Saba's reluctance to publish *Ernesto*, see Parussa in this volume, especially note 3.

10. C. C., "Ernesto, ovvero una casta storia scandalosa," *Paese Sera*, 3 March 1979.

11. Saba, back jacket cover.

12. Ibid., p. 9.

13. Umberto Silva, "Indovina che c'è sotto," *Il Messaggero*, 11 February 1979.

14. Tullio Kezich, "Peccati di un adolescente in una città fine Ottocento," *La Reppublica*, 9 February 1979.

15. Saba, p. 129.

16. No Author, "I traumi di Ernesto ragazzo 'pagano,'" *Corriere della Sera*, 2 September 1978.

17. Saba, p. 136.

18. Roberto Ellero, "Ancora la sconfitta protagonista di un film diretto da Samperi," *Il Messaggero*, 1 September 1978.

19. Saba, p. 61.

20. Vito Russo, *The Celluloid Closet* (New York: Harper and Row, 1987), p. 268.

21. Ellero.

22. Alberto Moravia, "La metà del signor Ernesto," *Espresso*, 11 February 1979, p. 82.

23. Saba, p. 161.

24. Dante Matelli, "Un amore, una stretta di mano e un matrimonio senza qualità," *La Reppublica*, 8 February 1978.

25. See Robert Aldrich, *The Seduction of the Mediterranean: Writing, Art, and Homosexual Fantasy* (New York: Routledge, 1993), pp. 15–20.

26. Brian Pronger, *The Arena of Masculinity: Sports, Homosexuality and the Meaning of Sex* (New York: St. Martin's Press, 1990), p. 135.

27. Saba, p. 30.

28. Ibid., p. 128.

29. See André Béjin, "The Influence of Sexologists and Sexual Democracy," in: *Western Sexuality: Practice and Precept in Past and Present Times*, eds. Philippe Ariès and André Béjin (New York: Basil Blackwell, 1987), pp. 201–17.

30. Doulgas Radcliffe-Umstead, *The Exile into Eternity: A Study of the Narrative Writings of Giorgio Bassani* (Toronto: Associated University Presses, 1987), p. 81.

31. Ibid., p. 77.
32. G. L. R., "Gli occhiali d'oro," *Il Tempo*, 27 September 1987; No Author, *L'Eco di Bergamo*, 21 October 1987.
33. S. R., "Noiret si perde per amore," *La Stampa*, 3 October 1987, 16; M. M., "Gli occhiali d'oro," *Oggi*, 10 October 1987.
34. Interview with Anna Maria Mori, "Una storia d'amore vissuta con paura," *La Reppublica*, 9 March 1987, p. 23.
35. Interview with Giuseppina Manin, "Incontri al Lido: il cast de 'Gli occhiali d'oro,' " *Corriere della Sera*, 4 October 1987.
36. Radcliffe-Umstead, pp. 79–80.
37. Wayne Koestenbaum, *The Queen's Throat: Opera, Homosexuality and the Mystery of Desire* (New York: Poseidon Press, 1993), pp. 220–21.
38. Giorgio Bassani, *Il Romanzo di Ferrara* (Milan: Mondadori Editore, 1980), p. 176.
39. Wayne Koestenbaum "The Queen's Throat: (Homo)sexuality and the Art of Singing," in: *Inside/Out: Lesbian Theories/Queer Theories*, ed. Diana Fuss (New York: Routledge, 1991), pp. 205–34; quotation p. 207.
40. Bassani, p. 175.
41. Laura Mulvey, "Visual Pleasure and Narrative Cinema," in: *Film Theory and Criticism*, eds. Gerald Mast and Marshall Cohen (New York: Oxford University Press, 1992), pp. 746–57; quotation p. 751.
42. Pronger, p. 181.
43. In stark contrast Montaldo seems to encounter no problem whatsoever in using more intimate shooting strategies for the asexual relationship between Fadigati and David, who alternate numerous close-ups in their shared scenes.
44. Paul Veyne, "Homosexuality in Ancient Rome," in: *Western Sexuality: Practice and Precept in Past and Present Times*, eds. Philippe Ariès and André Béjin (New York: Basil Blackwell, 1987), pp. 26–35; quotation p. 33.
45. Mario Mieli, *Elementi di critica omosessuale* (Turin: Einaudi, 1977), p. 153.
46. Ibid., p. 153.
47. Bassani, pp. 189, 193.
48. Veyne, p. 30.
49. Bassani, p. 192.
50. Marilyn Schneider, *Vengeance of the Victim: History and Symbol in Giorgio Bassani's Fiction* (Minneapolis: University of Minnesota Press, 1986), p. 95.
51. Bassani, p. 198.
52. Ibid., p. 234.
53. Ibid., p. 220.
54. Ibid., p. 225.
55. Ibid., p. 234.
56. Gilberto Perez, "*Umberto D.* and Realism," in: *Vittorio De Sica: Contemporary Perspectives*, eds. Howard Curle and Stephen Snyder (Toronto: University of Toronto Press, 2000), pp. 77–80; quotation p. 79.
57. Russo, pp. 347–49.
58. Saba, p. 113.
59. Ibid., p. 100.

10

Reluctantly Queer: In Search of the Homoerotic Novel in Twentieth-Century Italian Fiction

Sergio Parussa

When at the beginning of *Sodome et Gomorrhe* the narrator places himself on the staircase of the Hôtel de Guermantes, peers through the shutters, and witnesses M. de Charlus' encounter with Jupien, his distant and critical look begins to construct, before the reader's very eyes, one of the first fully developed gay characters in Western literature. In 1921 when Proust's novel was first published, homoeroticism was not a new narrative subject. Indeed, it had been a favorite theme of the late nineteenth-century aesthetic sensibility. Nonetheless, in writing *Sodome et Gomorrhe* Proust ventures into a new literary land: Not only does he tackle homoeroticism in an artistic form as had been done before, but he makes it the thematic center of a bourgeois novel. *Sodome et Gomorrhe*, unlike most novels published earlier, is not an erotic biography in disguise, nor is it a fictionalized account of a young man's erotic apprenticeship characterized by the expression of an idealized and asocial homoerotic desire. Rather, it is precisely through a nonidealized treatment of homoeroticism—by placing it within a social milieu, within the frame of a bourgeois novel—that Proust makes it the center of the narrative. In providing M. de Charlus with a name and a social background, with thoughts and emotions, Proust's novel undertakes the social construction of the homoerotic self and begins to acknowledge its existence as a social subject.

Nothing of the kind happens in Italian literature between the end of the nineteenth and the beginning of the twentieth century. Until very recently,

Italian literature has lacked a homoerotic novel.[1] Only after the Second World War did Italian novelists begin to create characters comparable to M. de Charlus, such as Doctor Fadigati in Giorgio Bassani's *The Gold-Rimmed Spectacles* (1958). Nonetheless, during the first half of the twentieth century some Italian writers—in an attempt to make of homoeroticism a subject suitable for the novel—created unusual narrative forms, a set of lyrical prose works that constitute a deviation from the narrative norm. With the term "deviation" I refer not so much to the presence of homoeroticism as a literary subject as to the consequences that such a presence has at the formal level. In these texts the fundamental structures of the traditional bourgeois novel—character, setting, plot—are changed, as if the very presence of a homoerotic subject modified the act of writing and altered the boundaries between literary genres. In other words, these texts do not belong to the genre of the bourgeois novel but constitute a marginal and scattered tradition, almost a separate alternative genre. The texts I will discuss in this article include prose works by Italian writers during the first half of the twentieth century or shortly thereafter: Pier Paolo Pasolini's early novels *Amado mio* (1947–1950), *Atti impuri* (1947–1950), and *Romàns;* Filippo De Pisis's notebooks and literary sketches, in particular *Ver-Vert;* Giovanni Comisso's *Gioco d'infanzia* (1931–1932); and Umberto Saba's *Ernesto* (1953).[2]

To begin, I should say that most of these texts were left unfinished, kept in drawers, or published only posthumously as if, among their authors, there was a certain reluctance to treat homoeroticism as a narrative subject. Such reluctance could be an effect of self-censorship, which seems to underlie all the arguments put forward by Umberto Saba to justify his inability to conclude and publish his homoerotic novel *Ernesto* (such as its supposedly difficult language).[3] On the other hand, self-censorship provides only a partial explanation. The fact that these texts were left unfinished also bespeaks of an inability to formally reconcile the novel as a genre with a certain kind of homoerotic inspiration. Pasolini's *Atti impuri, Amado mio,* and *Romàns,* as well as De Pisis's *Ver-Vert* and Saba's *Ernesto* are all failed attempts at writing novels of homoerotic content. Their inspiration—the lyrical representation of an ideal of male beauty and youth—seems to undermine the very foundations of the traditional bourgeois novel: character, setting, and plot.

These prose works are constructed around narrative figures that lack the social and psychological complexity of traditional characters and have, instead, the static, conventional quality of types. They are endowed with a limited number of physical and psychological traits that represent the extremes of a specific quality—innocence or guilt, purity or corruption, virility or femininity—and that tend to remain identical throughout the entire narrative. Consequently all the characters look alike, as if they were symbolic representations of an abstract quality, emblems of eros. They are repetitions of an idea of male beauty, projections and embodiments of the male homoerotic desire that inspires and shapes all these narratives. The treatment of onomastics provides evidence for this claim. Literary proper names often suggest character traits and can contain a reference to a character's narrative function. *Fosca* anticipates the dark and gloomy temperament of Tarchetti's heroine; Manzoni's *Lucia* evokes a pure and shining example of goodness; *Beatrice* refers to the heavenly beatitude that awaits Dante, just as *Laura* envisions the literary glory that Petrarca expects from his poetry. In our texts, this literary practice is taken to extremes as correspondence between name and narrative function is univocal. In Pasolini's *Atti impuri, Bruno* announces a dark-haired boy bearing a dark passion as *Desiderio* signals the character's exclusive narrative function as desiring subject. Similarly, in De Pisis's *Ver-Vert, Narciso* signifies nothing but the character's erotic quest for a beautiful youth in which to mirror himself. In both texts, proper names simplify and reduce the potential complexity of character to an erotic function. Names are not used to complement personality or to specify social or psychological realms; rather, they function to make explicit and exclusive reference to physical or moral qualities that the character represents.

This becomes even clearer when we note that characters in these works are very rarely designated with proper first names, which are often replaced by common nouns, nicknames, literary pseudonyms, or simple epithets that refer to some trait, often external, that exhausts the character's narrative role. Instead of Charlus and Jupien, Aschenbach and Tadzio, Lord Henry and Dorian Gray, readers encounter "fanciulli," "giovani," or "marinai" (boys, young boys, or sailor boys). As in antonomasia a proper name is substituted by a common noun in order to emphasize one specific quality, so in our texts a character's first name is replaced by an epithet to express just the specific quality that the character is called to represent. In *Ver-Vert*, De Pisis tells the erotic adventures of a character named Filippo. Most of the young and beautiful men that Filippo meets are referred to with epithets that describe only their erotic appeal, such as "le jeune Arabe" (the young Arab), "il bel dio bianco" (the beautiful white god), "il giovane soldato" (the young soldier). Similarly, and still antonomastically, a proper name is sometimes used to make reference to a general idea of male beauty and youth. Young and beautiful as an Endimione or San Giovanni by Donatello, De Pisis's characters are often referenced artistically by comparison to figures from paintings.[4]

Pasolini's works provide a wide range of examples for this process of denomination. In both his poetry and prose, first names, epithets, and nicknames often refer to characters' physical attractiveness as well as the state of physical and psychological innocence that most of them inhabit. In Pasolini's poetry, appellatives both in Friulan dialect (*nini, ninìns, fantàsut, fi, frut, frutìns, zòvin, zovinùt*) and in Italian (*giovinetto, giovanetto, fanciullo, fanciulletto, piccolino*) are used to describe beautiful young boys whose anonymity signals the lack of an inner life, of a conscience. Similarly, literary pseudonyms characterize Pasolini's early homoerotic novels. At the beginning of *Amado mio*, Desiderio spots a boy in the crowd at a country festival, Benito, and takes an immediate liking to him. When Benito vanishes from sight, the narrator comments: "Iasìs se n'era andato col suo nome ancora ignoto, né Benito, né Sardanapalo . . . e nemmeno Giuseppe, o Bepi, come la sua maglia voleva." (Iasìs had disappeared with his name still unknown, neither Benito, nor Sardanapalo . . . nor Giuseppe, nor Bepi, as his sweater suggested.)[5] It matters little whether his name is Benito, Giuseppe, or Bepi (as suggested by his provincial striped sweater): The narrator assigns a literary pseudonym, a nickname that endows him with the innocence of a Cavafy youth or the lust of a Dantean king.[6] These are precisely the two types of beauty that Pasolini's characters represent: pure, innocent ephebus and corrupted sensual youth. The name *Iasìs* alludes to the arcadian innocence of a young shepherd; *Sardanapalo* and *Bruno* in *Atti impuri* hint at excess and the obscurity of the erotic desire they excite.

The character Nisiuti in *Atti impuri* is no exception. Although he is one of the most developed of Pasolini's characters, he remains a type, the embodiment of the Greek ephebus, the hundredth personification of innocent but sensual youth. Such a type also signals the lyrical tone of this prose and the narcissistic quality of its homoerotic inspiration: lyrical prose that gives voice to an erotic search for identity by praising youth and beauty. In a passage from *Atti impuri*, the narrator wonders whether the young boy's erotic fantasies are inspired by an idealized image of himself, whether he evokes—as Narcissus before a sheet of water—his own image, that is, the image of an anonymous, divine boy as abstract as a transcendent Platonic Idea: "Probabilmente Nisiuti dopo cenato non si concedeva mai quei minuti d'ozio, dove creare, tra luce e ombra una sua immagine, divinamente anonima, di giovinetto." (After dinner, Nisiuti probably never allowed himself those moments of leisure where he might create, between light and shadow, a divinely anonymous image of himself as youth.)[7]

Thus these boys are not real characters, but variations on the theme of the *Giovinetto*, anonymous embodiments of an ideal preexisting beauty:

E Iasìs non era nemmeno più una persona: era il Giovinetto. . . . E davanti al Giovinetto che è senza volto e tutto corpo, tutto bellezza non esistono più freni. . . . Se poi egli, il Giovinetto anonimo dei canti anonimi, aveva trovato un corpo in quello di Iasìs, allora . . .

And Iasìs wasn't even a person anymore: he was Youth. . . . And before Youth—without a face, all body, all beauty—there are no restraints. . . . If then he, the anonymous Youth of anonymous songs, had found a body in Iasìs' body, well then . . .[8]

Ora questa maglia [Iasìs by metonymy] . . . non era che una variante, infatti se ne vedeva accanto una gemella.

Now, this sweater . . . was nothing but a variation; in fact, you could see an identical one next to it.[9]

The narrative even classifies boys according to their appearance—fair or dark, innocent or corrupt—in a significant correspondence between sensible phenomena and moral truth:

Armando rideva: apparteneva al tipo bruno di Caorle, con la testa grossa, la bocca carnosa . . . un vero selvaggio.

Armando was laughing: he belonged to the dark-haired type of Caorle, with a big head and thick lips . . . a true savage.[10]

Quei due rappresentavano, contrastando con singolare evidenza, le due diverse razze di Caorle: uno biondo, coi capelli a raggera doratissimi, il profilo corto, il viso già un poco deliziosamente rugoso; l'altro bruno, il capo grosso, la bocca rotonda e mal disegnata.

In striking contrast, those two represented the two races of Caorle: one blond, with a golden halo of hair, short profile, and an already slightly wrinkled yet delicious face, the other dark, with a big head and round, misshapen mouth.[11]

Finally, although different, all the boys are brought together by a noumenal collective eros of which they are the sensible phenomena:

Era quella doratura fallica che uno straniero come Desiderio annusa in ogni minimo fatto dei luoghi sconosciuti, quell'eros indigeno, collettivo, e quasi folcloristico, che si spezza e si rifrange come in prisma nella folla di ignoti vestiti a festa.

It was that phallic gilding that a foreigner like Desiderio could sniff out in every little corner of those unknown places; the native, collective, almost folkloristic eros that breaks up and refracts as in a prism amidst the crowd of strangers in their Sunday best.[12]

Setting and plot are treated similarly. If characters are reduced to types, settings become mere backdrops, and plots tend to repeat the pattern of erotic quest. The traditional setting of the bourgeois novel—the solid social background against which characters stand out and define their individuality—is either absent or dissolved into its very opposite, in settings that are the very negation of bourgeois society: Arcadian villages, urban outskirts, or exotic islands.

Similarly, events do not unfold according to a traditional narrative model. Even though the plot (*intreccio*) is sometimes very complex, the story (*fabula*) is reduced to its minimal elements. There is no progress from an opening phase of disorder to a final restored order, and in the moral or social development of the character there is neither improvement nor degeneration. To make use of a simile suggested by Pasolini's own writings, one could say that in these prose works events follow one another like altar-pieces: juxtaposed repetitions of a uniform model.

Giovanni Comisso's novel *Gioco d'infanzia* offers another example of a narrative in which characters, settings, and plots are diluted as a very result of the work's homoerotic inspiration. Written between July 1931 and April 1932, *Gioco d'infanzia* was published only in 1965: yet another example of significant delay in the publication of a homoerotic novel. It tells the story of Alberto, a well-to-do 30-year-old tired of his bourgeois life, who sets out on a journey to the east: "[Alberto] voleva godere con i suoi sensi illimitatamente, ma era difficile nella piccola città dove abitava, così aveva deciso di partire per l'Oriente." ([Alberto] wanted to enjoy the life of the senses without any limitations, but that was difficult in the little town where he lived, so he decided to leave for the East.) Alberto meets other fugitives on the voyage traveling to Ceylon in search of an elsewhere that might restore authenticity to their meaningless lives. He meets Hans (a young German on his way to Bangkok where he will convert to Buddhism), a seductive and mysterious sailor, and a melancholic Italian officer. Alberto shares with his fellow travelers a strong hatred and disdain for bourgeois society and imagines a murderous alliance that would free them from their social unhappiness:

> Alberto fremeva. Anche questa gente era degna di vivere, ma la morte era stata creata per loro per trasfigurarli. Si sarebbe augurato una tempesta, un naufragio pur di vederli diversi. Giunse a immaginare un'alleanza con il marinaio e con il tedesco per massacrarli a colpi di coltello e poi fuggire insieme in una barca per approdare a una terra selvaggia, senza possibilità di vedere più gente simile.

> Alberto was shaking. Even those people's lives were worth living, but death had been created to transfigure them. He wished their ship would end up in a storm and wreck just to see them changed. He went so far as to imagine an alliance with the sailor and the German to massacre them in a flurry of

knife blows and then flee together in a boat to some wild land where they would never have to worry about seeing such people again.[13]

But this narrative seed does not germinate: Events follow one another without causality; characters remain two-dimensional and move through settings that are nothing but vanishing dreamlands. Once more it is a certain notion of eros that prevents this narrative from becoming a novel. The idea of an asocial and idealized eros, in fact, cannot translate into a novel, only into lyrical prose. Where the author of a novel might depict the struggle between the aims of the individual and the demands of society and deploy their tragic or comic interaction, these authors can only raise an erotic hymn to beauty.

Indeed, in *Gioco d'infanzia* eros is intertwined with a desire to escape society, either through flight into a wild and exotic land of sexual happiness or through the memory of an erotically happy adolescence. Eros here takes the shape of two mysterious and seductive sailors and an Arcadian shepherd. The sailors—once more anonymous characters—are described only in terms of the erotic appeal expressed by their names and bodies:

> [M]a questi due marinai svelti ad ogni movimento della manovra, dimostravano oltre ad un corpo tutto equilibrio, un'allegrezza da fare pensare che l'uno con il suo coltello alla cintola e l'altro con il berretto da marinaio messo di sghembo, fossero sodisfatti del proprio aspetto come di una mascherata.

> [C]arrying out their duties with speed and agility, these two sailors—their bodies the very picture of harmony in motion, the one with a knife hanging off his belt, the other with his jaunty cap—gave off such an air of happiness they seemed pleased with their appearance like it was some kind of masquerade.[14]

> Il marinaio con il suo sguardo chiaro e con il rosso carnoso del volto sembrava nitido come un frutto. Per Alberto questo suo aspetto era quello stesso della vita.

> The sailor with his dazzling gaze and flush sensual features was like a shiny red apple. For Alberto, this was the image of life itself.[15]

This latter passage describes Mario, a young shepherd and childhood friend who is nothing but a fleeting appearance in the narrative, but his strength, harmless brutality, and wild sexuality remain impressed in Alberto's memory:

> Un giorno era andato con Mario a pascolare le pecore. Si erano distesi sull'erba vicino a un colle dove tutte le pecore stavano sparse. Un coleottero

dalle lunghe corna era caduto accanto e subito preso, si erano messi a osservarlo. Mario gli aveva girato due volte la testa e poi aveva scommesso che avrebbe ripreso a volare ancora, ma lanciato in aria cadde sulla siepe e non fu possibile ritrovarlo. Alberto si era accorto allora delle grosse mani di Mario e si era provato con lui a chi avesse più forza. Mario gli fu sopra, i loro volti erano rimasti l'uno contro l'altro, poi si erano ammansiti a un estro di piacere dato dallo stringersi. Rotolati ai piedi di un albero, Mario gli aveva scoperto il ventre, lo aveva toccato, palpato, gli aveva detto che era già uomo, le sue mani non cessavano di toccare: un godimento mai provato prima, fino ad abbattersi disteso contro l'albero, ferito dalla dolcezza. Ma subito preso dallo sgomento, si era rialzato, indispettito contro Mario che ridendo era scappato su per il colle a ricacciare le pecore verso il pascolo.

One day he went with Mario to watch the sheep. They lay down on the grass near a hill where all the sheep were grazing. A beetle with long antennae fell nearby. They grabbed it and began to inspect it. Mario twisted the bug's head around and bet it could still fly, but when he threw it up in the air it fell into the bushes and they couldn't find it again. Then Alberto noticed Mario's big hands and challenged him to see who was stronger. Mario was on top of him in an instant, their faces pressed against each other, but then they abandoned themselves to the pleasure of their embrace. They rolled to the foot of a tree. Mario pulled up Alberto's shirt and touched him, rubbing his chest. He told him he was already a man and his hands kept on stroking: he had never felt so good. He fell against the tree wounded with pleasure. But Alberto, a bit shocked, stood up all of a sudden upset with Mario, who had run laughing up the hill to herd the sheep back to pasture.[16]

Sexual freedom and happiness—the childhood games of the title—are only possible in the lost paradise of childhood or perhaps on a mythical and mysterious eastern island. Indeed, when the ship taking Alberto to Ceylon is about to sail across the Straits of Bab el Mandeb and leave Europe, civilization, and society behind, Alberto has a sudden recollection of Mario and their childhood games:

"Lo stretto di Bab el Mandeb: l'Europa si allontana." Pensò e rivide il suo vecchio atlante scolastico, la sua scuola, i compagni di un tempo, le finestre aperte sul cielo primaverile, i giorni di vacanza in campagna sulle colline vicine alle Alpi, aveva quattordici anni, tutto il suo corpo si rivolgeva in se stesso per trasformarsi.

"The Straits of Bab el Mandeb: Europe is fading away." He began to think and called to mind his old atlas, his school, his classmates, the classroom windows opening onto a Spring sky, summer vacation in the country on Alpine hills. He was fourteen and his whole body was turning inside out transforming itself.[17]

Ricordava e vedeva . . . i colori e le forme dei sassi del torrente: bianchi, verdastri, rossi, tondi e piatti, e questi li facevano rimbalzare sulle acque e il corpo nudo di Mario, quando li lanciava, pareva potesse scattare a volo con il sasso. "Lo stretto di Bab el Mandeb." Si disse . . . e con l'imagine del corpo agile di Mario si sentì scomparire quietamente nel sonno.

He thought back and could see it all . . . the colors and shapes of the stones in the stream: white, greenish, red, round and flat, and they skipped them on the water's surface and Mario's naked body, when he was throwing them, looked like it could take off in flight with the stone. "The Straits of Bab el Mandeb." He said to himself . . . and with the image of Mario's agile body he felt himself disappearing quietly into sleep.[18]

Significantly, Alberto does not *fall*, but quietly *disappears* into his sleep. While crossing the Straits of Bab el Mandeb, while thinking of Mario and of their childhood game, Alberto's self vanishes. At the end of his journey, Alberto's homoerotic desire reveals its regressive character: It is a return to an earlier and happier period of his life and an entry into a more primitive stage of social development. Only in an Eden of eternal youth or an exotic paradise, only in an Arcadian countryside or the wild life of the Roman suburbs, only where there is an overturning of common morality is homoeroticism possible. These authors' search for an artistic mode to give expression to homoeroticism and their inability or reluctance to locate an appropriate literary form mirrors just such a utopian notion of eros. As long as the homoerotic theme remains tied to an idyll of youth and beauty, full characters cannot develop, nor real social settings, nor fully developed plots. With the passing of time, Comisso became aware of these structural limitations and on at least one occasion expressed a desire to abandon the representation of characters deprived of an inner life, of a conscience:

Sarebbe per me un tradire il mio tempo se persistessi nell'esteriore compiacenza del paesaggio con figure d'esseri come elementi di esso, non viventi per un loro mondo interiore. Sento continua un'ansia di far vivere i miei personaggi futuri con una loro coscienza che non sia più fuori di loro, sopra di loro a muoverli come a un tocco di un filo, ma dentro di loro.

It would be a waste of time for me to persist in the exterior satisfaction of a landscape populated by figures of beings as mere elements within it, and not living for their own inner world. I feel a constant anxiety to make my future characters live with a conscience of their own and not outside of them or above them—as if they were being moved by a string—but inside them.[19]

More than 50 years earlier, André Gide was probably struggling with the same formal problems and wondering how to construct a homoerotic novel that would include the core of its erotic inspiration, namely beauty and youth. On a Wednesday evening in May 1921, after paying Marcel Proust a visit, he wrote in his journal: "When I ask him if he will ever present that Eros in a young and beautiful guise, he replies that, to begin with, what attracts him is almost never beauty and that he considers it to have very little to do with desire."[20] Despite Gide's request, Proust's *Sodome* will never be peopled with young and beautiful men because for Proust desire is not necessarily linked to beauty. As for youth, continues Gide in his journal, Proust said that—in order to complete the heterosexual elements of his book—he had transposed as young women (à l'ombre des jeunes filles) "all the attractive, affectionate, and charming elements contained in his homosexual recollections."[21] In Proust's narrative universe, homoerotic desire is separated from youth and beauty, which can only be articulated in a heterosexual vocabulary. Gide could not hide his frustration: "I tell him that he seems to have wanted to stigmatize homosexuality"; "I've read Proust's latest pages . . . with, at first, a shock of indignation." In December of the same year he adds: "I do not know any writing that is more capable than Proust's *Sodome et Gomorrhe* of confirming the error of public opinion."[22]

Perhaps Pasolini, De Pisis, and Comisso would have agreed with Gide and would have expressed a similar kind of distress. However one wants to judge Proust's handling of homoerotic desire, relevant to our discourse is the fact that his remarks imply a different notion of writing. Unlike most homoerotic novels published at the turn of the century, *Sodome et Gomorrhe* is not an erotic biography. Both in its conception of desire and the art of writing, it aims for a higher degree of complexity. It is precisely through the separation of desire from beauty and youth and through their transposition into a heterosexual world that Proust makes of his work a novel and of Baron de Charlus a real character. Paradoxically, it is not through the description of youth and beauty but through the treatment of the comic and tragic aspects of desire and its claim to universality that homoeroticism finally becomes the narrative core of a novel.

Can the scattered and broken narrative tradition that we have gathered and analyzed in this article be called "queer"? If "queer" is a critical notion that embraces literary discourses on identification and desire, on how homoerotic desire can express a search for identity and provide a means of identification, then the answer is surely yes. These are, in fact, discursive practices that treat homoerotic desire as a privileged mode of identification and, as such, help construct homoeroticism in Italian culture. Their relevance becomes even clearer if we consider that literary discourse (a common language and the shared set of values implied) has been fundamental to the shaping of Italian national and cultural identity. On the other hand, because of their depiction of an asocial and idealized eros confined to the realms of beauty and youth, these narratives paradoxically thwart the construction of a social homoeroticism and homoerotic subject. With their lack of narrative structure, flat characters, asocial settings, and broken plot lines—with, in a phrase, their narrative reluctance—these unusual, incomplete, impossible novels also testify to the resistance encountered by Italian writers who would bring homoeroticism into mainstream literary discourse. This resistance has contributed, ultimately, to the delayed, contradictory, and still problematic entry of homoerotism into the more general discourse of Italian culture.

Sergio Parussa is Assistant Professor of Italian Studies at Wellesley College. His publications include *L'eros onnipotente. Erotismo, letteratura e impegno nell'opera di Pier Paolo Pasolini e Jean Genet* (Turin:Tirrenia Stampatori, 2003), several articles on contemporary Italian literature, and a translation of a novel by Ginevra Bompiani (*The Great Bear*. New York: Italica Press, 2000). He is currently conducting research on contemporary Jewish Italian writers.

Notes

1. I prefer the term *homoerotic* novel to *homosexual* novel since the first gives prominence to the psychological aspects of the erotic impulse whereas the second describes only the biological and medical aspects. As such, *homoerotic* novel also better describes a group of literary texts that take the *Bildungsroman* (i.e., the psychological education of a young man) as a model. In this literary context, the use of the term *gay* novel would be inappropriate since it has social and political implications that are foreign to the time when these prose works were written.

2. This selection is somewhat arbitrary and serves the purpose of exemplifying the existence in Italian literature of a particular kind of homoerotic literature. It could be enlarged to include other texts.

3. Set in 1898 Trieste but written in 1953 and published only posthumously in 1975, *Ernesto* tells the story of the sexual initiation of a 16-year-old boy by an adult man. The novel's unfinished plot and delayed publication are good examples of the reluctance that characterized Italian literature, and Italian culture in general, in dealing with homoerotic themes.
   Saba's justifications for not finishing and publishing *Ernesto* are extensively documented in his letters. See Umberto Saba, *Ernesto* (Turin: Einaudi, 1975), passim: "Tutte le persone alle quali l'ho letto: Linuccia, Carlo Levi, Bollea e un giovane qui ricoverato dicono che è la più bella cosa che io abbia scritta. (Anch'io lo credo). Disgraziatamente è impubblicabile: per una questione di linguaggio. . . . La non pubblicabilità del racconto non sta tanto nei fatti narrati quanto nel linguaggio che parlano i personaggi. . . . Il più che si potrebbe fare sarebbe pubblicare o il breve racconto (se non farò altro) o il romanzo (se finirò

il libro) in un'edizione privata di pochi esemplari, e fuori commercio; e, naturalmente, dopo la mia morte. (Everyone I've read it to—Linuccia, Carlo Levi, Bollea, and a young patient here—says it's the best thing I have ever written. (I think so too.) But I'm afraid it's unpublishable because of the language. At most the short story (if I don't manage any more) or the novel (if I finish it) might be publishable in a very small private edition—and then, of course, after my death.)

"Disgraziatamente (non per i fatti narrati ma per il 'linguaggio') il racconto è impubblicabile." (Unfortunately—not because of the story it tells, but because of its 'language'—it is unpublishable.)

"Se quel racconto che è castissimo (ma di una castità che la gente non capisce) fosse pubblicabile (non lo è per ragioni di linguaggio) credo che, questa volta, farei i soldi." (If that story, which is very chaste but chaste in a way that people don't understand, were publishable—it isn't because of its language—I think this time I would make money.)

"Ernesto deve restare un 'libretto' se no quel mascalzone mi ammazza il Canzoniere." (Ernesto has to remain a 'libretto'; if not that rascal will kill my *Canzoniere*.)

Unless otherwise indicated, all English translation are my own. For more on Saba's reluctance to publish *Ernesto*, see Watson in this volume.

4. Filippo De Pisis, *Ver-Vert* (Turin: Einaudi, 1984).

5. Pier Paolo Pasolini, *Amado mio; preceduto da Atti impuri*, ed. C. D'Angeli (Milan: Garzanti, 1982), pp. 130–31.

6. The name Iasìs is taken from the poem "Tomb of Iasìs" by Constantin Cavafy. See also Pasolini, *Amado mio*, p. 154: " 'Il tuo nome non mi piace,' gli disse dopo un po', 'ti chiamerò Iasìs.' 'Chi era Iasìs?' chiese il ragazzo. 'Un amore di fanciullo, di cui tutti si innamoravano.' " ("I don't like your name," he said after a while, "I will call you Iasìs." "Who was Iasìs?" asked the boy. "A lovely boy who everyone fell in love with").

7. Pasolini, *Amado mio*, p. 97. It is interesting to note that this passage is an elaboration of an earlier poem, the Sapphic ode "Finita la tua cena, mentre il cielo." The translation of the same theme from verse into prose reflects the uncertain formal character of a prose work like *Atti impuri*, which falls halfway between prose and poetry, narrative and lyric; see Pier Paolo Pasolini, *Bestemmia. Tutte le poesie*, ed. G. Chiarcossi and W. Siti (Milan: Garzanti, 1993), II, p. 1256:

Finita la tua cena, mentre il cielo s'oscura sul tuo tetto e la campagna, esci di casa, forse, e impallidito ti guardi intorno.	Having had your dinner, as the sky darkens over roof and field, you step out, perhaps, and pale look around.
L'umile veste che ti copre il corpo essa pure si spegne: e tu appoggiato	The cloak of humility that covers your body it too begins to fade: and you lean

| ad un muretto, celi il dolce gesto | against a wall, you conceal the sweet |
| nel triste portico. | gesture in a sad doorway. |

Sotto il collo, nei fianchi, a mezzo il	Under your neck, along your thighs,
grembo	in the middle of your groin
si dissolvono l'ombre; resta solo	the shadows dissolve; all that remains
un rossore sul volto, perché inconscio	a red glow on your face, because
sogni lontano.	unaware you dream far away.

E' imminente la notte, e per miracolo	Night is imminent and by miracle
che quelle cose eterne, stelle, nubi,	those eternal things, stars, clouds
ti nascano qui intorno, e ne scolori	spring to life around you, and you
il corpo effimero.	discolor their ephemeral body.
	(trans. Cestaro)

8. Ibid., p. 167.
9. Ibid., p. 129.
10. Ibid.; see also p. 130: "Chini il ragazzo rosso fu subito classificato da quel primo sguardo." (Chini, the red-haired boy, was instantly classified by that first glance.)
11. Pasolini, *Amado mio*, p. 191. In *Romàns*—Pasolini's third Friulan novel—there is a similar classification of the local youth; see Pier Paolo Pasolini, *Romàns* (Parma: Guanda, 1994), p. 56: "Romàns è una specie di paese nel paese. I suoi abitanti hanno caratteri propri, fisici, anzitutto: sono biondi, d'un biondo tra barbaro e delicato, alti, solidi come pioppi, hanno una pronuncia strascicata, rude e vezzosa. Al contrario giù per Braida prevalgono i tipi bruni, con un'aria più svelta e moderna." (Romàns is a sort of village within the village. Its inhabitants have character traits all their own, mostly physical: they are blond—a blond somewhere between barbaric and delicate—tall and strong as poplars, and they speak with a drawl, rough and graceful. By contrast, down in Braida there are more dark-haired types, with a faster and more modern air.)
12. Pasolini, *Amado mio*, p. 191.
13. Giovanni Comisso, *Gioco d'infanzia* (Milan: Mondadori, 1965).
14. Ibid., p. 192.
15. Ibid., p. 231.
16. Ibid., pp. 267–68.
17. Ibid., p. 267.
18. Ibid., p. 269.
19. Giovanni Comisso, *Capriccio e illusione* (Milan: Mondadori, 1947), p. 18.
20. André Gide, *Journal 1889–1939* (Paris: Gallimard, 1951), p. 694: "Lorsque je lui demande s'il ne nous présentera jamais cet Eros sous des espèces jeunes et belles, il me répond que, d'abord, ce qui l'attire ce n'est presque jamais la beauté et qu'il estime qu'elle n'a que peu à voir avec le désir." English translations from *The Journals of André Gide 1889–1949*, ed. and trans. Justin O'Brien (Evanston, Illinois: Northwestern University Press, 1987).

21. Ibid., p. 694: "tout ce que ses souvenirs homosexuels lui proposaient de gracieux, de tendre et de charmant."

22. Ibid., p. 705: "Je lui dis qu'il semble avoir voulu stigmatiser l'uranisme"; "J'ai lu les dernières pages de Proust . . . avec, d'abord, un sursaut d'indignation"; "Je ne connais aucun écrit qui, plus que la 'Sodome' de Proust soit capable d'enfoncer l'opinion dans l'erreur."

11

Secret Wounds: The Bodies of Fascism in Giorgio Bassani's *Dietro la porta*

Derek Duncan

One of the oddest and most striking features of the ways in which fascism has been represented in the postwar period has been through its persistent association with homosexuality.[1] One of the earliest instances of this occurs in Roberto Rossellini's classic film, *Roma città aperta* (1945). This celebration of the Italian resistance under German occupation depends on a bold distinction that conflates ethics and sexuality. The political rectitude of the partisans is indexed by their heteronormativity while the evil Germans are predictably homosexual.[2] This scenario is quite typical of many areas of cultural production in Italy after World War II, in which representations of the fascist period very often were filtered or understood through some kind of synthetic relationship to homosexuality. The inescapability of homosexual characters in novels set during the regime by such major antifascist writers of the 1940s and 1950s as Pavese, Bassani, Moravia, Morante, and Pratolini belies the commonly held belief that until very recently homosexuality in Italy was unmentionable. Films made in the 1960s and 1970s that intensified and made ever more graphic the link between fascism and deviant sexuality extend this cultural narrative.[3]

For some this association has emerged almost organically from fascism's apparent obsession with the male body. In an interview televised in the U.K. in 1983, Alberto Moravia was asked what he remembered most about growing up under fascism.[4] He explained that as a sickly adolescent he lived a solitary existence, so his major preoccupations were personal ones relating to the state of his health and literature. Yet for him the regime was best summed up by its obsession with sport and physical fitness, factors that almost automatically debarred him from being a fascist. This obsession was embodied in the construction of the Foro Mussolini sports complex in Rome and, in particular, the Stadio dei Marmi, adorned with 60 enormous classically inspired statues of male athletes. The statues were paid for by each of Italy's provinces, indicating an unusual investment in the national body. They exemplify the fascist adoration of youth and the male form, yet subsequently their very grandeur has evoked contrasting responses. Felice Fabrizio argues that more than anything else these much imitated statues captured the "style of the period."[5] Carlo Cresti, the architectural historian, is suspicious of the excessive, overt, and ostentatious display of masculinity that the statues flaunt:

> È vero che gli ignudi maschi di marmo e di bronzo attiravano gli sguardi maliziosamente ammirati delle Giovani Italiane, ma probabilmente esorcizzavano anche le frustrazioni e le impotenze di tanti anonimi e gracili fascisti, e accontentavano le preferenze estetiche di qualche gerarca dai gusti particolari.

> It's true that the marble and bronze male nudes would attract the mischievously astonished glances of the Giovani Italiane [Female Youth], but they probably also exorcised the feelings of frustration and impotence of countless, unknown tender fascist youths, and satisfied the aesthetic preferences of any party official with special tastes.[6]

Cresti's dislike of the Foro is expressed through inverting the values that the statues were intended to represent. At best they can only compensate for the very absence of heterosexual masculinity in fascism.

Alberto Arbasino takes a different view of the statues' homoeroticism when he sees them as symbols of a lost—and much regretted—bisexuality that is often believed to have characterized Mediterranean societies.[7] The statues, therefore, are hardly fascist at all but rather the final resting place of a culture whose coordinates far exceed the regime's national and temporal frontiers. Taking a different line again, George Mosse, whose work has done much to advance an appreciation of the centrality of masculinity as a core fascist value, doesn't see any particularly homoerotic element in the statues.[8] His argument is that this was only a feature in protestant Germany, where sexual repression intensified erotic desire that could in turn then be perverted.

These retrospective perceptions all contain some kind of assessment of fascism more generally through its association with homosexuality: its corruption, transience, or relative insignificance compared to Nazi Germany. Yet, they all gesture to the fact that this cult of masculinity harbored some obvious contradictions. The public celebration and display of the male body raises questions of how men looked at each other. Sexual potency was lauded, yet contact with women was shunned. How close could men get to each other without the value of such relations being tainted with the very effeminacy they sought to flee? To what extent did the nature of fascism compromise the homosocial contract on which it was based by spilling over into the excluded realm of the homosexual?

Eve Sedgwick has warned against an overly facile reading of the flagrant homosociality of fascist social organization and its iconography as repressed homosexuality simply because characters encoded as homosexual in films such as *Cabaret* or *The Conformist* are used as mechanisms for rendering the perversity of the regime somehow intelligible. Rather than seeing the homosocial and homosexual as being particularly close under fascism, she argues for their utter irreconcilability:

> Fascism is distinctive in this century not for the intensity of its homoerotic charge, but rather for the virulence of the homophobic prohibition by which that charge, once crystallized as an object of knowledge, is then denied *to* knowledge and hence most manipulably mobilized. In a knowledge regime that pushes toward the homosexual heightening of homosocial bonds, it is the twinning with that push of an equally powerful homophobia, and most of all the enforcement of cognitive impermeability between the two, that will represent the access of fascism.[9]

Although her argument contests the commonplace implication that fascism was "really gay," she nevertheless sustains the notion that homosexuality (even as the butt of virulent homophobia) was what best characterized it. Fascism is now identified by its pathological disavowal of homosexuality's very possibility, most especially in relation to itself.

Before moving on to consider what gain is made through the enmeshment of representations of homosexuality and fascism after its fall, it is worth pausing to consider what empirical evidence there might be to suggest that homosexuality was central to the regime. In 1930s Italy did homosexual men in some sense achieve their apotheosis through the fascist party and the values it promoted? Conversely, to what extent can it be argued that fascism's distinctive note was homophobia, and if so, how was this translated into actual policy?

Only a limited amount of work has been done on how fascism dealt with homosexuality and less still on the experiences of homosexuals under fascism.[10] Patrizia Dogliani, in the only general history of fascism to devote any space to the issue, discusses it in a broader chapter on demographic and racial policy.[11] She observes that since unification Italy had never had specific laws against homosexuality, preferring a silence that relegated it to the private or religious sphere unless it somehow erupted in "atti lesivi dell'interesse sociale" (actions detrimental to the common interest).[12] In the late 1920s when the new penal code was being drafted, initial proposals to outlaw homosexuality were abandoned because of the belief that it was so little practiced in Italy. Additionally, there was the suspicion that to legislate against homosexuality would publicize it and result in its inadvertent promotion. Dogliani adds that it potentially damaged the virile image that fascism had of itself, but that in effect was considered so marginal to the fascist cult of masculinity that it could be dealt with on a local level by limited powers given to the police to admonish persistent deviants and eventually place them under house arrest or subject them to internal exile.[13] These penalties were imposed unevenly throughout the peninsula, although they were more rigorously applied after 1938 and the introduction of the Race Laws. Dogliani makes the almost inevitable comparison with the excesses of Nazi Germany, concluding that if Italy had wanted to pursue an equally draconian path "avrebbe dovuto in primo luogo, paradossalmente, rendere visibile ciò che per scelta politica secolare aveva reso occulto, e poi reprimerlo per farlo ridiventare occulto" (paradoxically it would first of all have had to make visible what had been hidden by political choice for centuries, and then repress it in order to hide it again).[14] The question of the visibility of homosexuality and its relation to public knowledge determines how fascist policy has been understood. Dall'Orto argues that fascism had merely retained the strategy used by the liberal state in allowing the Church the freedom to regulate matters deemed to be of private morality. Homosexuality constituted "il regno del non-detto, dei sussurri, degli eufemismi, dei giri di parole, dei volti nascosti: un mondo che c'è, però non esiste, perchè non ha il diritto ad affiorare alla realtà" (the realm of the unsaid, of whispers and euphemisms, of circumlocution and hidden faces: a world that is there but which doesn't exist because it isn't allowed to emerge into the light of day).[15] The effectiveness of this ploy illuminates the relative casualness with which homosexuals were targeted even in the late 1930s when homosexuality had been recategorized as a political crime. Dario Petrosino disagrees, however, over the question of homosexuality's (un)speakability under fascism. While legislators seemed to have been convinced that silence was the best policy, the press exercised an almost morbid interest in discussing it. Petrosino comments on the way in which the Italian press used a whole range of euphemisms to denote homosexuality, adding, however, that the phenomenon was most commonly displaced onto other societies. Almost randomly, it was a trait associated with Muslims, Jews, and the general decadence of American or north European cultures.[16]

Barbara Spackman makes a convincing case that links fascism's dream of "Autarchia" or self-sufficiency with its ingrained homophobia and xenophobia.[17] Through the earlier writing of the futurist poet Marinetti, she scrutinizes the ways in which the crisscrossing of national frontiers invites, even as it refuses, the transgression of boundaries of sexuality. Homosociality and colonial ambition depend on other men and other races yet abhor and distrust their proximity. It is noticeable that, more generally, questions of race or geographical location cause the silence around homosexuality to be broken. Petrosino notes that with the introduction of the codice Rocco "per la prima volta veniva tutelata il concetto di stirpe" (for the first time the idea of race was protected) and that after 1938 the criminal nature of homosexuality was judged in a political frame as "lesione del prestigio di razza" (offence to the prestige of the race).[18] Dall'Orto reflects that with the politicization of homosexuality, homosexuals had become "nemici della razza" (enemies of the race).[19] Carlo Scorza, the *ras* of Lucca, offers further insight into how the issue was framed: "Society today despises deserters, pimps, homosexuals, thieves. Those who can but do not perform their duty to the nation must be put in the same category. We must despise them. We must make the bachelors and those who desert the nuptial bed ashamed of their potential power to have children. It is necessary to make them bow their foreheads in the dust."[20] Here, the homosexual is not singled out but is only one in a range of generally undesirable characters. Why thieves, for example, should father fewer children than honest folk remains unexplained. Scorza's comments reveal that homosexual activity, however, was considered to damage the reproductive potential, or health, of the Italian race. Their crime was nonreproductive sex that contradicted the regime's express wish to increase Italy's population.

As the rest of this essay will revolve around the implication of homosexuality in some notion of race, it is worth trying briefly to define how I will use the term in this context. Recently, a lot of very valuable historical work has been done on competing notions of race during the fascist period and before. The specific contributions of Italian ethnographers, such as Paolo Mantegazza and Giuseppe Sergi, have been compared to those of their foreign counterparts, particularly as they fed into Italy's imperialist project in East Africa. There has been a broad tendency to accept the view that fascist "racism" imitated but differed from that of Nazi Germany because it distinguished groups according to some idea of national spirit rather than biology. The value of this emphasis is debatable because it detracts from the effects of "race" as a political weapon. Henry Louis Gates, Jr. makes the fundamental point that "[r]ace, as a meaningful criterion within the biological sciences, has long been recognized to be a fiction. When we speak of 'the white race' or 'the black race,' 'the Jewish race' or 'the Aryan race,' we speak in biological misnomers, and, more generally, in metaphors."[21] To argue that "race" is a metaphor is not to deny or underestimate the extraordinary power that the metaphor can wield as a principle of social organization. The fact that it lacks material substance means that "race is the ultimate trope of difference because it is so very arbitrary in its application."[22] It is this mobility that allows "race" to be deployed tactically.

Barbara Sòrgoni points to how in the 1930s fascism abandoned the scientific pretence of ethnography and its claims to knowledge with a deployment of racial categories that had overtly functional or political ends. As a means of controlling more severely its African colonies, measures were introduced that progressively segregated the "white" and "black" populations. These measures aimed particularly to control sexual and marital contact. Infringement of this legislation was again deemed to be a crime against "il prestigio della razza" (the prestige of the race).[23] Fascism's autarchic ambition moved ever more clearly into the territory of the "reproductive fantasy" identified by Spackman as the regime's sustaining myth. The imposition of a racial hierarchy instates a fear of difference, but perhaps more insidiously, a fear that the hierarchy might be reversed. In light of this, a number of commentators have concluded that racism as the fear of contamination was often motivated by the perceived need to exercise control over reproduction, over, that is, heterosexuality.[24]

Yet the terms are never so stable. Dall'Orto reports the case of one Otello A. convicted in Eritrea in 1938 for "menomazione al prestigio della razza, essendosi abbandonato passivamente ad atti di pederastia con indigeno dell'Africa Orientale" (undermining the prestige of the race, having engaged passively in acts of pederasty with a native of East Africa).[25] Here it is the Italian's "passivity" that warrants censure as an assault of the Italian race. This incident provides an interesting gloss on Robert Young's study of the racialization of desire that focuses on "hybridity" as the key term in nineteenth-century constructions of race, signaling a desire for/fear of the cross-fertilization of species. His argument compellingly places heterosexuality at the heart of the imperial project. The status afforded to homosexuality was contradictory. On the one hand, Young remarks that "same-sex sex, though clearly locked into an identical same-but-different dialectic of racialized sexuality posed no threat because it produced no children; its advantage was that it remained silent, covert and unmarked." Fears of "racial amalgamation" even led to the promotion of homosexuality in "the imperial game" that "was, after all, already an implicitly homo-erotic practice."[26] Yet, homosexuality was also viewed as a "degenerate product of miscegenation," the result of inadequately controlled heterosexuality that in turn weakened the race further. Both cause and effect, sexuality and race reach out to each other, never meaningful in themselves.

The idea of "race" that I want to work with here is relatively weak in that it does not attempt to engage in any direct way with the various ideologues and architects of racist policy who set out their precise albeit confused categories of racial difference. I want to follow the spirit rather than detail of the energies that favored such interventions and made them possible. "Race" expresses a desire to categorize and is a symbolic structure that lays particular claim to bodies in what might be termed both their synchronic and diachronic axes. The "raced" body exists in the present as a somatic symptom of the past. Its alleged, inherited inferiority is inscribed on the flesh. "Race" becomes the sign under which categories of difference that find their point of reference in some perception of the body are deployed. The point of this perceived difference is to remark a natural inferiority. As Gates suggests the power of "race" lies in the very arbitrariness with which it can be deployed. I think some notion of "race" is required to get around the obstacles of thinking about homosexuality in a historical and cultural moment when it was largely seen as a foreign practice: foreign to Italians and endemic in foreigners.

Until recently questions of race in Italy tended to be limited to discussions of Judaism and antisemitism. The idea of fascism as a historical parenthesis came in useful as a means of deflecting any accusation of more ingrained racism. The infamous Race Laws of 1938 could be viewed as the crystallization of a regrettable anomaly. This idea was bolstered by the belief that Italy's Jewish population identified very strongly with the unified secular state that had completed their liberation from the ghetto. Literary works such as Giorgio Bassani's *Gli occhiali d'oro* (1958) set in the 1930s seem to confirm this. The fact that the novella's first-person narrator is Jewish is only revealed halfway through the book when the fascist regime's antisemitism becomes too blatant to ignore. The narrator's initial silence about his difference from his Catholic peers is explained by the extent of his integration or assimilation. In a sense, the very Foucauldian narrative is about how he forcibly becomes Jewish as a consequence of the identity foisted upon him through fascist legislation. The narrator's growing isolation from his family and Catholic friends parallels an increasing intimacy with Dr. Fadigati, a respected physician who loses his social status as a consequence of flaunting his homosexual relationship with a young man at the family holiday resort of Riccione. Critics debate the exact nature of the apparent equivalences drawn between the two forms of marginalization, which, as they often point out, already have a shared history.[27] Lucienne Krohe sheds light on the nature of their relationship by juxtaposing her reading of this text with *Dietro la porta*, a later novel by Bassani that involves the same first-person narrator looking back at an earlier period in his life.[28] Krohe argues that *Gli occhiali d'oro* is structured around the narrator's continued denial of any sense of identification with Fadigati. Ironically, what his narrative reveals to the more astute reader is the disavowal of his own unresolved sexuality. Krohe finds evidence of this in *Dietro la porta*, in which the narrator at an earlier point in his life finds himself accused of homosexuality in a set of circumstances that he is unable or unwilling to elucidate. The accusation emerges as part of a complex enmeshment of identities and desires experienced by the narrator as he crosses a difficult adolescence.

I do not particularly want to contest Krohe's pathologizing of the narrative but would prefer to attempt a reading that is less bound to questions of individual psycho-sexual development and more open to broader questions of the intelligibility of cultural representations of homosexuality and race. Rather than looking at *Dietro la porta* as a retrospective anticipation of the psychological mechanisms that structure *Gli occhiali d'oro*, I want to dislocate this sense of direct dependency on the earlier text to examine its dependencies on the kinds of conflations of sexuality and race identified in fascist discourse. Additionally, I pick up on Judith Butler's point that "the analysis of racialization and class is at least equally important in the thinking of sexuality as either gender or homosexuality, and these last two are not separable from more complex and complicitous formations of power."[29] I would suggest that what Bassani presents in *Dietro la porta* is a racialization of masculinity that makes the accusation of sexual deviancy inevitable whether or not the narrator can in any sense be justifiably said to be homosexual. The conflation of discourses of sexuality, race, and social class works to produce a homosexual by default.

The novella is set in Ferrara between October 1929 and June 1930. The time and place are familiar from Bassani's other works. Typically, they focus on the Jewish community in Ferrara under the fascist regime and ways in which history overtakes the comfortable feeling of assimilation that Italy's Jews apparently enjoyed. The city itself is a strong, albeit claustrophobic, presence. Bassani's protagonists experience it as an alienating place. Its walls symbolize division and the impermeability of its borders is reflected in their loneliness and bleak interiority. Set some eight years before the Race Laws were introduced, *Dietro la porta* differs from Bassani's previous work because the question of antisemitism is quite explicitly raised at a time before it became an important plank of official policy: In fact, there is no overt mention of fascism. It is ostensibly a tale of schoolboy rivalry and envy, yet the narrator sees this brief period as the darkest in his life, emblematic of his subsequent experience of isolation and segregation, a "ferita segreta, sanguinante in segreto" (a secret wound, bleeding in secret).[30] The novel is haunted by this image of the wound in both literal and metaphoric senses although its exact referent is never pinned down. The reader knows that the narrator is Jewish from virtually the outset of the novel and so the plot does not turn, as in *Gli occhiali d'oro*, on its sudden revelation. Yet the information emerges elliptically in the form of a disavowal of antisemitism. He interprets the ambivalence of one of his friends towards him as envy for his luxurious home and devoted mother: "L'antisemitismo una volta tanto non c'entrava" (for once antisemitism didn't come into it).[31] Dismissed on this occasion, antisemitism is never far from the narrator's mind as he recounts the story of his academic sparring with Carlo Cattolica and his uneasy friendship with a new arrival at the school, Luciano Pulga. A situation of dependency is created between the narrator and Pulga, who the narrator thinks envies both his intellectual abilities and his family's wealth and social status. The narrator in turn envies Cattolica: "[I]l mio senso di inferiorità non scaturiva tanto dal confronto dei nostri rispettivi rendimenti scolastici, quanto da tutto il resto." ([M]y feeling of inferiority didn't spring so much from the comparison between our respective academic achievements as from all the rest.)[32] It is this "rest" that is particularly interesting. Cattolica's superiority is expressed through his height and the adult sophistication of his clothes. He has a girlfriend and even sports an engagement ring. The narrator despises the ring's vulgarity yet is in awe of what it symbolizes: "Forse per diventare uomini, o almeno per acquistare quel minimo di sicurezza in se stessi indispensabile a passare per tali, un anello così andava bene, poteva aiutare molto." (Perhaps to become a man, or at least to acquire that minimum of self-confidence necessary to pass as such, a ring like that one was just the thing, and could help a lot.)[33] Cattolica's ring confirms and enhances his heterosexual masculinity. Its visibility daunts the narrator, who does not seem to doubt the authority of the body acculturated in this way at least to "pass" as a man. The reference to Cattolica's fiancée is not developed, which suggests that the significance of this detail might lie elsewhere, perhaps in the racist fantasy of assimilation.[34]

The feminist philosopher Elizabeth Grosz has argued against the traditional dichotomy that pits the body against the soul or reason. The body is not just mute, brute matter, a hindrance to the eloquent intellect but an active term in how subjectivity is constructed. Grosz insists on the plurality of bodies and on their historical and cultural specificity: "The body must be regarded as a site of social, political, cultural, and geographical inscriptions, production, or constitution. The body is not opposed to culture, a resistant throwback to a natural past: it is itself a cultural, the cultural product."[35] The body therefore can never be natural if by that is meant that it can be free of meanings that are socially constructed. A sexed, raced, aged body is a body adorned. Identity is produced through the enmeshment of the body in cultural discourses and practices. Elsewhere she has written about the body as a kind of transitional space, "a hinge or threshold: it is placed between a psychic or lived interiority and a more socio-political exteriority that produces interiority through the inscription of the body's outer surface."[36] Identity is not simply imprinted on the body as in the metaphor of the blank page but emerges as a process of contestation, of which the body is the site rather than the product. It seems to me that this approach is helpful in coming to grips with a text that is so patently, yet incoherently, about bodies. I would like to return to *Dietro la porta* to try to respond to what it has to say about bodies, bodies that are located at a specific historical moment when quite particular notions of race and gender were articulated through the search for their corporeal inscription.

Cattolica's ring ostentatiously proclaims his heterosexual masculinity, for the novel's narrator at least, who is obsessively attuned to the signification of the body's semiotics. The narrator's own intellectual and social superiority to Pulga is emphasized through their physical difference. Smaller and weaker, even Pulga's handwriting is described as "feminine."[37] However, on one occasion when Pulga initiates a conversation about sex, the roles are reversed and the narrator feels "debole, passivo, impotente a reagire" (weak, passive, powerless to react).[38] Pulga expresses astonishment that the narrator had never masturbated and, after extolling its benefits, wonders if this failure has to do with his circumcision desensitizing his penis. On a subsequent occasion, Pulga unbuttons his trousers to show the narrator his penis then insists he do the same. Only very reluctantly does he comply:

> "Tutta qui la circoncisione?—sbottò [Pulga] poi a ridere. Lui aveva sempre pensato a una operazione abbastanza seria. Robetta, adesso se ne rendeva conto. In fondo che differenza c'era tra il suo e il mio?"

> "So that's all there is to the circumcision?—then Pulga burst out laughing. He had always imagined it to be quite a big operation. Now he realized it was nothing at all. Basically what was the difference between his and mine?"[39]

Racial difference is dismissed as Pulga is unable to accept the visible evidence of what distinguishes him from his friend.

The link Pulga makes between masturbation and circumcision is not a chance one, for its preventative effect was one of the reasons typically put forward for the continuation of a practice that was the focus of some controversy. Sander Gilman points out that, like many of his contemporaries, Mantegazza was especially concerned with the visibility of difference, hence his speculation that the original reason for the practice of circumcision was that "it was felt necessary to imprint upon the human body a clear and indelible sign which would serve to distinguish one people from another and, by putting a seal of consecration upon nationality, would tend to impede the mixture of races."[40] Mantegazza dismissed the hygienic case that held circumcision to ward off the evils of both masturbation and syphilis (with their implication of racial degeneracy), claiming that its true purpose for the Jews was solely to set themselves apart from the rest of humanity. One of the aims of making the penis visibly distinct was to ensure racial purity. The sight of a marked or unmarked penis would allow the woman, racially at least, to know what she was letting herself in for. It was therefore part of a reproductive fantasy. Yet he was also worried that the sight of difference might well incite a perverse desire for the other, hence actually facilitate interracial contact. The Jew's penis then became absolutely central to the assertion or ascertainment of difference, to his identity, and to the policing of the racial politics of reproduction.

On this level Pulga finds the narrator's circumcision an inadequate signifier. Its appearance belies its alleged import. In his study of narrative and the body, Peter Brooks explores the ways in which the novel as a genre makes curiosity about the body central to issues of knowledge and power.[41] The realist novel's emphasis on seeing as the principle means of acquiring knowledge meant that the body was subject to endless scrutiny. Any mark on the body (gender, race, physiological peculiarity) was read in order to be interpreted. Additionally, however, Brooks argues that the display of the penis is a particularly charged event in that it exposes the male subject to inquiry and risks transforming him into the object of knowledge: "[T]he gaze is 'phallic,' its object is not."[42] The narrator's penis (hence the narrator himself) is exposed to the evaluating gaze of Pulga and found wanting. An inadequate signifier of racial difference, it becomes a sign of a reduced masculinity.

Indeed, the narrator's primary understanding of the scene is not about race at all. His obsessive memories of the event revolve round the apparent absurdity that the puny Pulga should possess a penis of such inordinate size: "una *cosa* talmente sproporzionata: un che di gonfio, bianco, ma soprattutto enorme" (a *thing* so out of proportion: something swollen, white, but in particular enormous). He is unable to think of anything other than "quel sesso oscenamente, paurosamente enorme" (obscenely, terrifyingly enormous sex), as gaudy in its own way as Cattolica's ring.[43] The sight of Pulga's penis fills him with an overpowering feeling of disgust. He wants to put an end to his friendship with Pulga but needs to do so without being humiliated himself; "calare le braghe" (drop his pants) is the metaphor suggestively deployed.[44]

Their friendship as a result does deteriorate until one day Cattolica orchestrates a scene designed to convince the narrator of Pulga's increasing disloyalty. The narrator hides "behind the door" at Cattolica's house and listens to what Pulga, unaware of his presence, finds to "vomitare su di [lui]" (belch up about him).[45] The door the narrator hides behind is that of Cattolica's parents' bedroom. Described as a crypt and also a womb, the bedroom, the site of the "talamo" (marriage bed) is a specifically Catholic space.[46] The narrator notices an image of Christ as he hears Cattolica (previously compared to a medieval monk) replying "da buon cattolico" ("as a good Catholic") to Pulga's ramblings on metempsychosis.[47]

The antisemitic asides about his character, family's wealth, and his mother's sensuality are offensive enough. Pulga then recalls the time when he saw the narrator's "cazzo" (cock), which in spite of the circumcision "gli era sembrato proprio qualsiasi, normalissimo" (had seemed to him just like any other, totally normal).[48] What was not normal in his view was the violence of the narrator's response to seeing Pulga's penis, which could only point to the fact that he was "di sicuro un 'finocchio,' sia pure allo stato potenziale; un 'busone' in attesa soltanto di 'saltare il fosso,' e tuttavia ignaro (questo, il tragico!) della bella carriera che [gli] stava davanti, inevitabile" (certainly a 'queer,' even if he didn't realize it; a 'fag' just waiting to 'take the leap,' and still unaware—this is the sad thing!—of the great path that lay inevitably before him).[49] The narrator's penis appears normal, which is not to say that he himself is. Pulga is able to read beyond the signs offered by physical difference to produce another interpretation exceeding that available to the embodied self. In an earlier conversation the boys had already skirted around the topic of the narrator's racial difference, discussing his inability to do math in terms of the common belief (held also by his father) that Jews had a natural propensity for scientific subjects. Here too the implication was that the narrator in some mysterious way was not Jewish enough. Rather than confront Pulga, the narrator flees to wrestle perpetually with the dilemma of the closed door. But what exactly is the narrator's dilemma, the key to his "secret wound"? As stated, I am not particularly interested in what the text has to say about individual psychology but in the way in which the juxtaposition of certain elements makes the accusation of homosexuality almost inevitable.

The revelation of the adult mother's sexuality provokes a hostile reaction in the son. The pat Freudian theory of homosexuality is, however, only half-heartedly pursued. Pulga's description of the mother's sensuality dislodges this animosity from the conventional Oedipal paradigm. Said to be "magari un po' 'sfasciata' come sono sempre le ebree" (maybe a bit "flabby" like Jewish women always are), her sexuality is racialized by this reference to her body's morphology.[50] Conversely, the narrator's body is not distinct. Pulga needs to make the Jew different, yet the place where his difference is traditionally asserted and proclaimed turns out not to be different enough. It is Pulga who is different, identified by the horrid excess of his giant organ, entirely at odds with the rest of his body's lack of substance, inescapable even at the end of the novel when the narrator meets him at the beach. It is not only the narrator who feels disgust at Pulga's body.[51] Cattolica says that the thought of Pulga makes his blood turn.[52] He compares him to a mongrel, debased in his nature. Pulga is a "meteco," a barely tolerated outsider whose presence inspires unease. Cattolica's revulsion is again bodily: " '[S]arà perché non sono un bastardo e nemmeno un meteco, e le mescolanze non posso soffrirle, mi fanno venire una specie di pelle d'oca, io non sto bene che a casa mia.' " ("[I]t's probably because I'm neither a bastard nor a metic, and can't stand anything mixed, they give me goose bumps, the only place I'm happy is at home.")[53]

The home becomes a place that ensures freedom from racial taint as questions of geography and reproductive heterosexuality unexpectedly, but by now predictably, resurface. As indicated above, the first mention of possible antisemitism is bound up with what the narrator believes to be envy of his mother and his home, two of the things Pulga most violently mocks. While Cattolica defends the purity of his house, the narrator's mother's excessive sexual desire threatens to disrupt his. Yet the narrator had originally compared Cattolica's house to a brothel, and his conversation with Pulga that sparked the chain of events was about the goings-on in the cheap hotel where his family stayed, to all effects a brothel.[54] If Pulga is a "meteco" there is doubt cast too over Cattolica, whose name leads the narrator to suspect a Jewish ancestry. Proper bodily confines are also blurred as Pulga bitterly acknowledges that the way the narrator treated him turned him into some kind of slave "dal quale è giusto pretendere che 'offra il didietro ringraziando' " (that you can justifiably ask to "give you his arse and say thank you").[55]

It is hard to imagine that anyone would seriously support the view that *Dietro la porta* is about the fear of anal sex, yet there does seem to be a gnawing feeling of anxiety expressed about boundaries, identities, and places and their susceptibility to penetration. Grosz makes the point that a certain type of masculine identity depends on the confident assertion of its boundaries: "Part of the process of phallicizing the male body, of subordinating the rest of the body to the valorized functioning of the male penis, with the culmination of sexual activities and male orgasm, involves the constitution of the sealed-up, impermeable body."[56] This may offer an insight into representations of the ideal fascist body, yet for a number of reasons the bodies of Bassani's adolescents are subject to slippage and uncertainty. No one is quite what he seems and no identity is securely held. It is in this sense only that the narrator (or Cattolica or Pulga) is homosexual.

As a writer Bassani is recognized for a prose style that is allusive and reticent. His nuanced explorations of the searingly traumatic 1930s refuse to yield any absolute statement about the past or, indeed, about how it might be remembered. *Dietro la porta* is unique in Bassani's work in that it suggests that antisemitism was widespread and quotidian before the Race Laws were introduced. Its attention to sex and the way in which the racial question is bound up with questions of sexuality are also remarkable. The revealing of the two penises conflates and confuses questions of how race and sex are inscribed on the male body. In a radical inversion of expectation, it is Pulga's uncut penis that is made monstrous, unnatural on account of its size, whereas the marked narrator is able to "pass." In a distant way, Pulga's deformity recalls that of the enchanted "zeb" in Marinetti's colonialist fable *Mafarka le futuriste*.[57] In fact, a girl who allegedly waves suggestively to Pulga does so while leaning out of the "Pensione Mafarka."[58] Italy's colonialist enterprise is not referred to in any direct way in *Dietro la porta*, but the novel is abidingly concerned about domestic space, its proper habitation and infiltration. The boys, for example, show a very strong sense of Ferrara's symbolic geography through they way they interpret the locations of their respective houses and jealously control entry.

I would resist the claim that an understanding of this novel, and by extension *Gli occhiali d'oro*, rests on the question of the narrator's unresolved sexuality, if the implication is that he is *really* gay. A more challenging sense of the unresolvability of sexuality comes from dislodging its adherence to the identity or body of any single character. What Bassani's text points to, in my view, is the insubstantial nature of somatic readings that singularize the body and do not recognize it as a mobile zone of contestation. In Bassani's text the body and the meanings appended to its parts are mobile and contingent. They may be different but are never different enough to allow a single interpretation. As Grosz points out, the body stands at the confluence of a range of historical and cultural forces and represents a response to them. Identity is not written on the body in any securely intelligible way. Nor is space protected through some mechanism of expulsion because identities circulate and are inherently porous. Consequently, race becomes sex and there really is no place like home.

The queer historian Scott Bravmann says that in recent times the most valuable work in his field has signaled "a shift away from understanding lesbian and gay historical representations as literal or descriptive accounts of the past towards reading those representations as performative sites where meanings are invented."[59] It seems to me important to recognize the scant documentary value of writers such as Bassani when it comes to looking for information on the lives of gay men. What they do reveal, however, is the burden of representation that homosexuality sustains as the nexus of a complex, contradictory, and even incoherent set of invented meanings. By this I do not propose that they be seen as false, but rather overdetermined. Giorgio Bassani was Jewish although he wasn't gay. Like many of his postwar contemporaries, he wrote about fascism through the prism of non-normative sexuality. Contrary to the majority of them, he explicitly ruptures the convention that makes heterosexuality the touchstone of antifascism. What he does not do is attempt to clarify fascism's relation to issues of race and sexuality through explanation or even metaphor. His achievement is to act out for the reader their incoherencies. Sexuality, I would suggest, does not provide the thread of continuity that would allow the unintelligibility of both *Dietro la porta* and *Gli occhiali d'oro* to be resolved. What characterizes these texts is their author's attention to the different moments under fascism in which they are set; they are historically rather then sexually specific. In writing about the liminal experience of the abject body, Bassani proposes a refutation of binary models of identity that separate fascist and antifascist, Jew and Catholic, hetero- and homosexual. Without celebration, he pursues the incoherence of such logic at the level of the body, whose recalcitrant contours and permeable surfaces proffer material objection to discourses that aim to naturalize chance configurations of race, sexuality, and national identity.

Derek Duncan is Senior Lecturer in Italian at the University of Bristol. His research focuses on issues of gender and sexuality, and he has published widely on twentieth-century Italian literature and film.

Notes

1. Andrew Hewitt questions this recurrent association of fascism with homosexuality, tying it to broader issues of how the historical representation of fascism is actually made possible. He contends that the phenomenon has little to do with historical fact and everything to do with how fascism has continued to haunt subsequent generations so that homosexuality serves as a means of representing a political order that had literally become unspeakable. Although his invaluable study concludes with an analysis of Moravia's novel *Il conformista*, its primary focus is Nazi Germany, and it would be unwise to extend his argument to Italy without due attention to local circumstance; Andrew Hewitt, *Political Inversions: Homosexuality, Fascism, and the Modernist Imaginary* (Stanford, CA: Stanford University Press, 1996).

2. David Forgacs, *Rome Open City (Roma città aperta)* (London: BFI, 2000), pp. 47–48.

3. David Forgacs develops this point in relation to the further addition of homosexual S/M to fascism's gallery of perversion. He uses Julia Kristeva's notion of the "abject" to explain the inappropriateness of the straightforward equation of fascism with sadism: "For it hides the extent to which fascists demarcated between bodies, drew boundaries and expelled deviancy as abject, in order to establish a 'healthy' moral and political order that sought to exclude, in the name of religion or the state, all forms of 'perversion'. The irony is that in the economy of post-war representations fascism has so often been confused with that which it did abject in order to establish its own identity"; "Days of Sodom: The Fascism-Perversion Equation in Films of the 1960s and 1970s" in: *Italian Fascism: History, Memory and Representation*, ed. R. J. B. Bosworth and Patrizia Dogliani (Basingstoke: Macmillan, 1999), pp. 216–36; quotation p. 233. It is important to underline that abjection is not specific to fascism and has a more general application. See for example Jackie Stacey, *Teratologies: A Cultural Study of Cancer* (London: Routledge, 1997); David Sibley, *Geographies of Exclusion: Society and Difference in the West* (London: Routledge, 1995); Judith Butler, *Bodies that Matter: On the Discursive Limits of Sex* (London and New York: Routledge, 1993).

4. *The South Bank Show*, 4.12.83.

5. Felice Fabrizio, *Sport e fascismo: la politica sportiva del regime 1924–1936* (Rimini: Guaraldi, 1976), p. 147.

6. Carlo Cresti, *Architettura e fascismo* (Florence: Vallecchi, 1986), p. 83.

7. Alberto Arbasino, "Giovinezza giovinezza," *FMR* 26 (September 1984), pp. 96–98.

8. George Mosse, *Nationalism and Sexuality: Respectability and Abnormal Sexuality in Modern Europe* (New York: Howard Fertig, 1985), p. 174.

9. Eve Sedgwick, *Tendencies* (London and New York: Routledge, 1994), pp. 50–51.

10. All the work that has been done is indebted to the pioneering initiative of Giovanni Dall'Orto who, in addition to the essays cited here, has also collected the only oral testimonies of homosexual men from the fascist era; see Giovanni Dall'Orto, "Omosessualità e razzismo fascista" in: *La menzogna della razza: Documenti e immagini del razzismo e dell'antisemitismo fascista*, ed. Il Centro Furio Jesi (Bologna: Grafis, 1994), pp. 139–44; "Il paradosso del razzismo fascista verso l'omosessualità" in: *Nel nome della razza: il razzismo nella storia d'Italia 1870–1925*, ed. Alberto Burgio (Bologna: Il Mulino, 1999), pp. 515–28; as well as the many relevant articles and links on-line at *La gaia scienza*, http://digilander.libero.it/giovannidallorto.

11. Patrizia Dogliani, *L'Italia fascista: 1922–1940* (Milan: Sansoni, 1999).

12. Dogliani, p. 280.

13. This assessment supports the earlier work of Wanrooij, who nevertheless extends the policy of silencing sexuality in both liberal and fascist Italy to matters such as pornography and contraception, which was outlawed by the codice Rocco; Bruno P. F. Wanrooij, *Storia del pudore: la questione sessuale in Italia 1860–1940* (Venice: Marsilio, 1990).

14. Dogliani, p. 283.

15. Dall'Orto, "Omosessualità e razzismo fascista," p. 143. Not everyone would agree with Dall'Orto's assessment that homosexual practice was clamped down on by fascism, and some contend that it even thrived. His own work on homosexual men who lived through the period suggests that repression was sporadic. It has been argued that in many respects Italy's reputation as a sexual paradise was wholly justified, nowhere more so than in the camps set up under fascism to hone the bodies of its adolescent males. The work of writers such as Penna and Pasolini raises doubts about how repressed homosexual practice might have been. To find evidence for Cresti's point, however, that the fascist cult of the male body was promoted by a regime homosexual in its essence is more difficult to substantiate. Even if it is true that Augusto Turati and Giovanni Giurati, successive Segretaries of the PNF, were homosexual, the fact that they were both hounded out of their positions points to a climate of intolerance. On this last point see Massimo Consoli, *Homocaust* (Milan: Kaos, 1991), pp. 180–81.

16. Dario Petrosino, "Traditori della stirpe. Il razzismo contro gli omosessuali nella stampa del fascismo," in: *Studi sul razzismo italiano*, ed. Alberto Burgio and Luciano Casali (Bologna: Clueb, 1996), pp. 89–107.

17. Barbara Spackman, *Fascist Virilities: Rhetoric, Ideology and Social Fantasy in Italy* (Minneapolis and London: University of Minnesota Press, 1996), pp. 49–76.

18. Petrosino, pp. 93–94.

19. Dall'Orto, "Il paradosso del razzismo fascista verso l'omosessualità," p. 515.

20. Quoted in Victoria de Grazia, *How Fascism Ruled Women: Italy, 1922–1945* (Berkeley: University of California Press, 1992), p. 70.

21. Henry Louis Gates, Jr., "Writing 'Race' and the Difference It Makes," in: *"Race," Writing and Difference*, ed. Henry Louis Gates, Jr. (Chicago: University of Chicago Press, 1986), p. 4.

22. Ibid., p. 5.

23. Barbara Sòrgoni, *Parole e corpi: antropologia, discorso giuridico e politiche sessuali interrazziali nella colonia Eritrea (1890–1941)* (Naples: Liguori, 1998), p. 153.

24. For example, Richard Dyer writes: "All concepts of race are always concepts of the body and also of heterosexuality. Race is a means of categorizing different types of human body which reproduce themselves"; *White* (London: Routledge, 1997), p. 20. See also Anne McLintock, *Imperial Leather: Race, Gender and Sexuality in the Colonial Context* (London and New York: Routledge, 1995).

25. Dall'Orto, "Il paradosso del razzismo fascista verso l'omosessualità," p. 516.

26. Robert J. C. Young, *Colonial Desire: Hybridity in Theory, Culture and Race* (London: Routledge, 1995), pp. 25–26.

27. Eve Sedgwick explores the stakes involved in "coming out" and the relationship between sexuality and identity that such a gesture presupposes through a re-reading of the biblical story of Esther and her own decision to reveal her Jewishness; *Epistemology of the Closet* (London: Penguin, 1994), pp. 75–82.

This trope has been more extensively explored in relation to the question of Jewish identity and the move towards assimilation in Jon Stratton, *Coming Out Jewish* (London and New York: Routledge, 2000).

28. Giorgio Bassani, *Dietro la porta* in: *Opere*, ed. Roberto Cotroneo (Milan: Mondadori, 1998; 1st edition 1964). This edition follows the substantially revised text of 1980, which omits much of the more explicit sadism that had characterized the narrator. For some useful insights relating this theme to the psychology of the narrator, see Giusi Oddo De Stefanis, *Bassani entro il cerchio delle sue mura* (Ravenna: Longo, 1981), pp. 189–213 and Lucienne Krohe, "The Sound of Silence: Re-Reading Giorgio Bassani's *Gli occhiali d'oro*," *The Italianist* 10 (1990), pp. 71–102. I would like to thank Peter Kitchen for drawing my attention to this text.

29. Judith Butler, "Against Proper Objects," in: *Feminism Meets Queer Theory*, ed. Elizabeth Weed and Naomi Schor (Bloomington and Indianapolis: Indiana University Press, 1997), p. 24.

30. Bassani, p. 581.

31. Ibid., p. 588.

32. Ibid., p. 596.

33. Ibid., p. 597.

34. The slippages between gender and sexuality in the strategy of Jewish assimilation are discussed by Daniel Boyarin, "Outing Freud's Zionism, or, the Bitextuality of the Diaspora," in: *Queer Diasporas*, ed. Cindy Patton and Benigno Sánchez-Eppler (Durham and London: Duke University Press, 2000), pp. 71–104.

35. Elisabeth Grosz, *Volatile Bodies: Towards a Corporeal Feminism* (Bloomington and Indianapolis: Indiana University Press, 1994), p. 23.

36. Elisabeth Grosz, *Space, Time, Perversion: Essays on the Politics of Bodies* (New York: Routledge, 1995), p. 33.

37. Bassani, p. 619.

38. Ibid., p. 626.

39. Ibid., p. 632.

40. Sander Gilman, *The Jew's Body* (New York and London: Routledge, 1991), p. 95. Gilman notes that in Germany there had been quite general debate in the Jewish community over circumcision. This does not seem to have been the case in Italy where Mantegazza's ideas were dismissed as antisemitic: "Mantegazza si fece eco delle accuse dei nemici nostri, giungendo al punto di consigliare a noi l'abolizione della circoncisione" (Mantegazza reiterated the accusations of our enemies, even to the extent of advising us to abolish circumcision). This quotation is taken from an article published in the Piedmontese Jewish journal, *Il Vessillo Israeltico* 3 (1898), p. 121. I am indebted to Elizabeth Schächter for providing this information and reference.

41. Peter Brooks, *Body Work: Objects of Desire in Modern Narrative* (Cambridge, MA and London: Harvard University Press, 1993).

42. Brooks, p. 15.

43. Bassani, p. 636.

44. Ibid., p. 637.

45. Ibid., p. 661.
46. On the symbolic role of the marriage bed, see Wanrooij, pp. 97–131.
47. Bassani, p. 668.
48. Ibid., p. 637.
49. Ibid., p. 678.
50. Ibid., p. 676.
51. The feeling of disgust at the sight of the "abject" is defining in Kristeva's use of the concept that stresses the liminality of the border phenomena in a way often lost sight of by subsequent critics; see Julia Kristeva, *Pouvoirs de l'horreur* (Paris: Seuil, 1980).
52. Bassani, p. 660.
53. Ibid., pp. 660–61.
54. Ibid., p. 598.
55. Ibid., p. 675.
56. Elizabeth Grosz, *Volatile Bodies*, pp. 200–01.
57. In addition to Spackman already cited, see Karen Pinkus, *Bodily Regimes: Italian Advertising under Fascism* (Minneapolis: University of Minnesota Press, 1995), pp. 33–41.
58. Bassani, p. 696.
59. Scott Bravmann, *Queer Fictions of the Past: History, Culture and Difference* (Cambridge: Cambridge University Press, 1997), p. 6.

12

Transitive Gender and Queer Performance in the Novels of Mario Mieli and Vittorio Pescatori*

Marco Pustianaz

One of the normalizing effects produced by modern sexual discourse is the mutual implication of gender and sexuality, both regulated according to a seemingly natural, symmetrical opposition: masculine vs. feminine, homosexual vs. heterosexual. On the one hand, any overlap between masculine and feminine within the subject is prohibited by a strictly binary definition of gender; on the other, the very contact between male and female bodies is required by the regime of heteronormative sexuality. In other words, gender norms command that the two opposite poles never merge in order to avoid gender confusion, whereas sexual norms insist that they touch for fear of sexual perversion. Caught up within this apparent double bind, a heterosexual body is discursively produced.[1]

The binary logic of gender (and of the sexed bodies that embody it) is implicit in the very possibility of defining heterosexuality and homosexuality, quite literally "coming before" those terms. How else could we take for granted and natural the meaning of "same" (homo) and "other" (hetero) that allows us to talk of homosexuality and heterosexuality as though they referred to a preexisting reality?[2] Therefore, in their mutually sustaining and paradoxical logic the normative paradigms of gender and sexuality stabilize each other and patrol the borders, allowing those crossings that are natural and mandatory while disallowing those crossings that are unnatural and outlawed. As a result, we might view gender as a discipline of "intransitivity" over and against an ever-present "transitivity," if only as a threat to be averted.

The mutual implication and complicity of the modern discourses of sexuality and gender speaks on behalf of a socio-sexual ideology that produces both the heterosexual body and its obverse, the homosexual. In her ground-breaking essay "Thinking Sex" (written in 1984 after the beginning of the AIDS crisis and in the midst of the feminist debates on pornography), Gayle Rubin recalled that the two are inextricably linked to the point where it seems impossible to talk about one without using definitions set down by the other.[3] This ideological entanglement can be a problem for a gay and lesbian critique of hegemonic notions of sexuality, as one can run the risk of taking on board acritical assumptions about gender while trying to clear the ground for an autonomous inquiry into sexuality from the position of the sexual abject. Rubin's proposal could be interpreted as a way of resisting the above-mentioned implication and of calling for a methodological—as well as political—separation between the two spheres of inquiry.

However, I would claim that it might be no less politically effective to keep on working right in the middle of that highly ambiguous and densely patrolled terrain by following the omnipresent traces of the diacritical borders between the (two) genders and the (two) sexualities. The coupling of gender and sexuality as if they spoke the same language (in a way they have been doing just that) overdetermines their relationship and is at the same time normalizing *and* trouble-making. At times of heightened social and symbolic struggles, that seemingly ordered terrain (i.e., properly gendered, sexed and sexualized) gives way to other ways of reading, and the clear-cut intransitivity that spells the rule of the Law betrays the underlying transitivity that all the while underwrites it. The late 1970s in Italy were, I would argue, one such time; the two novels I am going to write about interest me in that they give ground to an outbreak of borderline subjectivities—in our case, mainly queer male subjectivities speaking compulsively about gender borders, with a consequent uncanny effect of suspension and even negation of those borders. These in-between bodies exceed the normative regime of intransivity that has produced both heterosexuals and homosexuals; and that is the main reason why I will often speak of them as being "queer."[4]

I have chosen to reread two novels linked to the Italian lesbian and gay rights movement of the late 1970s: Mario Mieli's *Il risveglio dei Faraoni* (*The Awakening of the Pharaohs*) and Vittorio Pescatori's *La maschia* (*She-Male*).[5] My reading will attempt to show how the social and political struggles of the 1970s that allowed homosexuals, in Italy as elsewhere, to find a voice of their own produced narratives of identity that are themselves "transitive" and "askew" with respect to normative binaries. These narratives play out upon a complex and overdetermined terrain where politics, gender, and sexuality all intersect. The queer effect that results from these intersections attained a level of productivity probably unmatched since by the lesbian and gay rights movement in Italy. Although the two novels are very different when it comes to representing marginal experiences, both manage to foreground homosexuality's uneasy relationship to hegemonic culture and in particular to normative gender binaries. They thus work in diametric opposition to the integrationist agenda privileged by the Italian lesbian and gay rights movement in the decades that followed.[6]

At the same time, these are texts that have as yet received no critical attention either from gay and lesbian scholars, Italianists, or feminists, as far as I can tell. What follows is by no means the naïve celebration of an early chapter from the lesbian and gay rights movement, which was, to be sure, rich in experimentation and full of hopes in the revolutionary potential of gay and lesbian subjectivity. If anything, my reading tends to raise suspicions about the ideological limitations that allowed some activists to posit—much too simplistically—a natural alliance between the feminist and the lesbian and gay rights movement. Still, my essay wishes at least to pursue the conversation. We had better not allow the two discourses to be locked away in separate cages, gender identity in one, sexuality in the other. A more transversal perspective will lead us to re-explore those critical paths already taken by women, gays, and lesbians in the past, wherever they were thrown together by the intricate interdependence between gender and sexuality. Above all, my reading speaks for a refusal to let silence engulf both the desires and the limitations of those who came before us.

Il risveglio dei Faraoni is the only novel written by Mario Mieli, the major radical activist of the early Italian lesbian and gay rights movement and author of one of the movement's relatively few theoretical works, *Elementi di critica omosessuale*, published by Einaudi in 1977.[7] Einaudi was in possession of a draft of his novel when he committed suicide in 1983. The book was published against the wishes of Mieli's family only in 1994 thanks to an editorial collective of former fellow activists with the support of the Centro di Iniziativa Luca Rossi in Milan.[8] The novel is both too complex and deliberately scandalous to be summarized in a few lines. In many ways, Mieli's novel applies in the extreme many of the notions about sexual liberation that had informed his earlier theoretical essay. This radical manifesto clearly announces its universalizing intentions with the title of chapter one, "Il desiderio omosessuale è universale" ("Homosexual Desire is Universal"). The novel pushes this universalizing gesture to the edge in a post-1968, pan-revolutionary utopianism that aspires to "The Reign of Liberty," which is for the novel's narrator (Mario Mieli, Maria, Franca, Jesus reincarnate, and so forth) the only true communism.[9] *Elementi* calls for the rehomosexualization of desire under the aegis of

Freud and his notion of the polymorphously perverse, not to mention all political and sexual practices that lead to the (re)conquest of Eros by overcoming the "forme coatte in cui si manifestano l'eterosessualità e l'omosessualità" (coerced forms in which heterosexuality and homosexuality are manifest).[10] In his concluding remarks, Mieli reiterates with a prophetic stance often typical of his writing that his utopian ideal remains the transsexualization of desire, picking up on the theories of bisexuality he found in Freud, Jung, and Reich.[11]

By establishing a paradigm of perpetual transformation, Mieli's theory of transsexuality strives to erase the psychic patterning of the Real, which is to say the dichotomy man/woman. Mieli emphasizes that for him desire is transsexual both in relation to objects and within the subject.[12] This means that the transitivity of desire can only lead to liberation once the subject actualizes within him/herself the fullest intersubjectivity. What develops is a kind of messianic and esoteric belief in the annihilation of alienated subjectivity—alienated by the God Capital—and the advent of communitarian nonidentity once "la conoscenza avrà annullato le barriere tra Io e non-Io, tra Io e altri, tra corpo e intelletto, tra il dire e il fare" (true awareness will have broken down the barriers between ego and non-ego, self and other, body and mind, word and action).[13] This perspective is particularly evident in the novel, which ranges from the theosophic to the pornographic.

Before looking more closely at the ways in which this liberation of the androgynous might also mask a cancellation of the feminine, I should emphasize that the revolution envisaged by Mieli has far-reaching, cross-disciplinary, and transdiscursive implications. Mieli is well aware of the intricately overdetermined nature of the Real as a normative system that has accrued and petrified in multiple layers over time. He works tirelessly in his writing to attack this norm. Thus homosexual liberation will occur in tandem with heterosexual liberation along with a more general human emancipation brought on by anti-individualistic communism; all this will happen by embracing "the revolutionary women's movement" as a powerful force for overthrowing the current phallocentric system.[14]

> Il crollo del sistema fallocentrico comporta il crollo del sistema capitalistico, che si regge sulla struttura maschilista-eterosessuale della società e sulla repressione-sfruttamento dell'Eros che garantiscono il perpetuarsi del lavoro alienato e quindi del dominio del capitale.

> The collapse of the phallocentric system will bring about the collapse of the capitalist system, built on the (hetero)sexist structure of society and the exploitation/repression of Eros, which in turn has guaranteed so far the perpetuation of alienated labor and thus the dominion of capital.[15]

Now, if the only reason for embracing the women's movement were to create some futuristic androgynous union—what Mieli calls "l'Uno"—we might object that women are just a means to an end in that they will eventually be superseded by the utopian Man-Woman. But my reading of Mieli's novel is less interested in the objective than in the actual labor required to undermine the gender system, which as Mieli points out is basically a repressive psychic mechanism.

In point of fact, we do not see the dismantling of phallocentrism by the women's movement in either *Elementi* or *Il risveglio dei Faraoni*, and I would say that the lesbian and gay rights movement in Italy has never quite meshed with the women's movement. Thus it might seem a bit absurd just to think oneself "beyond gender" on the assumption that male homosexuality plays no part in phallocentrism. Yet it is precisely this assumption that allows Mieli to construct homosexuality as a degendered/degenerating praxis. He writes of homosexuality as a chink in the armor of patriarchy and its norms. Inasmuch as homosexuality transgresses patriarchal law, it represents for society at large a hairline crack in the mirror. Homosexuals are thus in a position to question norms "scoprendo nella nostra vita un profondo *décalage* tra regole trasgredite e norme ancora accettate e la contraddizione che esso crea nel sistema dei valori correnti" (by discovering in our own lives a deep gap between the rules transgressed and the norms still accepted, and the contradiction this creates in the system of prevailing values).[16]

Mieli never strays very far from a naturalizing discourse according to which the Real represents the repression of the Natural: The Real is a broken mirror that Nature would repair. But homosexuality is a flaw in the mirror that patriarchal norms have *themselves* created by proscribing those desires that fall outside the objectives of a capitalist and phallocentric society. In this sense, homosexuality is not scandalous by nature but only "positionally," in reference to a societal norm.[17] That tiny fracture opens up the frightening but productive space of disidentification, which should be cultivated by all those practices or performances that call attention to the contradictions within the norm instead of covering them over. Thus the privileged, indeed necessary, strategy for undermining straight male identity becomes gender performance, which in Mieli's novel and the subcultural milieu it came out of takes the shape of a repeated manipulation of the feminine enacted by gay men. Mieli challenges gay subjects to transform the carnivalesque reversal typical of drag performance into a continuous degeneration/degendering of the masculine so that the very structures that at best give scope to a simple reversal come undone and are "con-fused."[18] This notion of drag as gender performance promoted by Mieli in the 1970s in Italy and elsewhere (Mieli had spent time in England

and was in touch with the Gay Liberation Front there) posits obligatory performance as the key to wearing down the normative male psyche until it reaches a state of joyous abandon, or "follia" (literally, madness).

Il risveglio dei Faraoni is part family saga, part mystical-transcendental tale. It is also Mieli's autobiography even though he aims to dissolve the identity of the protagonist. In actual fact, the reader is faced with a sort of self-negating autobiography whose narrative intentionally multiplies and fragments the various episodes that constitute it. The narrative is "anti-subjective" precisely in the sense that both reader and writer must learn to accept that the utopian Uno has many voices and that the self-centered individual has been atomized through polymorphous desire. The first chapter, "La casa d'Egitto" ("Our House in Egypt"), sets the stage for the narrative's true protagonist, the family. As Mario/Maria/Franca's point of view gradually loses focus and relinquishes self-centeredness, "he" begins to recognize the various individuals he has sex with (mostly, but not exclusively, male) as so many perverse reincarnations of (God the) Father, Mother (Mary), brothers and sisters, cousins and aunts—all those, in fact, who have informed his sense of self and made up the intricate web of his infant sexuality. It soon becomes clear that the real object of Mario/Maria's desire is to acknowledge incest as a model of circularity and reincarnation. Just as he represents a reincarnation of the Son, Jesus, so the family saga becomes the only possible narrative and his tale becomes the perverse rewriting of the story of the scriptural Holy Family.

Mieli's work is an antinovel inasmuch as it aims to disrupt the linear progression of the traditional heterosexual *Bildungsroman*, which tends to move from an original family to the maturity of its autonomous male subject, who will then reproduce a second family according to a continuous pattern that embodies the forward progress of History. True enough, Mieli's perverse homosexual plot is forced to acknowledge the transhistorical continuity of the family that has created him and that he continues to desire sexually in all its various members. Nevertheless, in this novel the traditional autonomy of the male subject, heterosexual maturity, the encounter with the Real, and the domestication of language are all undermined by a progressive loss of individual differentiation, by the unmasking of the Real, and by the autonomy of language speaking on its own behalf. Mario/Maria is continually having revelations based on linguistic anagrams, a clear sign of language's self-sufficient transitivity and metamorphosis. Although Mieli's antinovel is forced to acknowledge that its plot cannot create a family—that is, a new family in the traditional heteronormative sense—it still operates entirely within the confines of *the* family. The breach in the mirror of the norm must be taken to its logical conclusion: In the realm of the Real neither gender actually exists. Both are merely the result of a fiction that has become constitutive. As the engine of history and death, masculinity must be killed off, or more precisely, it must be made to commit suicide since it controls all means of representation.[19] In Mieli's personal mythography, the perverted queer male in some ways represents the revelation of Being. First, he must recognize that he harbors within himself the flaw in the mirror of normativity. He is therefore called upon to step forward as the only possible instrument for "degrading" normative masculinity and knocking it off its throne of privilege. The process of degradation takes various forms related to taboos of bodily cleanliness and purity. For the protagonist of the novel these episodes of corporeal degradation represent so many rites of initiation: coprophagy, masochism, the sacred alchemy of feces and urine. One of the first initiations takes place in the Brixton jail, as Mieli delights in rehearsing scenes reminiscent of de Sade, Genet, and Pasolini (the Pasolini of *Salò*):

[E]cco perché ero vestita diversamente dalla maggior parte dei prigionieri! M'avevan dato la divisa riservata ai poveri di spirito. L'iniziazione prevedeva che m'abbassassi al rango dei ragazzotti che da bambino, ad Alòr, guardavo e odoravo con distacco.

No wonder I had on different clothes from most of the rest of the prisoners! They gave me the uniform for the 'poor in spirit.' It was part of the initiation that I be reduced to the level of a teenage boy, the kind I used to look at and smell from afar when I was a little kid in Alòr.[20]

These initiations lead the protagonist to a whole series of revelations on the threshold of the otherworld—visions of his dead relatives, a séance, his watery rebirth in a bathtub. He overhears strange voices when people he knows are talking and realizes they are reincarnations from the past.

The hairline fracture in the mirror represented by homosexuality reveals a critical limen and calls for the political necessity of its reworking. In addition, rites of degradation signal the abandonment of self to a desire that for Mieli is always masochistic, the desire to be taken and subjugated. The explosive potential of such desire—or more precisely, the repression of such desire—constitutes in Mieli's opinion the founding myth of patriarchal history: the prohibition against men loving men. Thus when Mario has sex with the young man he recognizes as his own Son, it is as though a cosmic reconciliation has occurred; the symbolic recovery of incest restores peace between Father and Son and abolishes the primal Law of the Father:

Umbertine ed io ci abbracciammo sul letto. Fummo Caino e Abele, Osiri e Seth riconciliati nel pianto. Versammo torrenti di lacrime: io mi specchiavo nel volto del mio gemello solare, lui si specchiava nel viso mio, nel viso del suo gemello lunare. Eravamo neonati. Millenni erano trascorsi da quando uno aveva ucciso l'altro. Da allora per così lungo tempo l'umanità aveva pagato le terribili conseguenze del gesto fratricida e all'amore del fratello per il fratello s'era sostituita la guerra.

Umbertine and I held each other on the bed. We were Cain and Abel, Seth and Osiris reconciled in our grief. We wept torrents: I saw my image in the face of my twin, the Sun, and he saw himself in my face, his brother the Moon. We were like newborns. Thousands of years had gone by since one had murdered the other. And humanity had been paying the terrible consequences of that fratricide ever since. War had taken the place of love between brothers.[21]

It is extraordinary that from this scene of reconciliation between men Mieli is able to predict resurrection for all humanity, which "sarebbe tornata a gioire con tutte le specie viventi" (once again would live in bliss with all the other creatures).[22] Apparently, the only way to imagine and represent overcoming the binary self/other and thus liberating all men and women is by starting with a struggle entirely between males and through the subjugation of heterosexual to homosexual men.

Two aspects of Mieli's thought should be stressed once more: a link between the liberation of desire and the deconstruction of the male subject on the one hand and on the other a risky, somewhat paradoxical notion of a universality to which we must return by making use of the "woman" that exists in all of us. A number of issues arise here. How truly experimental are gay men as subjects that exceed the bourgeois economy of gender? How can we say that gay men are more dangerous and experimental than feminists? Is there some sort of tension or competition between these two revolutionary subjects, at once in excess and defective with respect to the normative gender paradigm? What kind of difference separates gay subjects from feminist subjects? In texts and narratives that claim to unsettle the formation of normative gender subjects, is there mutual recognition between these groups? To what extent? And between gay men and lesbians?

I believe that such questions are crucial because they acknowledge the operation of difference within the same public, political, and textual spaces where nonnormative subjects play out their disidentification from the gender system responsible for their existence. Mieli's "subject" recognizes the oppression inherent in masculine identification and thus in a sense stages his own deconstruction. *Elementi di critica omosessuale* embraces feminism as a partner in the struggle against phallocentric authority. Nevertheless, when Mieli actually tries to represent his degendered ideal, the male subject who surrenders power always comes off as more dangerous, tragic, and experimental than the feminist subject who can only grab power from someone else.

The most interesting aspect of Mieli's nonnovel, written by a nonmale nonsubject, is the dual importance of the body and language and, thus, of deconstructive practices on and through the body and language. The dismantling of male gender is always already prefigured in the original polymorphism, but in order to get back to this presubjective stage, before the binary oppositions of sex and gender were set in place, we must act in ways that will appear violent to the naturalized norm.[23] The queer male subject can recapture his original polymorphous state through theatricalized acts and interruptions: by staging rituals of degradation, by taking on nonmasculine gestures and habits, by wearing nonmasculine clothing, by adopting feminine gender in speech.

Mieli's transsexual ideology reduces gender to a mechanism of repression that, somewhat ironically, must be destroyed through performance by the only degendered subject who has the powers of representation at his disposal. Queer males are the only ones capable of taking power away from the masculine and opening the breach that will set in motion a liberating regression to the primal "con-fusion" of genders. The end of History coincides with a return to the primal scene, before the foundational prohibitions of culture—all of which, it seems, had to do with love between men—made slaves of us all, men and women alike.[24] We will thus reach a state of degendered transitivity via "suicidal" gender performances by queer males. Despite Mieli's declarations about the centrality of feminism, queer males end up stealing the stage of history from feminist subjects (even lesbians), who are left to undermine phallocentric authority from the wings. It is as though the offstage invisibility of the feminist subject provided a kind of counterbalance—a thoroughly gendered one, I might add—to the spectacular excesses of the feminized, effeminate fag in the spotlight.

In its theatrical undoing, male subjectivity takes over the entire scene of representation as the deconstructive performances of the degendered queer male subject grow more and more radical. In the end, liberation from the tyranny of gender is at best incomplete. One might even go further and say that the very space of representation has been reconfigured even more strictly as exclusively male, given its implicit rules of inclusion and exclusion. While it is true that this performativity is intended to dissolve gender, in effect the type of performance promoted by Mieli reinforces the notion that only one gender is present on stage—the male gender—the only gender that really needs to be dislodged.

The female gender in Mieli seems to exist basically as a set of degendering practices for the sole purpose of dismantling masculine identity, which remains the only gender capable of announcing the liberating end of History, just as it had been the only gender to inaugurate its bloody beginning. If History is gendered masculine, History can only be done away with by a male gender-traitor, the queer male subject. The queer male can act as traitor precisely to the extent that he plays the performative agent of the feminine, which logically speaking is outside of language and history, even outside the discipline of gender. This is why the queer male is a conflated subject, if you will. He is the key subject shouldering the burden of every possible representation, both of power and of power displaced. For Mieli gender is visible in its true repressive essence only at the moment of its parodic dismantling. Thus it is the queer male subject (rather than the feminist political activist) who can hope to bring about gender's demise from his position of power and through an insistent degendering performance.

Vittorio Pescatori's *La maschia* (*She-Male*) can be read both as a critical revision of Mieli's transsexual myth and as an ironic representation of his "impossibly" degendered subject position.[25] I have chosen to focus on the first novel of Pescatori's "Teo trilogy" because it was written around the same time as Mieli's text and because it allows for a series of reflections on Italian gender politics at a significant socio-historical moment, that is, the heyday of the experimental queer collectives in Milan that had split off from the Fronte Unitario (FUORI).[26] In Pescatori's short novel, experimentation with degendered subjectivity—far from being presented as a private experience—is firmly situated within specific marginal spaces where the dizzying plurality of sex/gender differences is a constant presence and makes a mockery of any homogenizing description.

While the story of Tea/Teo[27] and his/her continually shifting identifications can be read as a response to Mieli's transsexual utopia, *La maschia* is also a tale about the end of a queer commune in Milan and the complex system of alliances and oppositions that existed at the time.[28] In the spring of 1976, the Milan collectives definitively broke away from FUORI, the gay and lesbian group active in Italy since 1971, in the wake of the latter's recent association with the Partito Radicale.[29] Pescatori's novel deals with the question of differences *among* homosexuals and it unfolds on the basis of such differences, which have to do not only with political ideas but with how different groups of marginal subjects perceive themselves. The novel probes differences in self-perception and identification between *froce* and *maschie*, gays and lesbians, gays and women, liberated women and phallocentric men, and so forth.[30] Teo/Tea's story is narrated in the third person to deliberately ironic effect, heightened by the fact that the protagonist starts off as Tea, a pre-operative male transsexual, and ends up as Teo.[31] Analogously, Teo begins the novel by assuming the grammatical feminine and then switches to the grammatical masculine, though never consistently. These various transitions and interruptions, both bodily and linguistic, are important because the theme of imperfect or impossible gender identification characterizes Pescatori's work in a way quite unlike the fluid self-de(con)struction typical of Mieli's subject.

In Pescatori's novel, the queer males of the collective led by self-proclaimed empress Victoria seem to adopt the grammatical feminine as a matter of fact. By comparison, Tea takes on feminine pronouns and uses feminine forms of agreement as part of an analytic therapy that is supposed to bring him to a complete identification with the feminine, which in turn is an absolute prerequisite for his operation. The (male) analyst that guides him on this psychological journey has also recommended him to his current employer, the proprietress of a tearoom where Tea is expected to "succhiare femminilità e sentirsi donna, la più donna, donna-donna" (. . . soak up femininity and feel like a woman, all woman, a hyper-woman).[32] Because Tea desires other men, "becoming a woman" is imperative in order to repair the rupture created by a sexual object choice disallowed by the heterosexual norm. Thus a sex change is supposed to bring the queer male subject—who no longer identifies with the male gender—into the "regno della coerenza, togliendole di dosso quel qualcosa di non suo e di provvisorio che, nonostante l'incedere regale e i complimenti delle amiche, sentiva sempre incombente" (realm of coherence by getting rid of that something that didn't belong, something temporary that always felt like a burden despite her regal bearing and all the compliments from her girlfriends).[33] Since gender and sexuality are mutually implicated in the heteronormative system, sexual perversion can only be resolved by reestablishing coherence on the dual axis of the sex/gender system. In other words, the dysphoria of the desiring gay subject would be repaired by a process that simultaneously involves "being a woman" in the biological sense and "becoming a woman" in terms of gender identity. In a heteronormative economy of desire, a man is someone who desires (to possess) a woman. Tea wants to become a woman because only as a woman will s/he "have the right" to desire men. Thus the promised "realm of coherence" is predicated upon a chain of interrelated propositions continuously shifting across gender, sex, and sexuality. "Being a woman" will be Tea's final reward for a whole series of realignments to be achieved by a complex schooling in behavior, of which Tea is a most willing student.

If Tea's reward for the double process of "becoming a woman" and denying the existence of homosexual desire is "being a woman," the role of the analyst in *La maschia* reflects psychoanalysis's complicity with those ideological forces that have a vested interest in mending tears in the social fabric at any cost. It is the analyst who holds out the reward, in Teo/Tea's case, of becoming a complete and total woman, *donna-donna*. In order to repair the rupture between sexuality and sex, desire and the body, he makes use of social, political, and linguistic tools shaped by the normative gender regime. As for language, the new subject's acculturation as a "complete woman" is carried out under the strict supervision of gendered speech, which for Tea is meant to anticipate and foreshadow his future female body and is accompanied by a process of socialization as a woman. Indeed, Tea's insertion into the normative gender regime is described via a series of processes of which language seems to be the most intimate. The metaphor of "soaking up femininity," in particular, describes the assimilation of unity and consistency not so much in the subject's present identity as in regards to who s/he is supposed to become. Not unexpectedly, then, as a transitional subject in the tearoom where s/he is working, literally, to become a woman, Tea's primary concern is that of "passing": passing as a woman in the eyes of other women is the first step toward becoming one.

The gender education that Tea has undertaken is predicated on the principle of the female subject's blanket uniformity that assumes "woman" to be invariably Woman, always the same, day in and day out:

> Così Teiera si era ritrovata da un giorno all'altro nella necessità di essere sempre e comunque donna e non, come le succedeva prima, solo quando non ne poteva fare a meno. E, cosa più difficile, una donna comune, non un'adoratrice di Amanda, tutta specchietti, cosce e parrucche di fuoco, che rappresentava la schiuma della femminilità, il favoloso archetipo delle travestite.

> And so from one day to the next Teiera began to feel the necessity of being a woman always in every way. Not like before when she would feel that way only when she couldn't help herself. And the hardest thing was she had to be an ordinary woman, not some Amanda-crazed queen, all makeup mirrors and hips and flaming hair—the bubbling surface of femininity, fabulous archetype of divas.[34]

For Tea, becoming a woman involves a twofold process of subtraction: the castration of that superfluous "something that didn't belong" and the moderation of that absolute desire for femininity that had always inspired her dreams of drag, the fetishistic adoration of things characteristic of queens and divas, but not, alas, real women. Thus one of the first steps of her education in womanhood consists of simplifying what s/he wears at work, because a "hyper-woman," if truly and wholly woman, can afford to be understated and still be no less woman for that, even in dull, sensible shoes, regulation blouse and apron. Along with internalizing her new gender identity, Tea must give up those things that used to signify *outwardly* his desire for femininity. Paradoxically, the *maschia*'s passage to true gender coherence will occur only when s/he is able and willing to reject any excesses of femininity and all those feminine constructs (makeup, compact, wigs) characteristic of "Woman," the diva and the drag queen.

Initially Tea makes a distinction between herself and the queens in the collective precisely because s/he does not want to be identified as a homosexual. The range of subjective and social identities in Pescatori's short novel is dizzying and defeats any attempt at a normative reading according to binaries such as masculine/feminine, hetero/homo. Tea joins the squatter collective because as a transitional subject it seems that queens and outcasts are the only people able to accept her. The occupied building is itself characterized as a provisional, transitory space, traversed by a variety of marginal and experimental subjects. Tea shuttles back and forth between her daily socialization at work and her socialization among other marginal subjects in the collective. But s/he never stops feeling like something of an outsider both at work, as a faceless, ordinary woman, and in the collective with its endless political divisions: "Ma io che ci faccio qui? ma che cazzo vogliono da me? Transizione, ecco, un momento di transizione, quando sarò donna mi inserirò in un contesto eterosessuale e qui non mi vedono più! ma mi capiranno gli altri? Non sono omosessuale, sono donna!" (What am I doing here? What the hell do they want from me? It's a transition, that's all, just a phase. Once I'm a real woman I'll go live in the straight world and they're never going to see me again! But will other people understand me? I'm not a homosexual, I'm a woman!)[35] At the same time, Tea doubts that the straight world can ever really be hers. Significantly, the gender coherence promised her requires acceptance in a world that is not just feminine but primarily heterosexual. Gender coherence equals normative sexuality.

Tea is caught in the double bind of her attempts at normalization. S/he hopes to conform to a heteronormative system that, as we have seen, castrates some part of her desire. Worried by the occasional lapse back into masculine identity, s/he puts off his operation. Along the way s/he discovers the queer commune as the only possible space for her, albeit a space that is anything but stable and in constant transformation. Becoming a woman promises to resolve every conflict by granting her a normative identity as a straight female subject, even though her new identity would still continue to be marked by lack: first because Tea will be a woman but will have lost the desire to be one whenever s/he wants to, and second because her quest for selfhood will have been prompted by her abjected "deviancy" in the first place.

In Tea's laborious identification with the feminine gender we also see a complex linguistic process of subject construction, one that we can glimpse in the making, so to speak, and that takes a tangible, even monstrous, shape in a new "name." The hybrid grammatical term *maschia* is the unruly name (literally "against the law" of grammar and gender) s/he gets as a sign of lack and excess at the same time. When the terrain of gender identity changes from intransitive to transitive, not even naming agrees anymore. For this reason I have argued elsewhere that gender-bending nouns such as *maschia* operate less as nouns identifying subjects than as disidentifying nouns.[36] They become namings for a subject caught in between lawful, gendered names: We know, as Italian speakers, that there is no naming outside gender. As an "impossible" name, *maschia* can only be spoken in a tone of camp irony in order to exist at all.

As we know, Tea ends up stopping his male-to-female transition in its tracks, gives up his feminine-inflected name and goes back to the masculine "Teo," while also abandoning his analyst and forsaking his hyper-feminine performances. Despite all this, Teo does not simply return to masculinity. Having become Teo once again, s/he does not shed the hybrid noun *maschia* in the end. It sticks as the name that names his continuous quest for an identity that is always somewhere else. The noun *maschia* would seem to conflate genders as a two-headed Janus, a word facing both ways, but it also suspends genders: It is a name *in* transition, not just *of* transition. Teo's persistent state of transition continues to signal the loose ends and the inner fractures of gender identity. In fact, Teo's obstinate desire for some kind of stability will be projected onto yet another identification, no less problematic—this time with the Arab Middle East and the Third World via his new lover Habib.[37]

After meeting Habib, Teo finally carries out the crucial objective of identifying his desire as homosexual. He gets his Christian name back as masculine Teo and finds out that his desire for a man can indeed make him a man: "Più mi scopano, più divento uomo" (The more they fuck me, the more I become a man).[38] Accepting his homosexual desire, though, is not a permanent or satisfying solution. The decision not to go through with the sex change does not make it any easier for Teo to participate in the queer collective, just as it does not make it any easier for him to embrace a thoroughly masculine identification. It is precisely the new urgency of his desire for men that takes him further and further away from the queer communal space, as he goes searching for the elusive Habib in a whole series of marginal urban spaces where myriad hybrid identities intersect: in city outskirts, at train terminals, in railway cars home to illegal aliens, eventually in the Hammam baths.

Teo's desire for Habib confers on him for the first time a legitimate identity within a new configuration of desire that no longer obliges him to renounce masculinity: a male homosexual identity. At the same time, however, it creates a permanent sense of instability propelled by his subjection to desire, which metaphorically aligns him with a stereotypically female subject position, forever in thrall to man. Teo plays the part of the victimized housewife who stays at home all day to cook and clean. S/he actually builds a commemorative altar to Habib when he stops coming around. Most importantly, Teo begins to realize that the homosexual desire he has embraced now threatens a new tyranny by turning him figuratively into a desiring woman: a love slave forever subject to male desire (the odalisque described by the title of the second novel of the trilogy). If it is true that the more they fuck him the more he becomes a man, this can only mean that his masculinity depends on the continuous repetition of the sexual act. After all, he has not really gained any permanent or essential identity either as a man or as a woman. Once again he is the provisional gender hybrid, *maschia* or *uoma*, a human being gendered only in quotation marks[39] whose masculinity, now dependent on desire, must then be continually reaffirmed through sex.

For Tea/Teo such repetition is the only possible means to a stable identity, at least as an object of desire. At the same time, it is profoundly destabilizing because his very masculinity (or should we say *maschia*linity?) is the result—not the origin—of fulfilled sexual desire.[40] What becomes of his "becoming a man" during the periods between sex? Thus the endless repetition of sex comes to signal the inability to reach an identity not riddled with contradiction: "[M]a perché, perché bisogna sempre ripetere l'amore? Ripetere, fare dei multipli continui, ogni volta ho il terrore che sia l'ultimo, o che non possa essere più così bello. . . . [S]e si potesse fare una volta per tutte, poi rimanere sazi e abbracciati fino alla fine." ([B]ut why, why do I have to keep having sex? Over and over and every time I'm terrified it'll be the last or that it will never be that good again. . . . [I]f only I could do it one last time and be done with it, satisfied and in his arms once and for all.)[41] The more Teo gets fucked the more s/he becomes a man, but as long as Tea is not getting fucked s/he cannot become a man. By deciding against a sex change, Teo had opted to accept his homosexual desire, but the outcome is that gender has now become the site of constant turmoil, where norm and desire do battle, questions of identity are never fully resolved, and there is no "once and for all."

Teo's (re)appropriation of gay masculinity foregrounds instead the hybrid and incomplete dynamics that inform normative relationships among sex, gender, and sexuality. In this sense, the psycho-social experience of normative gender calls forth the *maschia* as an impossible but necessary third term, as queers are constantly called upon to fit a gender identity that forever slips their grasp. The daily domestic chores that keep Teo/Tea busy—patching, polishing, scrubbing—serve as a figure for the impossible job s/he is trying to do on gender, a task that holds out the equally impossible promise of perfect normativity. But his efforts to work on gender in order to straighten himself out, as it were, will never equal the job gender does on him or the demands it makes as a normalizing relay between sexuality and sex.[42]

Called forth as impossible subjects, Teo and the other queens in the collective take on a whole series of identifications they call their own. While no less impossible, these have the appearance of staged performances over which gay subjects harbor the illusion of complete control. I am referring specifically to the various strategies that call into question Teo's Orientalism[43] and Victoria's regal imperialism: Victoria is the queen and the guiding force of the impossible revolutionary space the queer collective calls the Winter Palace, eventually overrun not by proletarian masses but by the police. The impossibility of finding a harbor in gender coherence drives the queens in Pescatori's novel to seek new arenas by sidestepping the sex/gender system that has marginalized them as perverse subjects. What results is a proliferation of alternative identifications, especially ones that conjure up positions subdued or defeated by history and dominant culture.[44]

Although the relationship between (male) homosexuality and exotic identities remains a complex problem, La Maschia confirms at least the possibility that the two may interact with gratifying results. Pescatori's novel suggests that since gay subjects cannot fully participate in a heteronormative gender economy, they are able to displace their impossible disidentifications to alternative imaginary spaces. However deprived of authority and culturally marginalized, these spaces are nonetheless useful. Here the gay subject can reconstitute himself as a subject whose place is already marked out by other binary oppositions—as an actor in uncannily familiar psychic and social scenarios now freely desired, such as the master/slave relationship. Either as the empress Victoria or as the love slave Teo, the performative scenario in question here—not unlike the diva's—gives the performer imaginary control over his/her own contradictions. Neither Teo as love slave nor Victoria in imperial robes—one servant, the other master—repairs his fissured gender identity by translating it into Orientalism or imperialism. But both do manage to reinscribe the experience of disidentification as an experiment in camp, which is to say an identity performance that dislocates the "here and now" of politics for the "there and then" of . . .

Of what, precisely? If the pressing "here and now" of politics is camouflaged as the imaginary "there and then" of some "other" subjectivity, what sort of internal contradiction arises when, for example, the "other" is not only elsewhere, but right here in the flesh as well, standing in front of us? When, say, Milan is overrun with Arab immigrants, to cite an example of particular relevance for Teo? When his Orientalist fantasies are transformed into emotional and sexual experiences with Habib and sex with Arabs in the Milanese Hammam? The *maschia*'s dislocated identity repositions her as an imaginary subject empowered by certain fantasies that I see as deferred in space and time—one might say "obsolete." But the border between "here" and "there," "now" and "then" is no less transitive than the apparently natural border set down by sex and gender. Victorian imperialism is allegedly a thing of the past and so free for the taking, available for use by latter-day queens as a kind of "innocent" power play. Victoria takes a certain detached pleasure in identifying with a power that can now be hers because it really no longer belongs to anyone. Thus s/he can indulge with pure pleasure in an identity that no one will deny her because it has already been overtaken by history. Teo/Tea, as we shall see, will experience more radical displacements.

After the dissolution of the collective, Teo begins moving further and further away and will end up in Africa in the second novel of the trilogy. But even in the first novel politics and its effects of power return to invade those imaginary spaces that queers would appropriate for themselves, no matter how alien they seem to any normative system. The spatial and temporal alterity of Orientalism and Victorian imperialism is never external or extraneous enough to protect queers from everyday power struggles. Their performances are enacted in displaced, transitional social spaces that are never safe from contestation, both from within and without. The occupation of the building in Via Morigi by the queer collective is an important experience because it puts them in competition with other political groups. The queer occupation is explicitly compared to another by a revolutionary collective called "lotta dura" (hard struggle).[45] At a certain point, all the women leave "lotta dura" in mass exodus to join the queer commune. The episode serves to contrast two revolutionary strategies. One—gendered male and heterosexual—sees itself as uncompromising, hard-core, and pure in its revolutionary intent. The queer collective, on the other hand, reflects an alternate theoretical model according to which opposition to phallocentric authoritarian patriarchy can and should make natural allies of queens and dissident women (feminists who reject the hierarchy of normative gender). In point of fact, Pescatori's novel highlights the difficulties inherent in the overly facile assumption of cross-identification that underlies such political alliances as well as the limits of any alliance forged for purely strategic reasons. In this case, the *maschie* end up running the show and as a result ironically replay the hierarchy of gender differences from the position of male privilege.

I would like to linger for a moment on the issue of a difference between gay[46] revolutionary occupation and other contemporary models of revolution, a dissonance that positions gay men in opposition to the system while at the same time presenting a revolutionary model alternative to Marxism. Is it possible for a gay man to be a revolutionary political subject? Or is this a tragic oxymoron, especially in the 1970s with the growth of lesbian and gay rights movements in Europe and America? The contradictions were particularly evident in those countries where Marxism and Communist models of revolutionary struggle held sway, as social strife resulted in a strongly polarized view of establishment versus antiestablishment. Such a representation of power seemed to do away with any possibility of dissidence outside of overthrowing the system in revolutionary struggle, the logical and inevitable consequence of class conflict. At the same time the 1970s offered many attempts at political experimentation and redefinition of what might be considered political and revolutionary.

Can a gay man, then, be revolutionary? If so, how? When attempting to answer such questions, we must take into account the historical context of the 1970s homosexual movement, which in Italy, as elsewhere, defined itself as revolutionary (FUORI: Fronte Unitario Omosessuale Rivoluzionario Italiano). Like Molina in *The Kiss of the Spider-Woman* (the gay character here moves in a setting dominated by an idea of revolution as armed conflict, this time Latin America), the queens in Pescatori's collective experience a sense of impossibility when it comes to being truly revolutionary, in ways analogous to the inconsistencies they feel with regard to normative gender.[47] The point is not simply that revolution is gendered even in Marxist ideology (along with the revolutionary, the political activist, and the armed combatant). The equation between a "real" man and a "real" revolutionary is not simply the result of the macho connotations of warfare and political "activism."[48] Rather, the impossibility of being a "real" man instantly evokes the black hole of treachery, the cardinal sin in any revolutionary armed struggle and any war. The figure of the gay man as deserter and traitor requires no concrete evidence of treachery. Gay men are always already betraying gender, a betrayal that will always put them on the other side, and, thus, with the enemy.

As Mieli observed in *Elementi di critica omosessuale*, homosexuals already represent a rupture within the heteronormative system, so all they have to do is name themselves, make themselves visible and known in order to become revolutionary subjects.[49] For homosexuals simply becoming visible *is* their revolution. Nevertheless, such virtual revolutionary status is inevitably subjected case by case to all the ideological demands that define revolution not with respect to the virtual or contingent positionality of the subject, but in terms of choice of objectives, means, and policies that actually *count* as revolutionary.[50] In other words, the very terrain of the political and, no less emphatically, of revolutionary politics is demarcated discursively in ways that will include certain spaces and subjects as politically relevant while excluding others. In this light, the feminist dictum "the personal is political" must be seen as a way to include in "the political" subjective experiences and issues that had never before counted as political. In the same way, the homosexual is recognizably political from the moment he appears on the scene thanks to this extended notion of what qualifies as revolutionary, since gays and lesbians are defined by sexuality and bourgeois culture can imagine nothing more intimately personal. And yet Pescatori's *La maschia* would not suggest, as Mieli does, that homosexuals are a revolutionary thorn in the side of the establishment, an irreparable fracture that calls attention to and creates contradictions in the system. Rather it posits the no less scandalous idea that revolutionary identity—something his queer subjects would gladly embrace—actually underscores the irreparable lack that results from their betrayal of gender. These two fractures—between homosexuality and heteronormativity on one hand, between homosexuality and revolution on the other—can never be entirely reconciled. The revolutionary potential of gay subjectivity is doubly marked by rupture and thus branded antirevolutionary or at least unrevolutionary because it is transitory, doubtful, impure.

Perhaps it is no coincidence that the actual occupation of the so-called Winter Palace is never described, just as the novel never directly narrates the scene when the collective leaves the building.[51] Even though the entire story is narrated in the third person, it unfolds through the experience of Teo, who gets there only after everyone has cleared out and the police are sealing the doors shut. Such incomplete identification with revolutionary occupation is not limited to Tea but extends to all of the queens in the collective. We might even go further and remark that Victoria and all of her politicized companions speak of themselves as revolutionary and *not* revolutionary at the same time. Teo's betrayal of the collective's cause, owing to his desertion in search of Habib and "love," represents only the most obvious disavowal of the role of revolutionary subject. We find a similar ironic detachment in the political debates among the queens in the collective, with their hybrid mix of chat, gossip, and witty repartee. Indeed, gay chat of this sort is itself a kind of "impolitic" version of formal political debate.

We never see the queens engaged as activists in revolutionary political action or revolutionary struggle in the masculine sense. Besides,

[L]o sanno, lo sanno alla questura che siamo mansueti, che dal nostro gruppo può venir fuori non so, un Michelangelo, una Wanda Osiris oppure nella politica rivoluzionaria un . . . un Mazzini, ecco, o una Settembrini, tièh, proprio a voler spremere! . . . Sanno benissimo, 'loro', che siamo mansueti, che non rompiamo le palle, appunto perché ci siamo accettati e dichiarati. Le vere criminalesse sono loro, le Adolfe e le Benite, con tutte le loro gerarchesse, obbligate a scoparsi le donne sognando d'essere trombate come draghe da nerborutissimi sigfridi!

[T]hey know . . . they know perfectly well down at the police station that we're gentle people, that in our group they might find a Michelangelo or a Wanda Osiris or in revolutionary politics, I don't know, maybe a Mazzini or a Settembrini if you really want to push it! . . . They know that we're easy, we don't get in the way or piss anyone off, because we're out and we've accepted who we are. They're the real criminals, the big girls Adolphine and Benita and all their mincing fascist minions. They fuck women because they have to, but all the while dream of getting plowed by some buff Arian god, some Siegfried slaying dragons![52]

It would appear, then, that an occupation like the one that takes place in the novel has a character all its own. It comes off as somehow less revolutionary (even in its own eyes), if not downright counterrevolutionary, because intimately subversive of gender solidarity, that most intimate of bonds that takes the shape of a proletarian body always gendered male in the arena of class identity. Thus the queer collective's incapacity for violent action makes it untrustworthy for all those who see the solution in a violent overthrow of power. Paradoxically, if the revolutionary subject is also by definition a subject of conflict and battle, then pacifist queens can never bring about revolutionary action, that is, an action that is acknowledged as revolutionary by others. Gay revolution cannot escape the stigma of incompleteness and lack of recognition that also marks gay subjectivity. Not only does the above quote affirm that gay political practice is excluded from real (read: male) political struggle; it even seems to suggest that the more the gay subject accepts himself, the more pacified he becomes. The only gay subject roused to action would be one still fighting for acceptance, even self-acceptance. Those conforming to a normative model of political activism might after all be closeted queens, the kind that comes from trying too hard to pass as a man.

It may well be, then, that the contradictions inherent in the gay male subject find political expression in the very act of occupation, which also demarcates a rather ambiguous space. As Pescatori's novel progresses, the queer collective is continually trying to advance beyond its initial character as an ad hoc volunteer organization towards a more permanent structure complete with board of directors.[53] The organizing and running of the occupied space can be read as indicative of a negotiation of power that reflects queer positioning with respect to the heterosexual norm. Any political occupation requires taking over a space *within* the system, but squatters in particular choose a space that the establishment has somehow overlooked or neglected. Therefore, the political subject who chooses occupation as a strategy carves out a space within the very system s/he is fighting, a space that is best defined as "in-topian" and residual rather than utopian. Unlike revolutionary power struggle that represents itself as direct confrontation and sets about attacking the very site identified with power, the subject of occupation seeks out a space relatively devoid of power and moves in according to a logic of parasitic autonomy rather than direct opposition. The immediate objective is to take over a space neglected by the establishment and use it to develop alternative possibilities, like the liberating performances of Pescatori's collective. In this sense, occupation cannot be entirely assimilated to traditional notions of political activism because it relies on a fragmented and many-sided reading of political space.

I suggested above that Pescatori's novel implies a link between queens and obsolescence, which follows from their regal aristocratic fantasies. This makes the building occupied in the center of Milan particularly appropriate, for here Tea uncovers secret doors and hidden passageways, "marmi anneriti con rosoni al centro pieni di fiori dai colori tenui . . . putti, cieli blu, nuvole bianche e carri di Apollo" (soot-covered marbles with pale little floral designs gracing their center . . . little angels against a blue sky with white clouds and Apollo in his chariot) on the ceiling.[54] The aesthetic experience of marble and painted ceilings transports Tea towards a kind of ecstasy as waltzes begin to play faintly in the background. Soon the ecstatic identification comes to an abrupt end as the very degradation of the occupied building brings Tea back to the present, to the queen's everyday life and all her frustrated attempts to define an identity for herself. We find a similar sense of contradiction later in the novel when Tea follows Habib to the Hammam, where many of the same elements reappear (albeit in a somewhat more hellish context): architectural remnants, decaying memories of past sumptuousness, as well as a kind of artificial and decomposed Orientalism evoked by the textual allusion to *Aida*.[55] The residual quality of this purgatorial space represents an in-between that appeals to the queen as natural and unnatural at the same time. Just as the occupied building is the queen's fictional royal palace, a place where s/he can recover a legitimate political subjectivity "above ground," so the Turkish baths are her underground fictional Orient. Here s/he can fantasize about being lusted after by all the Arab men who congregate there and give in to her desire to be possessed by the Third World: "Il Terzo Mondo è sempre più pazzo di me!" (The Third World is crazier than ever about me!), Tea exclaims as s/he takes her place in the unlikely and utterly incoherent space of the Hammam, the place to which her desire has condemned her.[56]

This same incoherence and contradiction, I have argued, characterize the linguistic space carved out by the hybrid noun *maschia*. In Pescatori's novel, the experimental linguistic journey signaled by the transformations of the protagonist's name (from Teo to Tea and again to Teo) parallels a continuous search for hybrid social territory, politically and aesthetically dissonant, set in the very center of urban space and characterized by an aura of almost unreal decay. The devious path of grammatical gender in Pescatori's novel is similarly marked by an internal instability that makes the hybrid noun *maschia* a sign of disidentification, of suspended identity. Pescatori's novel thus bears witness to the sense of incompleteness and transitionality that has continued to inform the paradoxical status of gay subjectivity throughout the first century of its modern existence.

Marco Pustianaz (born Milan 1959) is Research Professor of English Literature and Theater History at the Università del Piemonte Orientale in Vercelli. His main fields of research are English Renaissance cultural studies, contemporary theater and gender/queer theory. Among his most recent publications in the latter field are the chapters "Studi gay e lesbici" in *Studi delle donne in Italia* (Carocci, 2001) and "Gay Literary Studies" in *Lesbian and Gay Studies. An Introductory, Interdisciplinary Approach* (Sage, 2000). He has coedited the volume *Generi di traverso. Culture, storie, narrazioni attraverso le discipline* (Mercurio, 2000) with feminist historian Paola di Cori and anthropologist Alice Bellagamba, as well as the forthcoming *Maschilità decadenti nella fin de siècle* (Bergamo University Press, 2004). A full biography is available at http://www.lett.unipmn.it/~janac/bio. htm.

Notes

* This essay is a revised and somewhat shortened version of "Genere intransitivo e transitivo, ovvero gli abissi della performance *queer*," in *Generi di traverso. Culture, storie, e narrazioni attraverso i confini delle discipline*, eds. Alice Bellagamba, Paola di Cori, Marco Pustianaz (Vercelli: Edizioni Mercurio, 2000), pp. 103–50. The English translation has been jointly undertaken by Gary Cestaro and Marco Pustianaz.

1. For a critique and commentary of the opposition desire/identification in Freud as a precondition of heternormativity, see Diane Fuss, *Identification Papers* (New York: Routledge, 1995), in particular the title essay, pp. 21–51.

2. The implication of gender in definitions of homo- and heterosexuality is discussed by Eve K. Sedgwick in *Epistemology of the Closet* (Berkeley and Los Angeles: University of California Press, 1990), p. 31; however, Sedgwick follows Gayle Rubin in preferring to keep distinct the two analytical categories; cf. note 3 below.

3. Rubin's seminal essay was first published in *Pleasure and Danger: Exploring Female Sexuality*, ed. Carol S. Vance (Boston: Routledge & K. Paul, 1984).

4. The issue of translation as well as the more general question of naming and especially self-naming deserves at least cursory notice here. The plurality of names designating "the homosexual" in the Italian texts I am commenting upon is an obvious reminder that no single name is felt sufficient by queers; no single signifier will do. It is not just a matter of translation, then, but of the experimental search for a multitude of other names that characterizes gay and lesbian subjects as, inevitably, language malcontents. In "Queer Epistemology: Activism, 'Outing', and the Politics of Sexual Identities," *Critical Quarterly* 36, 1 (1994), pp. 13–27, Simon Watney has written lucidly on the differences of naming and self-naming that have produced different generations of "homosexual subjects." "Homosexual," "gay," and "queer" refer only superficially to the same "thing." More precisely, they speak to the history and the different positions assumed in the power relationships implicit in the discourses that constrain our identity formations. In the case of Mieli and Pescatori's texts in particular, the presumably stable referent "homosexuality" is refracted through a wealth of different names. While we (the translators) have tried our best to avoid a facile homogenization of naming, the reader is well advised to have a look each time at the Italian term of the original text. I think that the Italian *frocio* (one of the many injurious terms used against male homosexuals in Italy proudly reappropriated by many of us since the 1970s), and especially its variant, reverse-gendered form *frocia* (in the feminine, as if to mimic a double insult), can sometimes be rendered as "queer" in English.

5. Pescatori's title is of course quite impossible to render in English. It represents the grammatical feminization of the masculine noun for "male" in Italian, *maschio*. The irony is that the very noun that refers to the male subject is thus queerly gendered as feminine! Since in Italian gender informs the very morphological structure of adjectives, nouns, and past participles, linguistic subversion has represented and still represents a key element of everyday queer practice. We have decided to leave *maschia* in Italian in the text.

6. Several recent reconstructions of the Italian lesbian and gay rights movement are at last available: Myriam Cristallo, *Uscir fuori* (Milan: Teti, 1996); Angelo Pezzana, *Dentro e fuori* (Milan: Sperling & Kupfer, 1996); and Gianni Rossi Barilli, *Il movimento gay in Italia* (Milan: Feltrinelli, 1999). The first two are personal memoirs. To speak of a "lesbian and gay rights movement" in Italy is a linguistic and political gamble. Rossi Barilli's book, for instance, hardly mentions lesbians. It is true that FUORI once included a lesbian group, but the story of the lesbian movement in Italy needs both a separate and integrated treatment within a wider narrative of the history of homosexual visibility. I have preferred to use "lesbian and gay rights movement" in order to acknowledge the presence of women, but it should be clear that the weight of the two terms is by no means equal.

7. *Elementi di critica omosessuale* (Turin: Einaudi, 1977), translated into English as *Homosexuality and Liberation: Elements of a Gay Critique*, trans. David Fernbach and (London: Gay Men's Press, 1980). All English citations are from this edition. Mieli began his political activity as a member of FUORI (Fronte Unitario Omosessuale Rivoluzionario Italiano) but later joined the splinter Milan

Collective (COM, Comitati Omosessuali Milanesi) when FUORI formally associated with the Partito Radicale in 1974. On the history of FUORI, see Barilli, pp. 46–89 and note 29 below. The entire corpus of Mieli's works, is being reissued as part of a major editorial venture by Feltrinelli publishing house. It will give all those who read Italian a much-awaited chance to reexamine Mieli's impact and relevance today. The *Elementi* has already been published: Mario Mieli, *Elementi di critica omosessuale*, ed. Gianni Rossi Barilli and Paola Mieli (Milan: Feltrinelli, 2002). This edition also includes valuable critical essays by Tim Dean, David Jacobson, Teresa De Lauretis, Christopher Lane, Simonetta Spinelli, and Claude Rabant.

8. Mario Mieli, *Il risveglio dei Faraoni* (Milan: Cooperativa Colibrì, 1994). The author's suicide kept the novel hidden until 1994 and it remains something of an underground novel to this day. As an editorial note specifies, Einaudi was left with uncorrected galley proofs. Their decision not to publish the book was due at least in part to the intervention of Mieli's family. A subsequent intervention by Mieli's family succeeded in getting the book off the market, but a few "pirate" copies are still available in Italian lesbian and gay networks. Thus an important experimental work of Italian literature from the late 1970s has remained virtually clandestine despite Mieli's own radical visibility. It too will be reissued by Feltrinelli.

9. *Risveglio*, p. 219, in a chapter entitled "L'Africa si muove" ("Africa on the Move").

10. *Elementi*, p. 236 (point three). The concluding chapter entitled "Fine" ("End") sets down nine points. Curiously, this section is missing from Fernbach's translation; English translations from this section are by Cestaro.

11. *Elementi*, pp. 235–37.

12. *Elementi*, p. 236 (point four). "L'Eros libero sarà transessuale, anche perché la liberazione dell'omosessualità e l'abolizione del repressivo primato eterosessuale-genitale avranno favorito e determinato la disinibizione completa e la liberazione della natura ermafrodita profonda del desiderio, che è transessuale (la psicoanalisi direbbe riduttivamente *bisessuale*) sia nei confronti degli 'oggetti' *che nel soggetto*." (Liberated Eros will be transsexual, because the liberation of homosexuality and the abolition of the repressive hetero-genital regime will have brought about total disinhibition and set free the profoundly hermaphroditic nature of desire, which is transsexual—psychoanalysis would say, reductively, *bisexual*—both in relation to objects *and within the subject*).

13. *Elementi*, p. 236 (point six). "Tutti gli esseri umani conosceranno se stessi, e non più dal punto di vista individualistico, che sarà stato superato, bensì da quello transessuale-intersoggettivo, comunitario: la conoscenza avrà annullato le barriere tra Io e non-Io, tra Io e altri, tra corpo e intelletto, tra il dire e il fare." (All human beings will know themselves but not in an individualistic sense. We will have done away with that. Rather in the transsexual/intersubjective/communitarian sense: true awareness will have broken down the barriers between ego and non-ego, self and other, body and mind, word and action.)

14. *Elementi*, pp. 236–37 (point seven). "Affinché si verifichi la liberazione dell'o-mosessualità, della transessualità e l'emancipazione umana, *è necessaria l'af-fermazione del movimento rivoluzionario delle donne.*" (In order to bring about homosexual liberation, transsexual liberation, and human emancipation, *we must embrace the revolutionary women's movement.*)

15. Ibid., p. 237 (point eight).

16. Ibid., p. 228; *Homosexuality and Liberation*, p. 225. Mieli speaks of homosex-uality as a whole, thus conflating gay and lesbian subjects as though they shared a comparable positionality. But the degendering practices he embraces, as I have tried to show, have such a transgressive impact because they are ascribed to *male* homosexuals. His focus is always on normative male identity.

17. On the "eccentric" positionality of the gay subject, see David M. Halperin, *Saint Foucault: Towards a Gay Hagiography* (New York: Oxford University Press, 1995), pp. 60–61.

18. At once confused and fused together.

19. *Risveglio*, pp. 65–86; the chapter entitled "Tentato parricidio" ("Attempted Patricide").

20. Ibid., p. 24. Notice that the narrator uses the feminine gender when saying she was clothed ("vestita") but keeps the masculine when referring to himself in the past as a *boy*.

21. Ibid., p. 268. Typically, the Father-Son relationship changes over into another male-male familial bond—that between brothers, whose archetypal feuds have given origin to (male) History as strife and bloodshed.

22. Ibid., p. 269.

23. In this sense Mieli's experimental linguistics might be compared to the *sémio-tique*, the pre-Oedipal order of language postulated by Julia Kristeva in *La révolution du langage poétique* (Paris: Seuil, 1974); *Revolution in Poetic Language*, trans. Margaret Waller (New York: Columbia University Press, 1984).

24. The influence of psychoanalysis is of course central (and explicit) in Mieli even when he opposes Freud or, more precisely, reductive post-Freudian the-ories. Of particular importance in this context are Freud's readings of the cul-tural foundations of society, from *Totem and Taboo* to *Civilisation and its Discontents*.

25. Vittorio Pescatori, *La maschia* (Salerno: Edizioni Sottotraccia, 1995); this vol-ume also includes the two subsequent installments in the Teo trilogy, *L'odalisco* (1989) and *L'animalo* (1995). *La maschia* was first published in 1979 by the publishing house of the alternative magazine *Re Nudo*.

26. On the history of FUORI and the Milan collectives see notes 6 and 7 above and Barilli, pp. 46–124. I am calling the Milan collectives of COM "queer" because they set out to radically subvert male gender identity in self-consciousness groups and drag performances as well as theater proper. The squatter's commune was "queer" in another sense. As described by Pescatori, it was home to a wide range of "outcasts" and marginal subjects: hustlers, drug addicts, runaways, pregnant women, homeless, queens, transsexuals (like Tea),

hetero-bisexuals, and petty criminals—a rainbow underworld presided over by gay queens!

27. Teo's names shift from Teo to Tea (and the corresponding nickname Teiera, "Teapot"), as he starts off as a male, pre-op male-to-female transsexual. The instability of his/her gender identifications (not of his sexuality, though) will bring about the gender-hybrid noun *maschia* as the best descriptive term for Teo. Such gender subversions are intimately connected to effects of subjectivity and are a crucial element in the text's continuous *différance*. We have chosen to alternate between feminine and masculine genders and have often opted for the pronoun s/he, especially when referring to Tea/Teo before he makes the decision to put an end to his sex transition. It should be noted that Tea speaks more or less consistently in the feminine. It is hoped that the pronoun s/he, while remaining faithful to Tea's linguistic usage, will also reveal the mark of the cut or fracture that typifies her being a subject in abeyance. Pescatori's text defies any attempt at straightforward translation. Nowhere is the queer subject more clearly shown as a subject fissured through desire and in language. The reader should also bear in mind that the default term most commonly used for the queers living in the commune is neither *gay* (a perfectly acceptable option in Italian as well) or *omosessuale*, but *frocia* (see note 4 above).

28. Mieli appears briefly on p. 27 of Pescatori's novel as "Mario, detto brevemente Maria, teorico ufficiale del movimento" (Mario—Maria for short—the official theorist of the movement).

29. FUORI had chosen to join the federation of the Radical Party in 1974. The party was led by Pannella and at the forefront of several libertarian campaigns in Italy. They had just led a victorious struggle for the right to divorce (a popular referendum took place in May 1974) and were at the time campaigning for abortion rights. The fourth FUORI congress was organized jointly with the Radical Party and the MLD (Women's Liberation Movement). As a result of the federation pact all local party branches became branches of FUORI.

30. None of these names should be interpreted as having a fixed or formalized meaning. The degendering of language in the queer commune can generate many such namings. There are many other instances cited in the novel, such as *le baffute*—literally, "mustache queens", masculine queers who are nonetheless gendered in the feminine here!

31. The narrative voice faithfully follows Teo's subjective point of view, but the third-person narration suggests ironic detachment and identification all at once. This is different from Mieli's narrative, in which the narrative "I" loses itself in the abyss of transsubjectivity.

32. *Maschia*, p. 9. On the relationship among transsexuality, sexual politics, and gender politics, see Bernice L. Hausman, *Changing Sex: Transsexualism, Technology, and the Idea of Gender* (Durham, NC and London: Duke University Press, 1995), which probes the medical and technological connections between transsexuality and the discursive construction of gender. For Hausman, the emergence of a transsexual subject in the last century is closely

tied to medical authority. It is interesting to read Teo/Tea's (dis)identifications as a way of interrupting what Hausman calls the "gender narrative," which naturalizes a "core gender identity" under the scientific supervision of psychology and medical technologies.

33. *Maschia*, p. 10.

34. Ibid., p. 10. The Amanda referred to in this quote is Amanda Lear (1946–), one of the most famous disco stars in Europe and most admired gay icons. In 1979 she was at the top of her success after three smash hit albums. She started out as a model in the 1960s and became close friends with Salvador Dalì; she has more recently hosted television shows and exhibited her own paintings! She was for a long time rumored to be transsexual and did all she could to play the part. Her singing was unusually throaty, her clothes over the top, from hyperfeminine to leather-dominatrix (as she appeared on the cover of Roxy Music's "For Your Pleasure" in 1973).

35. Ibid., p. 19.

36. Marco Pustianaz, "L'ombra dell'oggetto. Identità, identificazioni, disidentificazioni . . ." in: *Incroci di genere. De(i)stituzioni, transitività e passaggi testuali*, ed. Mario Corona (Bergamo: Bergamo University Press, 1999), pp. 9–45.

37. Indeed, *L'odalisco* finds Teo on assignment in Africa searching for Habib, whom he had met in Milan in the previous novel.

38. *Maschia*, p. 25. For further comments on this over-compensatory claim to masculinity cf. Pustianaz, "L'ombra dell'oggetto," pp. 29–32. While this remarkable statement would seem to win once and for all a masculine identification for the gay subject, once again it presents him with both fullness and lack. Teo's masculinity is always *in debt* to someone else, here to Habib.

39. See *Maschia*, p. 26, for *uoma*, the gender-reversed feminine form of the Italian word for "man," *uomo*.

40. See *Maschia*, pp. 51 and 53, where the desire to be sexually desired is defined as the one true obsessive need of all queens.

41. *Maschia*, p. 22.

42. A relay in the sense that it adapts each sex to his or her own proper sexual object and thus effects the necessary passage between them.

43. Following, in part, Edward Said, I mean by Orientalism a mode of representation that uses the Orient as an integral part of the constitutive identity of Western culture. In our case, even Western male homosexual identities set up a privileged relationship with Oriental (here North-African) sexuality. Racial fantasies and imaginary uses of the exotic play a crucial part in male homosexual relationships with non-Western alterity. Habib is just one instance of such an imaginary need at work.

44. See for instance the phantasmatic identifications with female movie stars that Teo experiences with increasing intensity after he has gone to live in Habib's village in Tunisia, itself more like a hallucination or mirage.

45. *Maschia*, p. 80.

46. It is hard to speak of a gay *and lesbian* occupation, as the lesbians in the novel do not live in the commune but visit regularly to perform all sorts of practical

and menial tasks. It will be apparent that neither Mieli nor Pescatori, in the texts cited, allow us to extend ipso facto the issue of revolutionary subjectivity from queer gay men to queer lesbian women. This is worth remarking in itself. For this reason, I am going to limit myself to some reflections on the status of the queer male vis-à-vis 1970s revolutionary politics without trying to include lesbian subjects where they are not written in the text. I am therefore registering here the use of *gay* in all its exclusionary force.

47. Hector Babenco's 1985 film *The Kiss of the Spider-Women* is taken from the 1976 novel of the same name by Manuel Puig. In the film, William Hurt plays the romantic gay idealist who identifies with various heroines of Hollywood melodrama, while Raul Julia is the pragmatic, straight revolutionary. Both are prisoners of the regime and powerless. As cellmates, they provide a study in contrasts between the political and the apolitical, between reality and fantasy in relation to power, and the problems that arise from placing the two in opposition. This is an important text on the relationship between the revolutionary subject and the gay subject, on the alleged activism of the former and pacifism/passivity of the latter.

48. In Puig's narrative, the political and the sexual are intricately aligned in terms like "active" and "passive."

49. That is, they are already virtual revolutionary subjects whose coming out brings about the full performative potential of an inner rupture, which, in political terms, can be named as "treason."

50. For a critique of the unquestioned priority of "the political" in gay and lesbian identity politics, see Diane Fuss, *Essentially Speaking: Feminism, Nature and Difference* (New York and London: Routledge, 1989), particularly pp. 105–07.

51. It is also telling that the queer revolutionaries never quite manage to imitate the language of Revolution proper. If anything, they speak the language of counterrevolution: The queer collective is occupying a "Winter Palace" governed by "grand empress" Victoria.

52. *Maschia*, p. 62. These words are spoken by various unidentified voices. Wanda Osiris (1905–1994) was one the most famous showgirls and singers of Italian revue and variety shows from the late 1930s through the late 1950s. But for gay men she is identified with her memorable entrances down elaborate stairways. The Neapolitan Luigi Settembrini (1813–1876) was one of the leading figures of the *Risorgimento*, the movement that led to the Unification of Italy in 1860. Imprisoned several times on charges of sedition by the Bourbon authorities, he became a senator in 1873. He is revered as one of the Italian patriots of the *Risorgimento* and author of a book of prison *Memoirs*. More to the point here, he also wrote *I neoplatonici*, a short novel centering on the mutual love between two young men set in ancient Greece; this text remained a well-kept secret until the manuscript was rediscovered and published for the first time in 1977 (Milan: Rizzoli). For further information see Stefano Casi, "Un patriota per noi: Luigi Settembrini" in: *Le parole e la storia. Ricerche su omosessualità e cultura. Quaderni di critica omosessuale no. 9* (Bologna: Il Cassero, 1991), pp. 49–70. Giuseppe Mazzini (1805–1872) was the

Risorgimento patriot who fought ceaselessly for a unified Republican Italy. While in exile, he founded the Young Italy movement and led the short-lived experiment of the Roman republic in 1849. After the Unification of Italy, he again went into exile in England, joined the First International, but sharply disagreed with Marx over the role of violence in revolutionary struggle. The ironic mention of Mazzini in the context of revolutionary politics is apparent here; moreover, his particular interest in the role of *young men* as the new political subjects of the *Risorgimento* can be read as charged with homoerotic affection. Adolphine (Adolfa in the original) and Benita are queer feminized nicknames for Adolf Hitler and Benito Mussolini.

53. *Maschia*, p. 28.
54. Ibid., p. 20.
55. Ibid., p. 82.
56. Ibid., p. 84.

Index

.